CHINA'S GLOBAL

REACH

MARKETS, MULTINATIONALS, AND GLOBALIZATION

GEORGE ZHIBIN GU

D1316006

TRAFFORD

Note for Librarians: a cataloguing record for this book that includes Dewey Decimal
Classification and US Library of Congress numbers is available from the Library and Archives
of Canada. The complete cataloguing record can be obtained from their online database at:
www.collectionscanada.ca/amicus/index-e.html
ISBN 1-4120-6911-4
Printed in Victoria, BC, Canada

Printed on paper with minimum 30% recycled fibre.
Trafford's print shop runs on "green energy" from solar, wind and other environmentally-friendly power sources.

TRAFFORD

Offices in Canada, USA, Ireland and UK
This book was published *on-demand* in cooperation with Trafford Publishing. On-demand
publishing is a unique process and service of making a book available for retail sale to the
public taking advantage of on-demand manufacturing and Internet marketing. On-demand
publishing includes promotions, retail sales, manufacturing, order fulfilment, accounting and
collecting royalties on behalf of the author.

Book sales for North America and international:
Trafford Publishing, 6E–2333 Government St.,
Victoria, BC v8t 4p4 CANADA
phone 250 383 6864 (toll-free 1 888 232 4444)
fax 250 383 6804; email to orders@trafford.com
Book sales in Europe:
Trafford Publishing (uk) Ltd., Enterprise House, Wistaston Road Business Centre,
Wistaston Road, Crewe, Cheshire cw2 7rp UNITED KINGDOM
phone 01270 251 396 (local rate 0845 230 9601)
facsimile 01270 254 983; orders.uk@trafford.com
Order online at:
trafford.com/05-1822

10 9 8 7 6 5 4 3 2

ABOUT THE AUTHOR

George Zhibin Gu obtained education at Nanjing University in China and Vanderbilt University and the University of Michigan in the United States. He holds two MS degrees and a Ph.D. from the University of Michigan.

Since 1990, he has been an investment banker and business consultant. He has worked for the last 15 years in the investment world with a focus on China. His work focuses on helping international businesses to invest in China and the Chinese companies to expand overseas. He has worked for Prudential Securities, Lazard, and State Street Bank, among others. He generally covers mergers and acquisitions, venture capital, business expansion and restructuring.

Also, he is a commentator on political, economic, and business issues. His articles or columns have appeared in *Asia Times, Beijing Review, The Seoul Times, Financial Sense, Gurus Online, Money Week, Online Opinion, Asia Venture Capital Journal,* and *Sinomania,* among others. He is the author of two additional books, *China Beyond Deng—Reforms in the PRC* (McFarland, 1991) and *Made* in *China – Players and Challengers in the 21ˢᵗ Century* (Portuguese edition, Centro Atlantico, 2005). He now resides in Guangdong, China.

CONTENTS

INTRODUCTION

This is an exciting time to be alive. The world has finally become a small place—a "global village" indeed. New York and Beijing are only 16-odd hours apart. A man steps onto the airplane for breakfast and lands on the ground just in time for dinner. How could any nation avoid globalization?

China is moving, finally! Dramatic changes have swept over Chinese life. Today the average Chinese lives in an environment dominated by openness, competition, and challenge. Engagement with the outside world has become a national passion. China has finally landed on a right path.

GROWING UP IN CHINA

This fast developing China is deeply felt by the entire world. For too long, China lived in isolation, which produced vast problems. Especially in between 1949 and 1978, the Chinese society and people were stuck in the mud. Getting out of the mud has been as difficult as moving a mountain.

I was born into the era that is now remembered as the Era of Vegetables. That time is still a painful memory. It involved the disastrous Great Leap Forward and the people's commune. From around 1959 to 1961, starvation occurred nationwide. Urban residents had insufficient food. Vegetables became a major element of their diet. The rural people suffered from famine. Youth today have trouble believing such stories.

Man-made disasters did not stop there. When I entered elementary school in 1968, the Cultural Revolution was already in its third year. It involved everyone, including 90-year-olds. My school had lots of damaged furniture and broken windows. Many of our teachers suffered both mentally and physically.

My age group could not have a normal growing environment. Looking back, I think what I missed the most was books. Great books can open many worlds. But those books that interested me often had torn or missing pages.

Luck was smiling on me nonetheless. I happened to belong to a fortunate age group. By the time of my graduation from high school, in 1978, the reform had started.

Since then, dramatic changes have swept over this ancient land— Chinese youth live in an increasingly creative environment. When I was growing up, life was so limited. I entered college in 1978. Before then, colleges had been closed for some 12 years. As if overnight, they reopened. Immediately schoolteachers became important again. Whereas only a few months earlier, urban high school graduates had been sent to rural regions to work, we could enter college.

In the first two classes that were enrolled, the students had huge gaps in age. Our oldest classmates had children who were just about the same age as our youngest classmates. We studied with an intensity that would surprise all students today. Our professors were impressed, naming us "the best group of students in a long time." At that time, applicants faced a cutthroat entrance exam. Much less than 1% of youth were admitted. Some kids who failed the entrance exam committed suicide. Today China has a much wider educational program than ever before with some 20 million students studying in college.

It was an era of dreaming and hoping. We were terribly interested in the outside world, in anything and everything. Nothing could stop us from dreaming of a new life. We quickly developed a mentality that everything in the West was great and everything at home was bad. The mood was very intense. That was the very starting point of China's opening to the outside world. In our high-intensity mind-set, we vaguely felt that bigger things would emerge. Yet nobody knew exactly what they might be.

GOING INTERNATIONAL

Over time, changes in China have gone wider and deeper. China has greatly expanded its sphere of activities. As for me, I went to study in the United States.

Today, all Chinese are eager to discover the world. Every Chinese student desires to study abroad. In 1981, the U.S. universities, among others, were eager to get Chinese students. That year I joined the first group of students to head for the outside.

When I landed in the United States, it was engulfed in its own problems. That era belonged to a rising Japan. Japan Inc. rolled over the entire globe, like thunder. Many U.S. businesses failed. This turn of fortune hit the United States hard.

The people of the United States had a moment of despair. They were forced into a painful restructuring. Self-determination paved the way. Very significantly, high-tech has suddenly emerged. High-tech has created a new turn of fortune in the United States, among other things.

I was there to witness all the changes. Since then, the waves of globalization have been wider and deeper. Globalization has swept over more and more nations. Willingly and proudly, China has become a new participant.

RETURNING HOME

In 1994, I returned to my homeland for business, representing an international investment bank. Since then, I have focused on business dealings between international multinationals and China Inc. I have gained firsthand experience with this new era. Especially since the mid-1990s, China's development has been picking up speed. More foreign multinationals and more Chinese entrepreneurs have emerged. They have promoted a high-speed growth.

Interestingly, this fast-developing land has become a magnet to the entire world. Countless foreign businesses want to share in its progress. They have added new fuel to the growth.

On various occasions, my international media friends and I went together to visit Chinese businesses. Such visits surprised many Chinese executives. Some said, "We thought that only international businessmen were interested in our work. Are people in general interested?"

As it seems to foreign reporters, outside observers are certainly interested in a rising China. In a way, watching China now is like reading the paths they themselves once traveled.

China has become a global theater—a theater of international ideas, dreams, and activities. A grand lesson from China is that no nation can truly develop without making itself open to the world. This massive international involvement is turning China into a nation called Global China. A new world history is being written.

THIS SMALL BOOK

The aim of this small book is to examine China's participation in the global economy today and possibly tomorrow. It focuses on those factors that are shaping the future course of global development.

Integrating China into the global economy has required huge efforts. But its progress is so impressive. In particular, we will examine the foreign business involvement: the motivations and expectations, successes and failures, and possible future courses.

A GREAT PARADOX

So far, China has experienced quick growth—a mystery to the Chinese, not just the foreigners. A great paradox is this: Despite vast economic progress, China does not have a new political-economic system in place. The old government-centered life continues to cause enormous pain. In many ways, it is like an old man who is still wearing baby clothes.

Despite all the imperfections, China's economy has achieved rapid growth. The first driving force is the private sector. Tens of millions of private businesspeople have come to life. They are most directly responsible for a booming economy.

The next driving force comes from the foreign investors and multinationals. Foreign businesspeople are widening the channels for China's global engagement. All such foreign involvement has greatly impacted global development, not just China.

Interestingly enough, the private sector and foreign businesses have coexisted with the state sector. This state sector is also moving forward, though slowly and painstakingly. Together these entities have created vast new business chains, thus a booming economy.

What could become the next level of development? China's ultimate goal is a modern nation based on law. There are still enormous obstacles in the way. The old political-economic framework is already broken, but a new one has yet to be created. China is going through a very painful transition.

The West took the modern path a few hundred years ahead of China. The various Western nations have resolved such issues as modern property ownership and a modern market order. China now stands at a crossroads.

The pace of change is extremely fast. True, China's development is only just beginning, but huge progress has been made already. It took thousands of years for the West to land on the modern path that it is traveling now. Why should anyone expect China to do so overnight? Even so, China is fast reinventing itself.

The history of this ancient civilization is one of immense achievement. For ages, China was the most advanced society in technology, the arts of life, and social harmony. Its contributions to global development have been huge. Yet in the last few hundred years, especially in Mao era, China has not been able to move ahead as before.

But the tide of fortunes is being turned around as now. Behind a fast-changing nation, China has a new lesson for the world: A burdensome large population can become a powerful and productive force if a fair environment is present. Today, tens of millions of entrepreneurs are charging ahead like bulls. This is opening a whole new world for China and beyond.

A COMMENT

When I had a draft manuscript of this book done, I ran into the following situation. One Chinese professor, with the best of intentions, told me that I should not write too much about things like corruption. I asked myself: Why not? The Chinese people are diligent and bright, and they deserve a much better life. What is holding them back from a more prosperous way of living?

But the real task for China is a mighty one. The old China was built around government. The government has always tried to arrange all things in order to make the population and the society to serve its needs. Now China is fast moving away from the old government domination. This new life is still full of difficulties, like those of an aquatic animal trying to resettle on the land. It just can't be that easy. Even so, China has taken one step, the most significant one, in this new direction.

Some people view China's new growth as the restoration of old wealth, but the truth goes much beyond that. Indeed, it is not for China to return to the past at all. China is on its way to becoming a modern nation. In particular, it will become an equal partner in the global community. China can only and deeply wish to share its progress with the world. The 21st century belongs to the world, not just Asia or China.

THE BIG PICTURE

China's big picture spans more than two millennia. For some 2,200 years, from the Qin dynasty to the Mao era, bureaucratic power only increased. By the 1950s, the entire private sector had been eliminated. Much beyond, for the very first time, bureaucratic power penetrated into the grassroots, which led to a perfect bureaucratic society. The key bureaucratic creations included the people's commune, the state sector, and an elaborate system against a free flow of goods, ideas, and humans. No citizens were left independent, not even artists and monks. As a result, the people, the society, and the economy must serve the government. But immediately, the economy was at a dead end. Furthermore, the whole nation was helplessly drawn into man-made tragedies, which include the Great Leap Forward, the nationwide famine, and the Cultural Revolution.

Since 1978, this bureaucratic power has been on the decline, finally. This has led to a sharply rising creative private sector as well as a booming economy. In particular, China has become a global theater with countless foreign businesses.

To contain this untamed bureaucratic power is the continuing goal for the Chinese civilization, as well as the most formidable. In the past two centuries, China has not really had any opportunity to resolve this issue with respect to its root causes. Instead, the tail has grown so big that it weighs down the body. Curtailing the bureaucratic power means nothing short of a true revolution. That is what is happening inside China right now.

Even bigger things are emerging around the globe. There is nothing less than a great convergence of civilizations. India, Brazil, Egypt, Russia, and China, among other developing nations, have reversed their historical paths. They have rushed to join in global development, bravely and whole-heartedly. At the same time, the rest of the world has had a direct involvement in these emerging nations. Because of all this, we are entering a new era in spite of all the new worries and conflicts. Though still in its very infancy, the convergence can only increase. Achievement of this great convergence of global civilizations is another true revolution in the making. Furthermore, if it is a true global revolution, it must resolve all the pressing issues that confront our world. The bombings of New York and London are powerful remainders of some of these problems.

This book is organized into four parts. Part I focuses especially on foreign involvement in the new Chinese theater. Part II examines China's new experiences with outside markets. Part III explores many aspects of China's unfinished business of reform. Part IV looks at future world prospects from the angle of global history.

ACKNOWLEDGEMENTS

Many friends have assisted my work. I am most grateful to all, especially Dr. Li Weiwei of Shenzhen, Mr. Li Le of Ningxia, Dr. Li Weimin of Beijing, Professor Tony Quan of Shenzhen, and Professor Qi Tongzhi of Nanjing.

I thank Professor Chen Ping of Peking University and the University of Texas for reading one draft manuscript and offering insightful comments. I am most grateful for the Afterword by the late Professor Andre Gunder Frank (who passed away in April 2005). I am also grateful to Mr. Jorge Nascimento Rodriques of Group Adventus for his encouragement. I thank Professor Joyce Sexton of University of Wisconsin at Madison for editorial help.

Chen Liang, the better half of my family, has gone through all the sacrifices. Without her, this project could have never been attempted.

I have also greatly benefited from giving lectures at various universities, companies, and government institutions in China. Here I wish to express my thanks to all, especially Beijing Air & Aerospace University, Peking University, Tsinghua University, University of International Business and Finance, Renmin University, Shanghai Jiaotong University, China Securities Daily, the State Center for Information of China, and Guoxin Securities.

I am alone responsible for any faults in this book.

GENERAL NOTES

1. Chinese names are different from English names. In this book, the Chinese family name appears before the given name.
2. One U.S. dollar equals approximately 8.28 Chinese yuan.

HEILONGJIANG

• Harbin

• Changchun

NEI MONGOL
(Inner Mongolia)

JILIN

• Shenyang

• Urumqi

XINJIANG

GANSU

BEIJING

LIAONING

• Hohhot Beijing •

TIANJIN

• Taiyuan HEBEI • Tianjin

• Shijiazhuang

• Xining

SHAANXI

• Jinan

SHANDONG

QINGHAI

SHANXI

• Lanzhou

• Zhengzhou

JIANGSU

• Xi'an

HENAN

• Hefei • Nanjing

SHANGHAI

XIZANG
(Tibet)

HUBEI

• Shanghai

• Chengdu

• Wuhan

ANHUI

• Hangzhou

• Lhasa

SICHUAN

CHONGQING

• Chongqing

ZHEJIANG

• Changsha

• Nanchang

GUIZHOU

HUNAN

JIANGXI

• Fuzhou

• Guiyang

FUJIAN

• Taipei

YUNNAN

GUANGXI

GUANGDONG

• Xiamen • Taichung

TAIWAN

• Kunming

• Guangzhou

• Kaohsiung

• Nanning

MACAU •

• Shenzhen

• HONG KONG

• Haikou

HAINAN

• Sanya

Part I

China as a New
Global Theater

1 AMBITIONS OF THE FOREIGN MULTINATIONALS IN CHINA

A rush to China is going on. Countless overseas businesses have reached this far corner in a hurry. By now, more than 400 of the top 500 global players are established in China.[1] From their perspective, China is becoming a gold mine.

A little story goes like this. One day at a New York airport, Bob sees his friend Joe carrying several bags. "Hi, Joe, where are you going?" he says.

"China."

"What's in those bags?"

"They're empty."

"What for?"

"When I return, these bags will be filled with gold."

TODAY'S VERSIONS OF COLUMBUS AND MAGELLAN

The very existence of multinationals means constant expansion, nothing short of it. Today, there is no place better than China for multinationals to display their ambitions.

Global multinationals are modern versions of Columbus and Magellan. They have new markets to discover, new treasures to explore, and new riches to earn. The world has become too small for their ambitions. China has become one last frontier. To the CEOs of Kodak, Nokia, Sony, Siemens, Unilever, LG, and Thomson, dominating in China would double their profits. It is natural for China to become a hot battleground as now.

The outside desires to tap into China have existed for centuries. In this era, vast opportunities have finally emerged. Millions of foreign businesspeople have followed in the footsteps of Lord McCartney, who led the first Western government delegation, with 600 officials and businessmen, to China in 1793.[2]

Over 200 years later, foreign businesspeople have succeeded where Lord McCartney failed. The British lord and his delegation brought to China many of the best goodies of the age, especially musical clocks, fast-firing guns, and telescopes, but they didn't interest the Chinese court much, except the musical clocks. Today, the world takes a different tack—a better one—and foreign businesspeople have better goodies. They have sodas, fried burgers, mobile phones, and cars. This time, they are winning in a big way.

In coastal cities, international players are already plentiful; inland, more players are rushing in. Making profits has moved to the far corners already. The foreign nationals have stepped into the most remote regions for the very first time.

But it took a long time for the multinationals to put China on their map. Throughout the 1980s, most could not really make up their minds. They were only watching with great interest. Some did mount small attempts. Now, they have gone to the other extreme. They are now chasing after each other's tails to enter China. They are eying the vast Chinese market with its fast-rising consumption. The only problem, seemingly, is that they have all come at around the same time, so that they must compete with each other head-on.

◌◌

In Hong Kong, a Chinese professional and the CEO of a small U.S. pharmaceutical company were chatting. "What do you do in China?" the CEO said.

"I help multinationals to invest here."

"Investing in China? The Chinese are too poor to afford our products. Maybe 10 years down the road."

"What products do you sell?"

"Pharmaceuticals."

"They are all here or coming!"

"Which companies?"

"Every big name you can think of."

By 2004, more than $560 billion had landed in China. Newspapers were flooded with these stories. August 4, 2003 was an average day. Several news pieces (including recent stories) appeared on the *Financial Times* Web site that day:

A giant European semiconductor company wanted to set up a plant in Suzhou (and a research center in Xian[3]).

Volkswagen was signing off on another joint venture deal in Shanghai after many previous deals.

An American auto parts company, which was part of Ford, decided to move its Asian headquarters to Shanghai.

Toyota was accelerating its jump into China.

Foreign and local auto players were fighting in China.

Nippon Steel was creating a joint venture with $377 million in Shanghai....

Well, they were all here or coming.

WHY ARE THEY HERE?

The question is certainly age-old, but people still ask: Why do businesspeople rush to new frontiers like China? The answer is always the same: They seek profits, nothing more. Multinationals must expand regardless of how big they already are. Their competition and their shareholders would never allow them to stop. Stagnation could mean nothing less than death.

Foreign businesspeople are excited to see that Chinese consumers are now loaded with cash—that they have big desires to improve their lives quickly and to enjoy all the modern goodies under the sun. Moreover, the Chinese consumers always love international things. This is pleasing to the eye of the outside business world.

Most foreign players come for specific reasons. Some are eager to find new markets, some to cut costs, and some to go after talented but poorly paid Chinese workers. Naturally, the smartest businesses want to do all these things. They all calculate how quickly they can double their profits.

Some are coming simply because everybody else is coming. Sheep love to follow the herd. If competitors were to move a step ahead, this would pose a threat. How could anyone refuse to come?

WHY CHINA?

A truth universally acknowledged is that it is much easier to share one's fortunes than miseries. The fast developing China means a booming economy at home. This is the most significant factor in making China a global theater.

With huge capital and tremendous resources, multinationals have vast choices. To be sure, they could go to any place on the globe. Today China has become a top choice. Why do foreign players want to bring their billions to China?

They have many reasons. A sound analysis will show that their reasons are valid.

Each nation has its unique advantages. In this era, China has been moving faster than most developing countries. To be sure, India has numerous advantages. Above all, India has a powerful army of IT professionals. But its growth in consumption is slower than that of China. India has less than 50 million mobile phone users. India is only beginning to show impressive results.[4]

China's consumption is growing fast. With 340 million mobile users by early 2005, China is already the number-one global market. A fast-rising income has led to explosive consumption. Like all consumers anywhere, Chinese consumers love modern goodies. In terms of consumption, China is well ahead of India and Indonesia, among other developing nations.

China's advantages manifest themselves in other ways. In terms of labor cost, many developing countries have lower pay scales than China. India, Vietnam, and Indonesia are some of these countries. But these low-income countries may not have a complete industrial and commercial range the way China does. In particular, their manufacturing capabilities are far less than China's. Each one of these countries can accomplish this or that, but each is far from being a true manufacturing center for the world. In this context, China has achieved more development in recent years.[5]

To be sure, development has also been rapid in numerous developing nations. Mexico, for example, also has impressive manufacturing capabilities, especially in textile and consumer products. But Mexico does not cover entire industries. Its pool of professionals is not as big as China's. In addition, it is a small market, and its growth has been far less than that of China.[6]

Many developing nations in Asia are attractive as well, but they also have many limitations. The city-state Singapore has an attractive environment. It has a legal and financial system that is more established than China's. Its government is highly transparent and effective. But its population size is less than half that of Shenzhen. The limitations are obvious.

Thailand has long been a favorite place for foreign investment, especially for the Japan Inc. But business scope is limited in Thailand and the market is small. Similar things can be said about Malaysia and the Philippines, among other Asian nations.

Maybe it is no accident that China has become a new business center. Numerous positive factors have helped China to achieve this end.

Fundamentally, China's new dynamic life has made the biggest difference. China's goal is to fully participant in global development. Improving living standards has been the number-one goal for all Chinese. They have made remarkable progress so far.

Surely enough, all multinationals study the global map, and they have countless nations in their sights. Finding the next gold mine requires huge efforts. Some have gone to Vietnam. But Vietnam has not reached the level of development seen in China. Also, there are enormous barriers, especially corruption, which has stopped many foreign investors from going there. True, corruption is also common in China, but opportunities are larger.

So far, China's reform has followed its own path, unique in many ways. It has avoided political chaos or social instability at large. This has been more than significant, especially in comparison to the former Soviet Union. The Soviet Union's reform has resulted in its disintegration and in chaos of historical proportions. This has produced further uncertainty for the resulting nations, Russia and the other former republics. Such political chaos has greatly limited healthy economic development up to now. In all such respects, China has been doing far better.[7]

Despite all the imperfections, China's carefully maintained stability has added much strength to the economic development. Above all, it has helped to link China directly to the world economy and development.

Vast changes have affected all aspects of China's society and economy. In particular, consumers have gained power. Explosive consumption growth is the single most powerful engine of overall growth. With all the explosive opportunities, how could businesspeople not come to share in China's progress? They have come, and their involvement has added fuel to a booming economy.

Having businesspeople come has required extraordinary efforts. It took global companies a long time to make up their minds. Prior to 1992, few came. If even some did, they were testing the water more than anything else.

But life is completely different now. Especially since 1993, the tide has gained momentum. China's determination to open up has reached a new height. Many global players have started to take the rush-hour train, one after another. All the foreign direct investments have been accelerating.

INFORMATION TECHNOLOGY PLAYERS FIRST

One exploding business is the IT industry. To be sure, with or without the WTO, global tech players are already in China. By now, China is already the second biggest IT market, only after the United States. No global player can avoid coming. Here everyone must compete with each other, and this competition has fueled further growth.

China's explosive consumption has become a magnet. These consumers are the biggest group in the world. They have gained huge disposable money. They are eager to improve their lives. If this consumer group desires foreign products, China is the perfect destination for global players.

Leading brands like Nokia, Motorola, Sony, Samsung, HP, and Ericsson would be 20% smaller without China. No global business CEO can afford to miss China. They all want their piece of the growing pie. Their shareholders, board directors, and employees, and especially their competitors, all demand the CEOs' presence in China. At the airport in Beijing or Shanghai, the nonnative person you bump into could be a CEO from London, New York, or Paris. Even SARS could not scare a businessman like Motorola's CEO. He came to Beijing in the middle of May 2003, at the very height of the attack. What a trip!

THE MOTOROLA CEO'S BEIJING TRIP

Motorola's CEO arrived in Beijing on May 16, 2003. The following day, he was easily the busiest person on earth. Besides meeting with numerous government officials—three groups in all—he met with the leaders of five Chinese telecom companies.[8]

The behind-the-scenes story is even more interesting. Motorola had revenues of $5.6 billion from China in 2002. It aims to reach $10 billion by 2006. It has already built a huge organization with some 12,000 Chinese employees. With its production in Tianjin and research in Beijing, among other places, it is trying to become a Chinese company, at least in terms of its local operations.

There should not be any doubt about Motorola's ambitions. After all, to the company management, it is Chinese consumers who have saved its fortunes. The positive effects are especially evident in the bear market for the IT industry at the present time.

By now, the fortunes of these global giants are closely tied to China.[9] In 2003 alone, Motorola sold 20 million handsets.[10]

So, the Motorola CEO had every reason to be here. His trip received much attention in China, especially considering the SARS attack. Media took the event very seriously and covered the CEO extensively.[11] To many Chinese, he presented a big gift just by being here for a couple of days. In this context, he outshone his competitors.

ONE BIG FACTORY-MARKET

By now, China has achieved a threefold role: as a fast-growing market, a huge manufacturer, and a top trading nation. Its innumerable players, both domestic and foreign, produce countless manufactured goods for global markets, China included.

One top Chinese TV maker, Konka, had cumulatively produced 50 million TV sets by May 2003.[12] Another leading TV maker, TCL, has been producing TVs only since 1996. In 2004, TCL produced around 17 million TV sets. Haier's sales reached 12.2 billion in 2004, only 200 million short to be included in the 500 club. This sharp rise in Chinese economic power has global dimensions.

This frontier market has become a dreamland. Many global brands can be found in Chinese stores already. But many popular U.S. brands, such as Maytag and GE home appliances, are not here yet. Chinese consumers wonder: Why are they afraid to show up? Are they not competitive?

In fact, many consumers are not aware of Whirlpool's two attempts to enter China over the last two decades. To what extent has Whirlpool tried to play over here? Its efforts have had a serious impact on the Chinese media. To many observers of China's home appliances market, no foreign player has ever tried as hard as Whirlpool. Nobody could have imagined how terribly Whirlpool would fail. It repeatedly failed in cities like Shenzhen, Beijing, Shanghai, and Guangzhou.[13]

But Whirlpool did not give up easily. Since 2000, the second try has been very fruitful. Yet Whirlpool's encounters made GE and Maytag less confident about coming to China. (In June 2005, Haier went to the US to compete to take over Maytag.)

China is a crowded market by now. It takes enormous effort to achieve success. The competition in most sectors is cutthroat. So far, international brands have shown mixed results.

By now, Siemens is one of the biggest international multinationals in China. It now has 30,000 Chinese employees and runs some 45 factories. Moreover, it has brought its entire business to China. The businesses range from telecom to home appliances, machinery, power equipment, medical equipment, transportation, and auto parts. Siemens' service businesses also include power operations and road management, among others.[14] It is well ahead of its major competitors, especially GE (see chapter 8).

INTERNATIONAL RETAILERS TREATED LIKE PANDAS

In this ancient land, 1.3 billion consumers are passionate about improving their lives now. They just love to shop for the best items in sight. Unlike Western consumers with credit cards, the Chinese buy large-ticket items with cash. Using credit is a new affair. How can foreign businesspeople not fall in love with them all?

Luck was with those international retailers who are already here. They have been operating in some of the biggest cities.[15] They include numerous international brands: the U.S. heavyweight Wal-Mart; the European giants Carrefour, B&Q, Tesco, IKEA; and Makro; and the Japanese Ito-Yokado and Jusco. They are set to stay here forever.[16]

The convenience chain store 7-Eleven is active as well. Its only problem, seemingly, is that it has countless copycats. Everywhere now, convenience stores spring up like bamboo trees.

Not every international retail giant has come over. The Chinese wonder: When will the rest come? Or are they making too much money elsewhere? But many Chinese retailers fear having more competitors. The smart ones are trying to move ahead fast, and they are learning fast. The less fortunate ones are in distress already.

ONE MAN WEDS THREE FOREIGN WIVES

Multiple marriages are perfectly legal as far as China's auto sector is concerned. How could it be otherwise? Owning a car has finally become a common dream. Today, an urban Chinese girl hopes to marry a man who owns a car. How could the auto market not be booming?

The cars on the roads in China are mostly foreign brands. Even if some Chinese auto makers are independent, their key technology is mostly imported. All international brands are manufactured by joint ventures, due to government regulations. China has tried to lift up its weak auto industry by bringing foreign players in. Foreign players must participate in joint ventures, and the WTO will not change this.

To all foreign auto players, China is the last frontier they must conquer. On the one hand, they have an overcapacity at home. On the other hand, China's auto demand has been growing fast. Over the five years, the auto market grew from 1 to 5.2 million.

This rush created some behaviors that are unique in the world. To many observers, the foreign auto makers are a bit crazy.[17] It seems to be no problem if several of them create joint ventures with one Chinese auto company. This is impossible in any other country, but it has already happened in China.

One big winner has to be Shanghai Auto Industry Corporation (SAIC). It has already wedded such foreign brands as Volkswagen, Toyota, and GM. Becoming a "concubine" is popular art with these auto giants.[18] SAIC has been highly successful in managing these eager brands. In 2003, the company made it into the global 500 club.

This rush has worried some Chinese. They feel that there may not be a way to create a truly Chinese auto company. Many experts claim that even if the foreign auto makers did not come, they would still take away most of the profits.[19]

Why? The Chinese auto makers are far from self-sufficient. They lack all the important elements. In particular, they don't have their own intellectual property. They have few advantages except government policies. Even with favorable government policies, they must buy technology and key parts from the outside world. Nevertheless, China has its arms wide open to all foreign players.

It is important to realize that a high degree of understanding exists between the Chinese government and foreign players. One Chinese researcher said to me, "Obviously, there is a working partnership already in place between the government and foreign businessmen. Under it, how could the foreign businessmen not make money in China?"

The evidence for this observation is strong. In particular, profits for the auto players have been abnormally high up to now—so high that they have shocked many Chinese. How could such a poor nation pay such high prices? One consumer wrote:[20]

"In celebrating China's 50 years history for auto industry, I am shocked to learn such numbers…Honda Civic with 2.3 liter engine manufactured in Guangzhou had a retail price 298,000 yuan ($36,000) in 2002. In Japan, the same model only cost 133,000 yuan ($16,100). Last year, the Honda joint venture in Guangzhou produced 32,200 cars with a profit of 4 billion yuan ($483 million) or 124,200 yuan ($15,000) per car."

According to this consumer, such fat profits do not lead to creativity: "I now realize that why China's domestic auto players are not trying hard enough…. In the first 30 years, China's door was closed; in the second 20 years, the auto men loved to count cash on the comfort bed. Who could feel sad to this kind of situation other than consumers?"

To consumers, the closed market has done more harm than good. In particular, the Chinese auto players have barely improved over many decades. Naturally, governmental protective measures may not have brought about the intended results. In fact, China's auto industry began 12 years earlier than South Korea's. But now South Korea is well ahead of China in every way. China does not have an auto company that is near the strength of Hyundai. This poor performance has been largely a result of closed-door, bureaucratic practices.[21]

By 2004, increased production had caused widespread price cuts, some as high as 30%. The auto market is beginning to enter a mature era. Even so, most foreign players are adding projects and hope to make it big over here. Fundamentally, it is a matter of survival, nothing less than it.

More Sectors, More Players

The herd mentality is certainly a driving force. In fact, following the herd is sometimes better than following one's own thinking.

A few international players develop most Western drugs. Naturally, their profits are impressive. Even these drug companies are moved by a rising China. They don't want to be left behind. They have rushed over together.

Their names are a who's who in the global pharmaceutical club: Merck, J&J, GlaxoSmithKline, Novartis, Zeneca, and Pfizer, among others. One important contribution from this group is that they have helped to introduce global standards in China. But they have brought over few really exciting drugs. Consumers ask: Are they bringing over the best drugs? If not, when are they going to?

The U.S. drug maker Pfizer was an early starter. Pfizer arrived in 1989 and has already invested some $500 million. It has brought more than 40 different drugs and intends to become a leading player. How does the company view China? Its China manager says, "China is a huge market and it is growing rapidly...despite enormous challenges, I am full of confidence in China."[22]

Infrastructure and Construction

The dramatic nature of the changes has given rise to countless delightful experiences. Returning students are often shocked with all the new things. Some can hardly recognize places they were once familiar with.

To many foreigners, China should really be called the "nation of cranes." This nation of cranes has attracted huge international interests. A booming economy offers vast opportunities for all hungry businesspeople, like the gold mines discovered in the Americas long ago. Countless Europeans took their tiny boats to sail in dangerous waters to get there. Naturally, only the fortunate ones arrived. But China offers bigger opportunities now.

All businesses are needed regardless of what they make or sell. Nowhere can they hope to make profits as quickly as in China. The construction business seems to be a hot area with fat profits for everybody so far, local or foreign.

The building of a strong infrastructure has been impressive. Hundreds of thousands of new towers, bridges, and expressways have appeared on the landscape. This gigantic change has surprised even many local residents. Many people who visited Shanghai only 15 years ago would likely now find the city completely new.

Naturally, all the foreign brands like GE, Caterpillar, ABB, Mitsubishi, and Siemens have already been very busy over here. How could they not be? They have been playing here for many years. And it is not just the big names—many small businesses have also rushed over. They have brought ideas, skills, technology, and more with them. No talent is too small or too big in the rebuilding of China.

For many decades, China's economy went astray under government domination. Shanghai, long the Pearl of the Orient, had lost its old glory. Its previous period of construction ended in the mid-1930s, just before the Japanese invasion. In the 1980s, when many cities like Shenzhen were doing great things, Shanghai was still filled with the old gray buildings. To many foreigners, the old Shanghai, before 1992, appeared frozen in time.

How could the Pearl of the Orient fall into a secondary place in Asia? For the first 37 years of the 20th century, Shanghai largely dominated business and finance in all Asia. Compared to Shanghai, the other major Asian cities like Hong Kong, Taipei, Singapore, and Tokyo were nowhere near in significance. When Shanghai lost its influence, these cities gained new power.

Indeed, Shanghai is the Chinese city that foreign people are most familiar with. When one U.S. citizen visited Tokyo and Shanghai in 1991, he reported his impression that the war had ended in Tokyo 50 years ago and in Shanghai only yesterday.[23]

One editor of *Fortune* magazine had a similar reaction: "Shanghai did not look like a big city: there were only about 100 cars running on the streets and one hotel for foreigners. What a pity for Shanghai!"[24]

Things have turned around since 1991. The rising tide has finally touched Shanghai. A brand-new city has come to life. Thousands of new towers, hotels, and roads have emerged. The urban size of Shanghai has doubled. Hundreds of thousands of new cars are on the streets. Shanghai has again become a pearl in Asia.

In this growth era, China's people have gained enormous confidence. They tell each other often that they can create prosperity as well. Many elderly men and women in the cities are fascinated with things new to them, the way children are. To the Chinese youth, even the old imperial palaces in

Beijing look dull today. The young people love the new glass towers. Within a short time, the old China has already acquired new clothes. Creating wealth has meant creating countless new towers, roads, and bridges as well.

Venture Capitalists Don't Hide

Among humans, the venture capital people are said to have certain special features. For one, they can smell the direction of the wind. Their whole game boils down to being a step ahead of the crowd. Timing is everything. Being early makes all the difference.

Many of them are already in China. There are several kinds of venture capital people. The first group is people in the investment arms of global multinationals. The next group comprises people in venture management associated with banks and financial companies. Independent money management companies are the third group.

Among all the players, the Japanese venture group Softbank stands out. It has made billions outside of Japan. How did it do this? It took a stake in a startup, Yahoo. With billions in profits, Softbank hopes to double. China is the next strategy.

It would surprise a newcomer to see how big a crowd the venture capitalists already are over here. Attending their annual meeting is always a big event. The meeting is held in Hong Kong each year. The location is usually the Marriott. All the familiar brands show up, ranging from global banks to private partnerships and multinationals. Many have been here for more than a decade.[25]

What has made them come? It is mostly the fact that every competitor is also coming. Well, people enjoy doing things their neighbors do. They all come, full of dreams and ambitions, with billions of their clients' money.

Especially in a bear market, with the NASDAQ having fallen for several years, China has remained a bright spot. It is still booming, despite the SARS and bird flu wars. Where can the smart money go?

Why do investors put billions in the hands of these venture managers? They must be reading a lot about what is new in China. They are eager to share in the growing pie. In some ways, the herd mentality has played a role. Someone is surprised to discover a nice sailboat in his neighbor's yard. Once he finds out that the money came from a joint venture in China, how could he not be tempted? Soon the venture managers are loaded with billions with which to try their luck in a new gold mountain.

They are all here or coming! China's rising economy has become a magnet. Has the desire to reach China worked into their blood? Or is it that their competition is here already? To be sure, each venture manager has a particular story to tell.

Anyway, they have all helped to turn China into a global China, a place for business dealings and moneymaking. Rain or snow cannot stop them. Even amidst SARS in the spring of 2003, numerous foreign players registered new companies. In 2004, more international businesses arrived. They created 47,300 new companies.

MORE MIDDLEMEN THAN ACTUAL PLAYERS

A booming economy demands the blessing of professional middlemen, the more the better. They are all here - bankers, lawyers, accountants, public relations specialists, and ad agents. Surely middlemen are among most diligent people anywhere.

Many land developers in particular, foreign and Chinese, have tried to meet the demand. They have created numerous buildings, specially designed for the middlemen. In the same buildings, all the familiar international brands are crowded onto one floor or another: an exhibition hall for the global brands. Reading the names is reading a list of the shrewdest businesses: names like Morgan Stanley, Citibank, JP Morgan Chase, Clifford Chance, PricewaterhouseCoopers, UBS, HSBC, and Deutsche Bank.

In Shanghai, more than 40 foreign law firms have set up shop. They are banned from practicing local law for now. This has not done much harm, as they are extremely inventive. They simply hire local lawyers to take care of their business. This has worked well for them, and their profit margins can be as good as anywhere outside.[26]

China has offered foreign nationals countless special treats, even for things related to living. There are specially designated office towers and living places. The foreign nationals may eat in the same cafes, drink in the same bars, and sleep within the same compound. How could some not feel as though they were being treated like pandas?

The untold truth is that foreign professionals watch each other closely. They are afraid that competing parties are doing better. They are even more afraid that their clients might jump ship. In a way, they would prefer to have an elevator of their own if this were at all possible. Then they would feel more secure in their quest to collect all the dollars under the sun.

These overseas professionals have local competition as well. Thousands of homemade middlemen are busy providing the same services. Like some Wall Street personalities, many Chinese dealers have risen to top positions through mailrooms. Better still, some have driven taxis in Shanghai and Beijing. They tell investors: Who knows better about the town?

THE BUSINESS OF CHINA IS BUSINESS!

China is changing rapidly. It turns out that commercial life has universal features. Even a new slogan is familiar: The business of China is business. When a nation of 1.3 billion chooses a new direction, the world must feel it. A vast number of young Chinese desire an entrepreneurial life; even many retired people are eager to try it out.

Such things would be contrary to the wildest imagination only 30 years ago. When I was growing up in the 1970s, China was completely different. At that time, the very best students pursued mathematics and science. Becoming an engineer or scientist was deemed glorious. Scoring high in mathematics and science would immediately invite admiring smiles from your female classmates. But life has changed now, and the focus is more on wealth-related activities.

Today, many of the brightest kids have different goals. They want to become a boss. The most popular words now are Gates and Soros. Nobody knows how many students write about such goals in their diaries. How exciting it is to be a kid living in China today!

And there is more: Time has become more valuable than ever before. A huge poster hangs in a major square in Shenzhen: "Time is Life! Empty Talks Destroy Prosperity!" That is how the Chinese feel and act now.

Naturally, all foreign businesspeople are determined to share in China's progress. Naturally, they are tightly hooked into China. How can anyone keep out the Nike, Coke, and McDonald's people if a nation of 1.3 billion loves their products? This itself shows the nature of global business. A regional boom belongs to the entire world.

In May 2003, one event caught media attention. It had to do with allowing selected foreign investors to trade in the Chinese stock market along with

Chinese. This was certainly a big step taken to link China's financial market to the outside world.

To the disappointment of many banks, only two foreign investors were selected as first announced in the spring of 2003. Their names were Nomura and UBS, and these bankers must have felt lucky. Being in China first meant more clients for them to acquire, which would translate into more profits as well. This small setback for competition banks must have produced many phone calls from New York, London, and Tokyo to their China representatives: Why are we behind?

Government officials love to see competition. The more players fight with each other, the more important the officials become. Humans are about the same everywhere. Bureaucrats, big and small, all enjoy being important. How could Beijing be different?

Given all this, many foreign businesspeople are determined to make it big over here. They have tried hard to become influential players in this far corner. By early 2005, 27 global investment brands had acquired licenses to trade. They have brought more than $3.6 billion in cash with which to play.

Naturally, these investment banks are never satisfied. They all desire to do more. They see gold mines in the Chinese financial market. In addition, there are vast opportunities for hot IPOs, as most Chinese companies are eager to get listed in the international stock markets. In all ways, becoming a leading player in China could double their profits. Despite regulatory concerns, they have been letting everyone of importance in Beijing know their intentions. These developments have been gathering steam over time.[27]

SPOUSES AND CHILDREN

Millions of foreigners now reside in China. This has given China a new flavor. In greater Shanghai, there are around 40,000 Japanese citizens.[28] But it is not just the Japanese—foreigners come from around the globe. All major cities have set up services to take care of their needs. There are all sorts of new service centers tailored to meet such needs. These are not just the usual business services for businesspeople. They are also aimed at helping the children and families.

With countless foreign kids in China, their education has become a new business. There are many creative solutions. Numerous special schools have emerged. Such schools teach in English and other foreign languages. They usually have higher fees. They have also attracted many well-to-do Chinese families who compete to send their children to these schools to gain an international experience.

Everywhere, businesspeople are smarter than just about anyone else. The Chinese are no different. They have been inventive in attracting foreign guests. One Beijing businessman has created an entertainment house: The traditional roasted Peking duck is served on the table while the Peking opera singers perform, singing and dancing on the stage. Business has been terribly good, as the establishment has become a must-see for many foreign guests.

WELCOME!

The word "welcome" has become most popular. The Chinese people are truly delighted to have all foreign nationals come. Deep down, they are aware that China is moving in the right direction. This is the very first time in recent history that China has made gains in a global context. It is exciting that great human interactions are going on. This is the most positive aspect of globalization. No one is happier about it than the Chinese.

Today, millions of foreign nationals live and work in China. Beijing alone has more than 100,000 foreign nationals. Many work for international companies; some study or teach in the local schools and universities. Increasingly, many foreigners work for Chinese companies. Often they can get higher positions than at home. China's businesses, educational units, and government agencies have an ever-increasing demand for foreign professionals. Their pay is always higher than the local standards.

In 2001, some 446,000 professionals from about 80 foreign countries and regions (including Hong Kong and Taiwan) were working for Chinese employers. About 42% of these worked for more than a half year. They were employed by either business organizations, governmental units, or educational centers. They became part of a new China.[29]

More interesting developments in this direction have occurred. Numerous regional governments such as Guangdong, Shanghai, Tianjin, and Beijing have tried hard to widen channels of communication with the outside world. In particular, they have created international advisory boards. They invite numerous foreign CEOs, researchers, and experts to be their advisors. Regular meetings are held, and these foreign advisors love to offer suggestions. Their comments are usually widely reported in the media.[30]

Such foreign involvement has added color to Chinese life. The foreigners bring all kinds of dreams and ideas here. They help China become more open and international in many ways. All in all, China's new development has involved the entire world. What is most impressive is this: All such progress has taken place within a short time.

2 CREATION OF A GLOBAL MANUFACTURING CENTER

This is a very creative era for China. The nation has become a highly dynamic and vibrant place as if overnight. One most unexpected outcome is the existence of a new manufacturing center, coming to life seemingly from nowhere.

STOCK MARKET WITH NO CHARTER

Events in China tend to happen in somewhat the same way the stock market did. The stock market was in operation for five years before a legal charter was introduced. At only about 14 years old, the stock market has involved the entire society with 71 million investment accounts. Some people say that if it had required a charter in the first place, they would have had to wait many years for its birth.

Moving China forward will demand much more. An old Chinese saying goes, "Things one dearly wishes for never occur, while things nobody expects do happen." The development of China as a manufacturing center has been more by accident than by design.

Arrival of Indian Companies

There are many countries with a labor pool cheaper than China's. Nevertheless, foreign multinationals see many advantages to being in the Chinese market. Even thousands of Indian businesspeople are here.

Highly attractive to the Indian businesspeople is the fact that China is not only a huge market, but also a business center. It is a place where all the industrial parts and components makers are concentrated. Moreover, quality is increasingly measured by international standards. This creates a favorable environment for manufacturers in particular. India's labor is cheaper than China's, but already numerous Indian manufacturers have come to China. Many Indian companies have set up factories or are planning to move over soon.

Strange? To be certain, the Indian businesspeople are among the cleverest people around. Rarely are they willing to take risks, and they do their homework carefully before they come. One Indian manager said that it is more convenient to operate a factory in China than back home in India.[1]

Doing business in China has other advantages. For many businesses, the herd mentality plays a role. Businesses go where their competitors go. Taking part in a fast-developing China may offer benefits. So these Indian companies, with the hope of reaching global markets, have first set up factories and shops in China.

One Indian company is more deeply involved in China than others. This company produces Internet televisions and other electronics goodies. Setting up a plant in China has meant many things for the company. The number-one reason for starting up in China is that China already has the market. China is developing fast, and the Indian products can be sold to the Chinese consumers.

The second reason is that producing such items is more convenient and cheaper in China than in India. There are more parts suppliers in China. Quality can be better ensured as well. There is a strategic aspect also: When the Indian market is ready, companies can expand back home.[2]

A manufacturing center requires many elements. Lacking any of these elements, it will not work. China has already established vast business chains. It has all the key ingredients that make a manufacturing center effective and attractive to all participants. Most strikingly, as already mentioned, the center has come to life more by accident than by design. Like trees and grass, it thrives on its own merits.

A strong feature of China as a new manufacturing center is that it has directly involved global markets. Its emergence is very different from that of Japan as a world business center. Japan's development has been largely a Japanese play. For China, the entire world has been involved directly.

ONE U.S. BANKER'S DISCOVERY

On one business trip, a U.S. investment banker and I traveled together. My colleague had been in Tokyo for many years. The place we went to see was Wuxi, a city about two hours west of Shanghai. This was his first trip to China. His eyes were very busy. A few minutes after we entered the city, many small shops showed up along the roads. His eyes opened wide: "Look how many tiny shops! This is quite unthinkable in Japan."

"Why?" I was curious.

"The Japanese only want to work for big companies and hardly anyone wants to venture out by himself."

"Why so?"

"The Japanese are very diligent people, but they really aren't willing to take risks. They are afraid to venture out on their own. They prefer to team up together. They feel that is the way for them to succeed. Obviously, the Chinese are more adventurous."

"Well, the Chinese must venture out on their own. They have no choice."

New entrepreneurs are not just in Wuxi, but everywhere. There are nearly 40 million today. Once they were free to pursue independent interests, they displayed the true colors of entrepreneurship. They have changed many things in China already.

One Chinese researcher said to me, "Deep inside, the Chinese are true entrepreneurs. But they need a fair space to gain development."

True, the Chinese people need a more liberal environment so that their creative energy can be properly employed. China's reform has lifted countless man-made barriers up to now. As if overnight, tens of millions of entrepreneurs have shot up like wildflowers.

Tens of Millions of New Businesspeople

The rise of private businesspeople in China is one of the most dramatic developments occurring today. It has produced vast changes. The influence of this group can be felt thousands of miles away. Many of the made-in-China products are produced by this group.

They come from all sectors of the society, especially the lowest levels. By the end of 2002, about 24 million independent vendors were in existence. Each employed about two people on average. There were about 2.5 million private companies in total. Each of these employed about 14 people on average.[3] By now, there are around 40 million private businesspeople, who employ nearly 50 million people, 25% of China's non-farm workforce.

In many small cities and rural regions, the private sector has become the leading player. In many cases the private sector has taken a giant step forward at the expense of the state sector. Countless state companies are gone by now.

In Wenzhou, Zhejiang, innumerable farmers have become new businesspeople. They have invented many trading platforms, selling items from buttons to toys to clothes and machinery. Buttons, especially, are an enormous business.[4]

Now, almost every industry involves private businesses unless it is one of those covered by an entrance ban. Some key sectors such as telecom, postal, rails, and banking are still off limits. Even so, private businesses deal in most things under the sun. They are most visible in the manufacturing, retail, construction, and service sectors.

To date, these are mostly small businesses. The biggest companies are still in the state sector. The four state banks, two oil and petrochemical companies, and several telecom operators are already in the global 500 club. As of now, China has 15 companies in the club; they are all in the state sector (see chapter 10).

Small does not mean insignificant. The significance of private businesses is in their vast numbers and in the fact that private businesspeople are willing to take risks. They are full of the "can-do spirit." Otherwise, their businesses could not have come to life.

Most new businesses started with tiny things. Almost all high-profile entrepreneurs of today had humble beginnings. They were empty handed when they tried to venture out. They had to sell their furniture and watches to raise seed money, mostly relying on the extended family network. There are plenty of rags-to-riches stories. These businesspeople are making history in their own way. Together, they have opened a new chapter for the nation and beyond.

In the initial stage, in the late 1970s and the 1980s, the rural regions achieved more freedom ahead of the urban regions. Today farmers have much more freedom than before. They became the first group of new businesspeople.

Relatively speaking, urban changes have taken more time to develop. People in the cities have the highest salaries. It is difficult for them to drop these jobs to venture into the unknown. Rural people have less to lose. Interestingly, rural China was first to embrace the new commercial wave. As a result, tens of millions of farmers have become businesspeople. As a group they have unique characteristics. Most have limited business experience and little education. They have been learning along the way. Naturally, failures are common.

BUTTONS CREATE A NEW INDUSTRIAL TOWN

Big events often happen in unexpected ways. Who could have anticipated that tens of millions of small vendors in China would help to create the new business center? Yet this is what happened.

In many coastal regions, new businesses jump out of the ground like mushrooms. In some villages and towns, hundreds of small businesses focus on making items such as buttons. Buttons are small, but everybody needs them. Making buttons has transformed many rural families into urban entrepreneurs. In the process, many people have become millionaires. A number of rural towns in the province of Zhejiang are leading the way. They have produced millions of entrepreneurs in all business sectors.

The biggest button market is in the city of Wenzhen. This once-small rural town has become a vibrant business center. The button manufacturing and marketing began with two brothers. In 1979, while the brothers were traveling, they found some bags of discarded buttons. They brought the buttons back to Wenzhou and sold them at a place called Qiaotou. On making a profit, they set out to manufacture buttons themselves.[5]

Business boomed. Quick profits created excitement in the villages nearby. All the neighbors started to manufacture buttons. Very soon, many villages joined in. Gradually, such businesses went beyond their immediate region. Production outpaced the needs of the businesspeople in the surrounding regions and it was necessary to go out to find more buyers.

These marketing efforts have reached all China. They have also reached the overseas markets. Buttons offered in these markets are the cheapest anywhere around the globe.

Now the Qiaotou button market is the biggest market of its kind in China. Currently it takes about 60% market share. The thousands of suppliers there have also attracted buyers from overseas. Many clients come from places as far away as Latin America and Africa. Buttons have become an industry of $314 million.[6]

Businesses are naturally contagious. The button suppliers have extended their service to the bigger business chain of the fashion industry. They have tried hard to protect their businesses. One way is to offer the lowest possible price. By doing so, the suppliers can increase their market share and create barriers for other players who are trying to make entry into this business. The button business has become a big business on the local level.[7]

In Wenzhou, the button industry is only one bright story. In fact, Wenzhou is home to a vibrant private sector. Tens of thousands of private businesses dominate the local economy. They are best known for producing all sorts of consumer products. In the 20 years following the reform, the size of the private sector grew 251 times. Its influence has gone well beyond the immediate region.[8] Its products have reached around the globe.

Today, China is being taken over by the great waves of private initiatives. As a direct result, countless rural villages have become new industrial towns. These developments have rapidly changed China from a traditional farming society into a modern industrial and commercial society. Just as significantly, the private sector has become a leading force in wealth creation.

JINJIANG, FUJIAN: BIGGEST EXPORTING CENTER FOR SPORT SHOES

Jinjiang is a little-known city in the coastal province of Fujian. It has become the biggest export center for sport shoes.[9] The city now has some 3,000 shoe makers. More than 10 nationally known brands are located there. They employ some 350,000 workers and produce more than 500 million pairs annually.

These products have reached the global markets. The companies have more than 200 international offices. They have direct links with more than 50 countries. They have recently set up a shopping center in Hungary.

In addition, this new industrial city is a major center for making clothes, zippers, and toys. Its development is partly the result of outside investments. There are numerous Taiwanese businesspeople in the city, since it is close to Taiwan. To date, about $352 million in investments has come from Taiwan.

Interestingly enough, many export-oriented companies have expanded their businesses along the way. They make many other consumer goods, especially clothes. Some have become active in marketing products within China as well. This has brought additional benefits—more profits at home.[10]

RAPID DEVELOPMENT DRIVEN BY SHORTAGES

China's fast-improving living standards have surprised not just outsiders, but also the Chinese. Foreigners often ask me, "What is the biggest driving force in China today?" My answer is consumption. China had a shortage-ridden economy for a long time. Shortage can be a powerful engine in a new environment.

How much has China changed? Older citizens remember the empty shops in the old days. In the Mao era, everyone needed a bike to go to work. Yet one had to fight to buy a bike. Things like simple medicines were almost out of reach. These types of shortages were produced by an economy that was government centered for many decades.

I nearly fell victim to this shortage-ridden economy. At the age of one, in 1962, I got meningitis. Around that time, after three year-long periods of starvation, things had begun to improve. As a top 10 city, Xian had many large hospitals. But they did not have sufficient pharmaceutical products. There were hardly any antibiotics available. A couple of large hospitals refused to take me in on the grounds that I was too ill to be cured. Some doctors even suggested that my mother stop feeding me. My parents did not follow their suggestions. They continued to try to get help. Finally I was taken in by one hospital—Xian Children's Hospital. I was given injections of salt and glucose only. Fortunately, I soon returned to health.

Since the mid-1990s, China's shortage-ridden market has finally turned around. The situation is now the opposite: Supply has exceeded demand for most manufactured goods for the first time in recent history. Certainly the old shortage environment paved the way for this reversal.

Looking back, one is easily impressed by the vast new development. Market needs have been growing along with the rapidly rising income. All this has created a huge space for new businesses to grow in.

By now, millions of businesses exist to serve market needs. This is instead of government—a thing of the past—and represents a change in history. These new businesses have helped to form complete new business chains. In the process, they have taken full advantage.

China's new engagement with the outside world has become another powerful engine. Foreign companies have added much to the business chains. With their involvement, China is able to produce the cheapest products for the world markets today. What is most surprising is that this has happened within such a short time.

Among all products, the durable products and consumer electronics have been the most strikingly successful. In this sector, China has created numerous consumption records.

All things considered, foreign companies have played an impressive role. They have been most effective in integrating China into the global economy. They have been most significant in distributing products to the outside markets. Wal-Mart alone spent about $18 billion in 2004. Philips had $9 billion in China business. Both LG and Siemens reached $10 billion or more. By 2004, China had surpassed Japan in trade. But it came out in a natural way.

What has China really gained so far? It is already the biggest producer for some 100 manufactured goods, covering numerous industries from chemicals to home appliances and electronics to household products. In 2003 alone, China produced 65 million TV sets, 22 million air conditioners, and 180 million handsets.[11]

All this business has involved foreign parties by the hundreds of thousands. Many products are manufactured by international operations or joint ventures. For example, tens of millions of cameras are produced by the Japanese and Korean factories over here. These products are sold globally.

China has become a manufacturing center for the cheapest products in the biggest volume. Though the center is still in its very beginning stages, it can only grow, as the benefits extend well beyond China. Many new business phenomena are being propelled by their own merits.

BUSINESS ELEMENTS, STRONG AND WEAK

China's expanded economy demands all kinds of participants. To be sure, to make huge business chains work, each and every element must be present. One element is the suppliers of parts and components. There are countless numbers of these now. The story in China is different for other elements, particularly technology.

Innumerable plants have shot up like bamboo trees. They operate around the clock. Their services are highly competitive, even by international standards. They can ship out any product you want at any time.

Most Chinese businesspeople are still weak. They must rely on the oldest trick: hard work. This is necessary especially considering that China's commerce is in its very beginning stages. Moving to higher levels will take much more time.

International behemoths such as GE have more choices. GE does not want to engage in business that returns less than 10%. The Chinese players do not have this luxury. In many ways, Chinese CEOs have to work harder and smarter than international CEOs such as Jack Welch. Foreign companies may not succeed here as the Chinese do with the same resources.

Chinese companies continue to be seriously lacking in numerous business elements. One of the biggest is cutting-edge technology. The lack of essential technologies has become a bottleneck for the economy.[12]

Examples are plentiful. China is the biggest TV producer in the world, yet most value-added parts come from international suppliers. These components are controlled by Texas Instruments, Philips, LG, and numerous Japanese companies.

This technological gap has created tremendous disadvantages for China Inc. Indeed, the dominant positions of the United States and Japan rely mostly on their rich intellectual knowledge. China Inc. has made tremendous progress, especially in the manufacturing sector. But it has a long way to go to catch up in technological development.

Nevertheless, China's fast-expanding manufacturing capability has made a huge difference already. For example, India does not have the booming manufacturing industry that China has. I asked one Indian businessman why. He replied, "It takes tremendous time and effort to build a factory. To Indians, it is easier to trade products. So we have more trading companies than manufacturers." But the Chinese businesspeople love to build factories. At the same time, their trading skills are improving as well.

China is now a leader in producing motorcycles. In 2002, China produced 12.36 million motorcycles, some 50% of global production. There are more than 100 Chinese motorcycle manufacturers. They don't yet own key technologies. This has created major difficulties for them.[13]

The chairman of TCL feels his company's limitations in numerous ways. The company's goal is to become a Chinese Sony or Samsung. Getting there will not be easy. The chairman is well aware that his company is far behind in intellectual development, with the consequence that it must follow the technical standards set by a few international companies. This gap creates tremendous limitations for the company. "Even if we achieve high volumes, we are still confronted with problems to reach higher."[14]

One person's shortage often becomes another's opportunity. China Inc.'s lack of intellectual products has created opportunities for global players. They have all rushed in to sell technology and chips. Naturally, they can make more profits than the Chinese manufacturers.

Slow intellectual development has limited China Inc. in significant ways. The Chinese businesspeople are certainly aware of their weaknesses. One executive describes the situation many Chinese companies face now: "Businesses would die if they have no basic research and development program; they would look for death if they do."[15] This is the conundrum posed by China's shortage of technology.

A CROWDED MARKET

The new business chains are already vast. China's resources, especially in the manufacturing sector, are on bright display. But by all standards, competition is most formidable.

At the same time, all businesses, foreign or domestic, are in the same boat as never before. They must increasingly rely on each other to make chains work. Making this business hub function has involved most nations, if not all.

On the supply side, very interesting developments have taken place. As in any other market, no player can truly dominate. In each and every business sector, there are numerous competing parties. In short, China has become both a global market and a world factory. Newcomers are shocked to see how crowded the market already is.

For some time before the mid-1990s, a number of overseas companies brought out-of-date technology to China. Some sold it successfully. Today this is no longer possible. Even with the best technology and products, many companies cannot be successful. There are just too many players in every sector. This is a significant aspect of the Chinese theater.

With all the players fighting in one market, reactions are bound to occur. As one result, the end-product players have experienced considerable development. It has become easy to produce end-products.

Surely enough, the traditional domination by a few brands is decreasing around the globe. Most products can be produced in numerous countries. It no longer takes much effort to set up a factory to make products of any sort. For example, it doesn't take much effort to create an air-conditioning manufacturing facility. China now has some 400 makers of air conditioners.

恓恓

One Chinese company has walked a unique path and stands above the crowd: Galanz. Galanz is a private company based in Guangdong. For well over a decade it has focused on producing microwave ovens. Like the personal computer for Dell, the microwave oven has until recently been Galanz's key product.

Galanz is already the biggest global microwave oven maker, with around a 40% share. The company's strength lies in its concentration and cheap cost structure. Its strategy is to make the cheapest products without sacrificing quality. Pricing competitiveness has made Galanz the leader not only in China, but also globally. In the past there were hundreds of small domestic players. Most of them are gone now. Even some international players have stopped selling microwave ovens in China.

Galanz's pricing advantage has also attracted numerous international players. If it takes $90 to produce a microwave in the United States or Europe, it takes only $30 for Galanz to do so. At the same time, Galanz can meet all client requirements, including quality, timing, and delivery. Thus has Galanz made itself "the manufacturer of the world," as its slogan goes. About two thirds of its products are targeted at outside markets[16] (see chapter 10).

CONVENIENT SETTINGS

China has become a new wonderland for global business. A remarkable element of the recent progress is a fast-improving infrastructure. By now China has constructed some 30,000 kilometers of highways and roads. All ports operate around the clock. They have become an integral part of the new business chains.

Over the years, ports in Hong Kong played a key role in linking China to the outside world. For many decades, most international trade with China went through these ports. This has started to change.

Rapid development has given rise to numerous new ports. Ports in places like Shenzhen, Tianjin, and Shanghai have become significant. Among other factors, pricing and efficiency are key.

The mainland ports have numerous advantages over Hong Kong now. Outstanding among these are tremendous pricing advantages and time efficiency. Charges at the mainland ports may be 40% cheaper or less. In Shenzhen, which borders Hong Kong, handling a container may be $230 cheaper than in Hong Kong.[17]

Moreover, the mainland ports are closer to the users. Also, much effort and time are saved in not having to deal with border crossing. Clients can avoid the complex paperwork between Hong Kong and the mainland.

These advantages have already altered the shipping map in the region. But the Hong Kong-based shipping players have choices. For example, they can easily expand into the mainland. This is what the Hong Kong-based company Hutchinson has done. It has been active in buying into major ports on the mainland. In so doing, it has been able to remain a leading global shipping player.

All such necessary services have effectively helped the business chains. Significantly, these things have been developing naturally. With all participating players, both domestic and international, China has greatly expanded its economic sphere. This extensive global involvement has become a top strength behind China as a new manufacturing center. Indeed it is a marvel that China has built this new business center so quickly.

INGREDIENTS OF A MANUFACTURING CENTER

To be sure, a business chain requires not only products and capital, but much more. It demands active participants, efficient organizations, an extensive distribution network, and responsible business partners, among other things. Effectiveness is harmed if any single element is missing.

China is becoming a global manufacturing hub. No planner could have invented the business chains that now exist. All of these things have emerged in the marketplace, naturally and accidentally.

Building a tower takes millions of tiny things. It is these tiny elements that produce a big tower: China is becoming a huge manufacturing center for the globe. By 2004, China had surpassed Japan in trade.[18] This new status has had everything to do with the new hub that China has become.

EXPLOSIVE GROWTH IN CONSUMPTION

China's consumption growth is extremely impressive. It has changed this once poverty-stricken land beyond imagination. And consumption will create more changes in China and beyond.

It is consumption that shapes the market in any nation. It happened in the United Kingdom some 200 years ago and in the United States 100 years ago. It is happening in China now, though in a different context. As one example, drug retail chains have existed in United States for some 70 years. In China, they have been around for only 10 years.[19]

In 2003, China added 95.45 million phone users, both wireless and wired.[20] In the 1970s, China had very few phones, and most citizens never used them. Even in the big cities, only institutions, shops, and factories had phones. Back then, phones used only five digits. But that era exists only in memory. By the end of 2004, there were some 314 million wired phones in China. By now all cities have upgraded to seven or eight phone digits. Wireless handsets use 11 digits. Having a vast population can have vast advantages.

The number of handset users is even larger—by 2007 it will be at least 500 million. This industry is the hottest business in China at the moment. There are more than 40 licensed players, as well as additional players in the form of OEMs or other specialized types of companies.

Naturally, competition is very intense. Tens of billions of dollars are involved. Though the Chinese companies began to manufacture mobile phones only in 1998, they have shown strong growth. In 1999, they had a market share of around 3%, but by 2003 they had over 50%. By 2003, some Chinese players had overtaken Motorola and Nokia. Ningbo Bird was a leading challenger. In 2003, the company surpassed both Motorola and Nokia to become number one. In 2004, another Chinese concern, TCL, overtook Ningbo Bird. Currently TCL is seventh in the world in the mobile sector. But also in 2004, Nokia retook the number-one position with $3.3 billion in goods sold in China and $3.6 billion in exports.

Who will become next year's winner? It is hard to say. This simply shows how hot the competition is in China today.

The competition is hot in all industries, not just the mobile phone sector. No business player, foreign or domestic, can be certain of future outcomes. The Chinese market changes more quickly than most in the outside world— so fast that no one can be sure who the winners will be.

FUTURE TRENDS

The new business center that is China has come into existence as something of an accident, but it is reaching a more rational level. However, there is no established model for China to copy directly. So far, things have been moving forward on a trial-and-error basis.

Most significantly, this center has directly involved global business. It turns out that one of the most powerful links between China and the global market is this new hub that brings capital, people, technology, goods, and ideas together. Yet its development is only beginning and can only grow. It may take less time to move to higher levels than one might think. The process is unavoidable. New phenomena that meet needs have a momentum of their own. Because of this, "International Inc." will become even more significant.

This center is highly expandable as well. Players are adding new elements with the hope of getting more out of it. Also, new technology can show up in China at almost the same time as anywhere else.

Furthermore, the center has changed China's domestic market into an international market. It has thus helped China become more open. In fact, China is now more open and more dynamic than many nations, such as Japan. At the same time, it is becoming more competitive.

It is worth noting here that the great benefits to all participating parties will hardly decrease as a result of the 2% increase in the exchange rate for the yuan announced in late July of 2005. In fact, in many ways, an increased yuan value could help China become more competitive and more efficiency driven in the long fun.[21]

All the effects associated with the center have just begun to occur. There is huge room for improvement. At the same time, growth will bring a greater interaction of ideas, standards, and human beings coming from everywhere around globe. The center is like a plant that has all the water, sunshine, and nutrients it needs in order to grow.

3 ALL PLAYERS ARE IMPORTANT

Today China is the biggest new frontier for international companies. In many ways, the Chinese market has a more international flavor than many other markets around the globe. Many unique characteristics have evolved along the way. Countless international businesspeople are singing their favorite songs and doing their traditional dances—all in one theater. So far, some have danced better than others.

Up to now, the "Overseas Chinese Inc." has been the biggest investor in Mainland China. The United States is in second position, followed by Japan and numerous European nations and South Korea.

Businesses from Hong Kong had an early start. Most if not all of the factories in Hong Kong have moved over the border. Today, about 240,000 Hong Kong residents work and live in China.[1] Their employers are mostly small and midsize companies. They mostly focus on low-end consumer products. Their strengths are best shown in their vast numbers.

China's expanding market has created tremendous opportunities for the global giants, especially in capital-intensive and high-tech sectors. These giants have made a huge difference in connecting China to the global markets.

Overall, on a global basis, the U.S. companies as a group are the biggest. The power of the United States is the most influential in many markets. In China as of now, U.S. players are just one among many foreign business groups.

Relatively speaking, the Koreans are more active today than the Americans. To the Koreans, coming to China is a necessity, for their home market is small. They aim to use China as a new engine for growth. But the U.S. companies have a huge market at home. They are less willing to venture out. Except for a few large players and high-tech companies, most sizable American companies have only 10% or less international business. This is quite different from the situation for many leading companies in Europe, Japan, and South Korea. They may have much bigger international sales than their U.S. counterparts.

In China, many Korean companies have been latecomers in relation to Japanese and Western companies. But they have made great strides. Several are already household names, especially LG, Hyundai, and Samsung.

LG has been a star performer. By 2003, LG had invested $2.4 billion in China. The company has become a leader in the consumer electronics and home appliances sector. Its China business reached $8 billion in 2003 and $10 billion in 2004.[2] LG is still expanding its investment programs and hoping to make China its second home.

Samsung is another success story. Its product lines—semiconductors, mobile phones, consumer electronics, and home appliances—fit China's needs.[3] By now Samsung has transferred most of its personal computer manufacturing to China.

What underlies the success of Korean companies is a combination of good timing and the right products. Above all, the Koreans are committed to China for the long term. The Korean success has inspired envy among international competitors.

In fact, Korean companies now treat China as their own production center as well as a big market. The average monthly salary for a manufacturing job is $1,524 in Korea, but only $115 in China.[4] In addition, China is a huge market, much bigger than Korea—something the Korean companies cannot ignore. They intend to move most of their production from Korea to China, increasing the efficiency and profitability of expanding around the globe.[5]

It seems that the Korean giant Samsung has found jade in China. Samsung intends to make China its biggest market, hoping to reach $14 billion in sales by 2005. To this end the company has been adding new programs. This has already made Samsung a leader in China. The Korean giant will become even more powerful, for it has found a big space in China.

How do Chinese consumers view foreign players in general? They seem to pay less attention to national origins than one might think. In many ways, they are rather indifferent to nationality. To consumers, all the foreign players are important.

In the auto market, all the American players are in China today. As is true internationally, GM and Ford are only two players among many in China. The largest player so far is Volkswagen. Volkswagen has been operating in China since 1985. But GM set up its Shanghai joint venture only in the late 1990s. Volkswagen has kept its leadership role by expanding its programs and adding joint ventures. In Volkswagen's global sales, China now accounts for about 20%. Volkswagen is adding 10 billion euros and wishes to make China a center of its global business.[6]

Moreover, GM confronts numerous competing players in its price range. Honda and Toyota are two of these. Korea's Hyundai landed in China in 2002. Hyundai hopes to make China its biggest market and is now in a hurry to achieve this goal. So far, progress has been huge. In 2004, Hyundai sold 150,000 cars in China, making it one of the top four car makers here. Another U.S. giant, Ford, does not want to be left behind. Its most recent project was to build an auto factory in Nanjing in partnership with Japan's Mazda and a Chinese company. At the present time, all global auto players are busy. They expect China's auto market to reach 10 million by 2010, from 5.2 million in 2004.

All in all, China has become a new arena for global business. All multinationals have taken their unique roles. They are all important for now, and they all want to become even more important. In order to do so they must fight hard with one another, besides China Inc.

INTERNATIONAL BANKS

In the banking sector, there have been numerous restrictions for foreign banks up to now. Even so, many international players are eager to establish a foothold. Since late 2004, because of the WTO accord, lifting of these restrictions has begun.

There are numerous international banks active today. Both Citibank and HSBC are aggressive players. They are competing with each other head-on. Nobody wants to be behind. Both banks are trying to bring their entire business lines over. Their eagerness and ambition are matched only by the degree of surprise on the part of the Chinese banks. Both players are household names already.

One strategy for both banks is to buy into China. In particular, Citibank bought a small stake in a small retail bank in Shanghai, the Pudong

Development Bank. The time was January 2003.[7] Citibank is also involved in buying nonperforming bank loans, among other things.

But HSBC had already done several deals. One was a minority stake in a small retail bank, the Commerce Bank of Shanghai. The other deal was bigger: a $600 million investment for a 10% stake in the second largest Chinese insurance company, Pin An Insurance. HSBC has recently become even more active. In late 2004, it took 19.9% stake in China's fifth largest bank, China Communication Bank. Between 2001 and 2004, HSBC had spent $2.7 billion buying into Chinese financial assets. To the Chinese public, HSBC seems ambitious and aims to build a financial megastore inside China.[8] China was HSBC's birthplace, and the company has tied its fortunes to greater China in a big way for well over a century. Now it is trying to double its fortunes in a hurry.

Naturally, many competing banks have taken similar actions. The herd mentality plays a big role. More international banks are trying to tap into the enticing Chinese market. One popular strategy is to buy stakes in Chinese banks, which is the quickest way to get established. The executives are busy visiting potential targets.

In investment banking, even bigger international crowds are already here. All the global investment houses are active, but nobody dominates the market. So far, the European houses have been as active as the U.S. ones. Building up a China business is a passion for them all, one that could translate into fat profits. These companies understand better than some others that a rising economy must produce giant opportunities. For example, just helping Chinese companies get listed in the overseas capital markets will generate fat profits.

Often it is the Chinese who select international investment houses to make deals with. This is partly because China's government wishes to have all the brokers come but does not wish any of them to dominate the deal flows. In particular, one broker would never be allowed to take all the hot IPO deals. So far, this has worked well. The international brokers must fight with each other for the most attractive opportunities.

INTERNATIONAL LISTINGS

One strong interest on the part of China Inc. is to enter the international capital markets. New York is now the global financial center that gets the most attention from China Inc. From this standpoint, the U.S. and global brokerages have an edge. Naturally, the U.S. investment banks face strong competition from the rest of the crowd. They are all interested in making profits by enlisting Chinese assets in overseas markets.

So far, numerous leading members of China Inc. have been listed in New York. These include China Mobile, China Unicom, China Life, Sinochem, and PetroChina. The company with the biggest listing so far is China Unicom, the second largest Chinese mobile phone operator, which raised some $5 billion in New York and Hong Kong.

New York remains a favorite choice. To the Chinese, raising capital from the international capital markets, especially New York, is considered a high honor. If international investors are willing to buy their shares, they must be doing something right. This adds much to credibility at home as well.

Up to now, Hong Kong is the most significant capital market for China Inc. outside the mainland. More than 300 mainland-based Chinese companies are listed there. Together, they have raised more than $115 billion.

So far, the Chinese companies are much less knowledgeable about the European and other financial markets. These regions also want to deal with Chinese companies and hope to get them listed on their trading floors. Business officials from numerous international financial capitals frequently come to China to attract potential Chinese clients. Up to now, New York and Hong Kong have remained the key choices. Singapore ranks as the third most popular choice, as more than 60 Chinese companies are listed there.

CONSUMER VIEWS

Basically, Chinese consumers treat all international companies equally, without trying to distinguish much as to their national identities. Consumers simply refer to all of them as foreign players.

As always, consumers today view international brands favorably. As long as products and services are of high quality and reasonably priced, they can be sold widely. The Koreans and Japanese may prefer domestic brands out of national feeling. The Chinese are very open in this respect.

In their daily lives, the Chinese consumers are more like U.S. consumers. To be sure, they are more global in their attitudes, which may surprise many foreigners. They buy countless foreign brands every day. They are generally interested in all things. One might say that the more foreign a product looks, the more eager the Chinese are to try it.

At this time, consumer taste is changing rapidly. In the past three decades, Chinese consumers have become more rational in many ways. Only the best products with reasonable prices can be sold. For a time in the past, consumers rushed to buy foreign brands almost regardless of these factors. Many foreign products have experienced a very short cycle from excitement to disappointment.

Some French liquor companies have had a great time for a number of years. For a while, XO bottles were the highlight of business gatherings. But now, they face more competitions from both domestic and international players.[9]

Consumers may favor international brands for many reasons. The key reason is their quality. This has gotten the multinational companies really excited. Some players even try to bump up price tags just to show that they are the best. Local players have quickly caught on to this trick. In one common situation, a shirt is selling in a shop for $5 and nobody wants it; then the price is raised to $50, and people buy. But the old shortage economy is a thing of the past. Today, merchants must fight hard to get consumers. Chinese shoppers are entering a stage of maturity.

4 LEARNING—A BIG INDUSTRY

China is now deeply caught up in the passion to create wealth. Gaining knowledge and professional training has become a national pastime. Learning is a hot industry as well.

DEMAND FOR EDUCATION

It is not just young students who are going to schools now. Continuing education and professional training attract all professionals and business executives. In a way, these people are competing with the young students to upgrade their knowledge. The fees can be unusually high, but professionals and executives are willing to pay.

Business education is new to China. There is a tremendous demand. People have a general conception, rightly or wrongly, that getting an MBA is a straightforward way to become a top business leader. This common desire has created a large opportunity for schools to make a healthy profit.

Many schools charge $6,000 or more for an MBA program. For an EMBA program, tuition can go as high as $30,000. In one case—in Shanghai—a school charges tuition of $40,000. Yet applicants are not lacking.[1] Many businesspeople feel that these programs can somehow pass along certain secret weapons. Naturally, some students may be disappointed. But still, many are more than willing to try. After all, not getting all the right information can be disastrous in the business world.

The market for an EMBA program will total more than $120 million over the next five years. It is little wonder that so many universities are competing with one another. Some top universities even demand that their students come from sizable companies—street vendors are not welcome.[2]

These fees are extraordinarily high especially when one considers the average income. On an income basis, China's education is much more expensive than in the United States and Europe. Yet applicants flood the top Chinese schools. Some classes are taught in English. Many businesses sponsor their top employees to attend these schools.

The Chinese students are known as hard workers. Some business management classes are taught in English. Many of the teachers have studied abroad. There are also numerous international teachers.

In these classes, the students are of widely differing ages and experience. The younger ones are in their twenties and the older ones in their fifties. Teaching these classes is not at all easy. The students can be very demanding. They are eager to get the best education. This can impose enormous burdens on teachers. Conflicts and problems have arisen from such strong desires. As an example, some students in one school demanded the removal of an international professor because he did not fulfill their expectations. It did not matter that he was doing his very best. The students felt and hoped that taking action would help them get the most from their educational experience.

Nowadays, dramatic changes in the business world make this new education a must. Many top business executives go back to school. In all major universities, special classes are designed to serve only general managers, CEOs, and chairmen. These classes are often offered in the evenings and on weekends. The students come from all regions of China.

In the classrooms, lively discussions are common. Interestingly enough, many case studies focus on global multinationals rather than Chinese companies at home. In a way, Chinese businesspeople know more about foreign companies than they do about the counterpart Chinese companies. In particular, many textbooks are authored by international experts.

In addition, a large number of foreign businesspeople, professors, and researchers are invited to give lectures and participate in special events. Usually the audience is large. Audiences are eager to learn any secrets the speaker may have to share. Somehow, many students feel that foreign businesspeople and experts have the most valuable secrets. The more experienced professionals and researchers realize that what they teach may not be directly applicable to China, for China faces different realities. There are really no ready recipes for immediate solutions to the problems China confronts today.

A Top School

Chinese learning institutions are eager to attract students. They have all been highly innovative. One top school in Beijing has designed very creative programs. The students are all chairmen, CEOs, and other top executives of Chinese companies.[3]

Program

Financial Markets
Strategic Management
…

Corporate Restructuring
Management Buyout
…

Venture Capital
Mergers and Acquisitions
IPOs at Home and Abroad
…

Students

Chairmen, Presidents, and Other Decision Makers

Aim
To help decision makers better understand modern management, especially through knowing financial and investment tools

Time

One year
Classes offered on two weekend days each month

This program has attracted immense interest. Even some businesspeople from Taiwan, Hong Kong, and Singapore, among other places overseas, have attended. In doing so, these overseas businesspeople hope to get to the powerful circles of the business community.

INTERNATIONAL INVOLVEMENT

China's educational demand is so high that it has attracted extensive international involvement. Many foreign institutions have been long established here. There are still some regulatory barriers. Even so, these institutions have made impressive progress. For now, they have a significant market share, especially in professional and vocational education.

Most international programs are offered through joint ventures. By 2002, China had about 712 international educational programs set up in this form. The international partners come from all over the world, but mostly from developed nations. Among the partners, 154 are from the United States, 40 from the United Kingdom, 58 from Japan, 12 from South Korea, 24 from France, and 14 from Germany.[4]

India's top software training and consulting concern, NIIT, is also active in China. Its chairman told me that he is very satisfied with his work in China. He hopes to add more locations and programs. Things are getting very interesting for India Inc. Many leading Indian IT companies are rushing over. Now that they have conquered the United States and Europe, China is their next target.

There are huge markets for all these parties. The success of the early players is generating more interest in the outside world. More and more educational organizations are coming. Interestingly enough, many lesser-known brands are more active than the famous brands. This may start to change, as many leading names can no longer sit still and watch others having a great time.

Many of the schools offer high-quality programs. They are attractive to Chinese students and professionals. Gaining an international education is viewed as a privilege. So these foreign schools have plenty of advantages.

But there are also cases in which programs and teaching quality are questionable. In fact, some who have joined the gold rush have abused the system. Schools have targeted millions of eager students. Getting a proper certificate is a high priority for young people and professionals. A foreign education certificate is certainly desirable. But there are also many reported abuses.

Recently, a newspaper investigated a particular foreign "university." It had been in China for some years and offered MBA programs. Hundreds of students had paid for the programs. But the reporters discovered that this operation was anything but a university.[5]

China's fresh experiences with the outside world have many facets. Despite a few rotten apples, China is excited about having all the foreign involvement. This popular desire underlies China's dreams to become a truly open society and an equal partner in the global community.

5 THE OFFICIALS' GLOBAL REACH

As never before, Chinese people are passionate to discover the outside world. They want to learn more about people elsewhere, their lifestyles, desires, and cultures, and especially about the way they think. The Chinese want firsthand experience above all. Countless Chinese are visiting other countries. They have quickly turned into popular global travelers.

OFFICIALS LEAD THE WAY

In this era, it is government officials who lead all the reform actions, including global traveling. They all enjoy seeing new places. Naturally, this has opened the door for the average citizen to travel as well—something that is clear to the global traveling industry.

Especially of late, the Chinese have taken the top position with regard to global traveling. Many countries want more Chinese visitors. Many foreign travel promoters are rushing to China. One major event took place in Beijing in August 2003. A large crowd of foreign officials and businesspeople came to promote travel.[1] They attracted huge numbers of people.

There are sound reasons for global travel on the part of government officials. Competition to attract international investment in all regions is high. Various regions compete with each other by providing the very best they possibly can. It is common for the officials to go abroad. They spend much time making business presentations and meeting potential investors, among other activities. This has become part of daily life for many Chinese officials today.

Before the mid-1990s, Chinese officials and businesspeople faced a difficult overall situation. They had few international connections. Very limited channels were available. This did not keep the Chinese officials from reaching out. But they had to rely on informal sources that might not be suitable by professional standards. If they didn't have the right contacts, they might get help from Chinese overseas.

Over the years, many managers of leading Chinese restaurants in New York's Chinatown have become good contacts. They have built relationships with numerous high-profile officials and businesspeople from China. There are many delightful stories about Chinese officials who have visited the United States.

An amusing incident occurred in New York in 1992, involving the top managers of Three-Gorge Dam. This project is easily one biggest investment project in the world, as it involves tens of billions of U.S. dollars. But the project needed extra capital, so the leaders went to New York, the financial capital of the world. Yet they did not know whom to talk with. In the end, they showed up at a retail investment seminar given by some stockbrokers who wanted to attract more retail clients.

Since then the situation has changed for the better. The role of these self-made middlemen is decreasing, as more direct contacts are in place. The Three-Gorge Dam leaders no longer meet with retail stockbrokers. Top international investment banks and multinationals flood their offices in large numbers. The only problem is, seemingly, how to keep some of them out.

In daily practice, these government officials are formidable figures in Chinese society. They are people who sit up high in the golden temples waiting to be entertained. In the view of the public they often act like demi-gods. It takes a tremendous effort for Chinese businesspeople just to meet them. Yet they love to meet foreign businesspeople. They are curious about what the foreign businesspeople desire. Accordingly, they want to do their best to meet foreign needs.

Such openness on the part of Chinese officials represents a significant change. It has made a vast difference in attracting investment from the outside. The officials have proven themselves as far as connecting China to the outside world is concerned, and China has gained more channels to the rest of the world.

These developments have made the Chinese businesspeople rather envious. Naturally, all regions within China work hard to improve their business environment. Regional competition has become a driving force in reforming China. It has had a direct impact toward creating a better environment in general.

Guangdong has experienced true development especially over the last three decades. For a long time before 1980, many inland cities, such as Xian, Wuhan, and Chengdu, were more advanced than Guangdong in investment generally. Today, it is the other way around. Guangdong has stepped ahead of all the other regions. Behind this achievement is the fact that Guangdong has obtained huge outside investments. These investments have come not only from overseas, but also from inland regions. Many Chinese companies in the inland regions have invested heavily in Guangdong. In particular, thousands of inland government units and agencies have created countless businesses in Guangdong. Innumerable office towers and hotels have inland names such as Anhui, Sichuan, Shanghai, Tibet, and Jiangsu.

In general, coastal development has been a step ahead, having relied on privileges granted by Beijing. Development on the coast has also created vast differences in development among the various regions of China.[2]

In general, there have been two major development stages. In the first stage, between 1979 and the early 1990s, Guangdong became China's frontier with respect to dealing with the outside world. Guangdong was able to attract investments from Hong Kong in particular. In the meantime, inland regions rushed there as well. This created new business centers in Shenzhen and Zhuhai.[3]

In the second stage, since 1993, China has become a hot destination for international multinationals and investors. Guangdong has attracted even more capital. As a result, it has become a commercial hub not only for China, but also for Asia.[4]

Many other regions have also made impressive progress. In some ways, Guangdong's role is no longer as significant as it was in the 1980s. In other ways, its significance has increased. Its export accounts for some 40% of China's export, for example.

The numerous rural towns of Guangdong have become vibrant business centers. Small old towns such as Shenzhen, Zhengdai, and Dongguan have all become major manufacturing centers for China and beyond. These new cities are flooded with foreign plants and offices. Their products are sent around the globe.

As far as business is concerned, Shanghai long ago lost its old glory. It was once the dominant manufacturer and supplier. This status has changed in the reform era. New industrial cities in Guangdong have emerged as highly popular manufacturing hubs. Moreover, these new industrial cities have gained global recognition. Goods produced there reach faraway markets. These cities are on the map of the global business world.[5] But many old factories in Shanghai are now in distress.

ABOLISHING BUREAUCRATIC TRICKS

Even with all the dramatic changes, China has yet to build a modern political-economic framework. Issues like modern property ownership and rights and wrongs in the markets are yet to be resolved. In this respect China is going through a painful transition today.

China has had strong bureaucratic domination over the ages. This tradition means that the government can lay down demands at will. Citizens are subject to government's demands concerning whatever they desire to do. Handling bureaucratic issues is the most onerous job for anyone in business.

This state of affairs is certainly nothing like that in the United States. The government has many tentacles. The decision-making power is largely held by the government. In the reform frontier city, Shenzhen, building a hotel requires 105 official approvals.[6]

Naturally, market dealings easily turn into bureaucratic dealings. All businesspeople want to gain true independent space. Yet the foreign companies have had more influence on the official world.

Shenzhen's new reform has this general background. Within, its businesspeople and residents demand to lift further the manmade barriers. Externally, it has countless competitors from other cities.

Shenzhen's old policy advantages are no longer as significant as they once were. Furthermore, it now faces rising salaries and high land prices, among other difficulties. Even in the immediate region, several much smaller cities that used to be rural towns have emerged as new manufacturing centers. They produce entire lines of products. They are especially strong in consumer electronics, home appliances, and clothes. Moreover, they have lower labor and land costs. Many new foreign players have chosen these small cities instead.

This is all worrisome to the Shenzhen officials. Also, there are lessons to be learned from the bordering city of Hong Kong. Hong Kong has lost much of its old vigor. In fact, it has not fully recovered following the collapse of its real estate and stock market in 1997. Shenzhen is eagerly learning from these lessons. Refusing to be another Hong Kong, the city is increasingly willing to move ahead by improving on its general environment. As a major measure, the city has reduced troublesome bureaucratic requirements. After two rounds of reform, its 1,100-odd approval demands were reduced to only 325.[7] In 2004, the city attempted the third round of reform, and the approval demands were further reduced to 239. This is still not enough in the eyes of many businesspeople and citizens. [8]

The city has an active international community. By now, more than $50 billion international money has been invested in the city. But many outside businesspeople are still dissatisfied with the countless bureaucratic hurdles, but few have directly raised their voices. Yet one business association from Taiwan came forward. It represents thousands of Taiwanese businesses in the region. The association was highly critical of the city's business environment, including a worsening investment environment, excessive governmental fees, and troublesome administrative demands. Such widespread complaints have worried the local officials. Through lengthy processes, the city government has been trying to gradually reduce its rules.[9]

To be sure, many inland regions are taking greater steps to move ahead. They view Shenzhen as a mere opportunist. What does it have that they don't have? Very little except privileges from Beijing. With these privileges, the city has been able to attract money from overseas. It has attracted even more money and resources from inside China. The combination of these factors has quickly built this booming city of more than 7 million residents as of today.

In the view of people inland, it is their turn now. They are increasingly confident that they can do better. In their opinion, the only difference is that Shenzhen has more private businesses and foreign investors. Therefore they are eager to follow the example.

This increased regional competition is very healthy for overall development. To show its commitment, the Shenzhen local government is now trying to sell more of the state sector companies under its control. But many inland cities are taking greater steps in this new direction. Many inland government officials wish to turn all their state sector companies into private companies. They are keen on this new effort and are already ahead of Shenzhen in this respect.[10]

At the same time, a broader reform is taking place in the inland region. In efforts to reduce bureaucratic rules, many inland cities are already trying hard to move ahead. This has created a lot of pressure on the Shenzhen government circle. Overall, its advantages are less visible today than a decade ago.

INTERNATIONAL FIRST

"Ladies first" holds true in many nations. In China today, it is "international first." This idea has many practical meanings. Suffice it to say that "international first" is a common mind-set.

In order to attract international businesses, all sorts of measures have been adopted. In many ways, international businesspeople are treated better than their domestic counterparts. This is against the principles of global norms. Yet the public has shown little surprise about it.

I often have opportunities to bring international businesspeople to China. We travel to various regions and meet officials and people in business. On one occasion we arrived in a major inland city and were received warmly by the local officials and businesspeople. Then we spent the next two days pursuing our activities.

The officials were eager to present the city in the best light. They talked about how much they had improved the investment environment in the city and about their sincere hope that the foreign guests would enable them to improve more. Their talk was no-nonsense, straight to the point. "Whatever you need to have success, we will try our best."

One of the factors the officials mentioned was the enormous efforts the local government had made to try to improve the investment environment in the city. The government had tried hard to increase efficiency and provide the best services possible. In particular, if an outsider player wanted to register a company, it would take only an hour or so.

All the services were picture perfect. Everything could be done within one building. All the relevant government agencies, the business administration, the tax bureau, the banks, the tariff department, the environmental control office, and the employment commission and many others were on one single floor. The new building was conveniently located as well.

Later, I asked a local businessman, "How long does it take a local person to register a company?" He smiled, "One month at least, and it all depends."

I asked, "How come they have to wait that long? Can't it be done in one hour in the same building?"

"No, that place is only for international players. All local businessmen must run around to different places all over the city."

"Why don't they use the Internet? With the Internet, these things can be done much quicker."

"Well, you don't understand the games here. The Internet destroys jobs. Jobs are in great demand, especially these government jobs."

What about jobs for the other 1.3 billion people? Would their lives be affected by these government jobs? After three decades of reform, China still lacks a mechanism for a cooperative relationship between government and business at large.

In Japan, there are strong ties between government and business. The Japanese government tries hard to assist businesses. In China, the relationship between the state and business is often problematic. Indeed, China's businesses must expend huge efforts to cope with bureaucratic obstructions.

Once I mentioned this issue to a Chinese researcher. He raised his voice: "How can you say that? Don't you know that the government can be highly efficient if it chooses to? It can be as efficient as any government anywhere!" Then, what is the problem?

In Shenzhen, the local government has recently set up an Internet registration system. Again, it is designed for the international players only. One month after its initiation in mid-June 2003, about 99 international companies had registered on the Internet. How about the local people? They must continue to go through all the ropes.[11]

In the eyes of Chinese businesspeople, their international counterparts are treated like royalty. Creating a friendly environment continues to demand a huge effort.

ᘏᕬ

Bringing in foreign investment has been a key strategy. For an emerging market like China, this certainly requires extraordinary effort. There are numerous tax breaks, among other things. In addition to many types of preferential treatment, Beijing is willing to do even more to accommodate the foreign needs.

China's government officials are eager to learn new tricks. In many ways, they have become masters at pleasing the preferred audience.

Spending public funds on traveling by government officials has constantly troubled the public. But it has also produced positive results. Chinese government officials have visited more foreign countries than anyone else. Such new experiences have helped to improve things at home significantly. Many Chinese critics claim that the officials waste big public money on their trips. In truth, these foreign travels can hardly be said to be without merit. In fact, many trips are well worth what they cost.

NEW YORK VERSUS BEIJING

Many benefits have followed from official trips, directly or indirectly. For example, many officials are impressed by the free access to Central Park in New York. They have brought home the idea of more free parks.

They are learning fast—faster than many school kids. Many new ideas have been transplanted to China from overseas. As one result, countless public parks are now open for free. Some cities have more free parks than others, maybe because the city officials have traveled more often. It is common now also for officials to compete to plant more trees. This must be partly a result of their global travel. At least in this regard, the travel money is well spent.

How big an impact has the outside world had on Chinese officials? It must be tremendous. In fact, the efficiency and competitive spirit of the international Inc. has deeply affected Chinese officials at home. In particular, the service style of McDonald's has impressed them. Many officials are improving upon the achievement of McDonald's.

In Beijing, the local officials are displaying what they have learned. They have been busy creating a more attractive environment. In particular, they have worked hard at building nice public restrooms. As if that were not enough, they have ordered all retail shops to make their restrooms free for tourists. This is something most of their international counterparts are not able, or willing, to do.

In terms of public housing, the Chinese officials are doing better than those in New York, according to one *New York Times* columnist.[12] In New York, the local government does not use a market economy for housing. Instead, the city has imposed serious restrictions on rents for commercial spaces. Only one-third of the city's 2 million rental apartments are free of some kind of price restraint. In some buildings, people live in similar apartments but pay dramatically different rents. In others, according to *The Economist,* lone elderly people sit in huge apartments, knowing that moving to a smaller place would mean higher rent.[13]

The system in New York City has limited the interest of real estate developers in building rental properties in Manhattan and other districts in the city. Consequently, there are great shortages of appropriate rentals for the millions of residents there. At the same time, commercial office space is overbuilt. Yet not many investors have tried to turn empty office towers into rental apartments. This is a result of the administrative rental control.

China's reform has already changed the old urban free-housing system. Now, every urban resident must take care of these things on his own.

In addition, there is no limitation on rental properties in terms of pricing in the New York style. Chinese land developers fight with each other to build millions of apartments in all regions. Not only do these land developers become prosperous, but countless Chinese consumers also have a great range of choices of apartments. In some ways, apartments are overbuilt, especially at the high end. Only now has this begun to cause concern in most cities.

This strongly contrasts with the housing situation in New York. Therefore it was natural for the *New York Times* columnist to use reform in China as an example. He suggested that the New York officials might learn something from their Chinese counterparts. After all, reform is contagious. Students and teachers must learn from each other now and then. How could it be otherwise?

In many areas, Chinese officials need to learn more from the foreign mayors. Very often Chinese officials misunderstand the needs of outsiders. They may even create embarrassing situations for foreign visitors. This has certainly happened in the past. In major cities, for example, some sections of the best hospitals were designated exclusively for foreigners. Even some Chinese dignitaries had problems visiting. Now, China has gained more international experience and these government officials are doing better in more ways.

6 "CAPITAL IS NOT ENOUGH"

Consumers in many emerging markets enjoy quality foreign brands, and so do the Chinese. Even so, not every foreign player has succeeded in China so far. The imperfect marketplace aside, many failures have originated with the foreign players themselves. This is evident by the fact that countless foreign players in China are successful.

A deeper analysis would show that not every international player has operated correctly. Players may engage in practices that are outside of the norm. Instead of creating sound organizations, some players have opted to take shortcuts. This has brought about adverse results.

No Shortcuts

Some companies have tried to get quick results without doing the needed work. Not all of these companies are startups. In fact, they can be global brands.

A regional head of a global company once asked a business advisor for help. His company was trying to sell telecom products in China. So far, results had been lackluster. "Do you know people in high places over there?" the manager asked.

"What do you want?"

"We want to sell our products."

"Well, in that case, you have many options. The best way is to set up a marketing network."

"We want quicker results."

"Well, you must create an organization," said the advisor.

...

"Well, I think our company can demand a higher price for our products."

"Why?"

"We are a big company."

"May I be direct?—all your competitors are already there. Many have been there for two decades. Your idea may be interesting, but it may not work, not even with my relationships."

Surely, all successful multinationals must go beyond pure relationships. How could it be otherwise? They must do all the right things—they simply have to build a business here in China the way they have in their home markets. How can they leap to profitability without this type of foundation?

China is certainly an emerging market in many ways. Even so, for the most part foreign multinationals do not really need to invent new tricks. Why are they successful at home? They are successful simply because they have done all the right things. So why shouldn't they do the same in a new market like China?

Happy companies are all alike, while failed businesses all have different stories to tell. Should China be an exception? Not really. So far, some multinationals have done better than others. The successful ones have all done similar things: For example, they try to offer quality products with competitive pricing, have strong marketing and brand promotion, and, very significantly, hire the best-trained employees. Any shortcuts may only lead to failure. Yet this does not stop international players from repeating the same mistakes.

Chinese consumers are favorably inclined toward foreign brands. They love quality products and service at competitive prices. They even think that it is fair to pay a higher price for international brands. Moreover, they are easily led to believe that foreign multinationals offer superior products and services. This popular attitude has been decisive in helping the foreign players.

But it is important not to try to generalize this too much. Consumers also demand higher standards from foreign businesses. After all, the prices are often higher. In return, consumers want better quality.

Numerous examples show that consumers often make tough demands, especially of international brands. If they have some quality issue with an international brand, they may raise their voices unusually high. This noise may get louder when their complaints are ignored.

ONE LESSON TO REMEMBER

Overall, leading international brands are attractive to China. Yet one giant Japanese company ran into an embarrassing situation some years ago. It happened on the island of Hainan in the late 1990s. A tiny matter triggered a big incident. A consumer bought the company brand TV, but soon had problems. He returned the TV set to the store immediately. The store contacted the company representatives in China. Though all this occurred within the warranty period, the Japanese offices demanded that the customer pay an extra charge. The consumer as well as the store managers rejected the idea.

Soon this tiny matter took a nasty turn. After rounds of talks, the parties came to no solution. The store soon announced a boycott against selling the Japanese brand altogether.

It did not stop there. Very soon, hundreds of stores nationwide joined the boycott. This public demonstration immediately attracted the attention of the offices in Japan. Company senior executives flew in. Immediately, the right steps were taken to end the public relations nightmare and thus the matter came to a peaceful resolution.

In fairness it must be said that more quality and service problems exist with many Chinese brands. Such problems are widespread. Why did so many retailers take such a dramatic action against the Japanese player?

A number of factors are involved. China's consumers appreciate many aspects of international brands. Above all, they like the quality and the service. They generally feel that the multinationals are better.

Why not? After all, most international brands have a higher price tag. The Japanese brands, especially, sell at much higher prices than the domestic brands—usually 30% or more higher. Consumers still want to pay for them. They naturally expect better service in return.

PROTECTING BRAND

As always, multinationals pay utmost attention to protecting their brand images. How could they not? They work harder at this than most of their Chinese counterparts, to be sure. After all, the brand image is their lifeline.

In a number of ways, many Chinese companies have not done as well. In fact, some players try to take shortcuts. Recently, a bureau of the Beijing municipal government made a shocking finding in checking into the local market for kids' shoes. Out of 60 Chinese brands, only 25 were qualified.[1] Why was there no public outcry against these players? Well, this is Chinese life today.

In practice, any demonstration against a domestic company may not produce any real effect. The store managers in this case were well aware of this reality. But they wanted to show their commitment to their customers. They understood that a foreign multinational would have to take them seriously. How could a giant company afford consumer dissatisfaction?

All this provided the right background for action. The store managers saw their opportunity: It was their moment to show their best intentions regarding the needs of consumers. So, things took their natural course. After one store made such a commitment, hundreds more joined in immediately. Teaching a small lesson to a multinational company is a good way to achieve a big outcome: reminding all businesses, international and Chinese, of the importance of consumers.

There should not be the slightest doubt that the Japanese businesspeople are great lovers of quality. They have created giant businesses based on quality products. However, this incident showed that they had not provided enough training for their employees and associates, to say the least. So a lesson or two were needed.

Consumers now treat this Japanese company like any other. Since the incident, they have been buying the same Japanese brands as before. It has been a good lesson for the Chinese companies as well. They have been improving professional standards in noticeable ways. No hard feelings on the part of the consumers—they are just the very best people under the sun.

A U.S. BRAND SELLING FOR PENNIES

All things considered, not every foreign brand can command a higher price. Even some popular international brands have experienced failure.

Some international companies try to sell their products without doing the right things. In one case involving a U.S. beauty products brand, the U.S. company has exported products into China. But it has done little else. There is no brand promotion at all. In the end, the products just sit on the shelves.

I ran into these products when I walked into a chain store in Shenzhen, run by a Hong Kong company, and saw this particular brand of beauty products sitting on the shelves. It surprised me that the store was discounting them for pennies on the dollar. How could I not be curious? This small example has much to say about doing business in a foreign place, or any place. It shows a lack of understanding on the part of the producer and sellers.

Without the right marketing, how would consumers know what to buy? Easily understood, best brands in one market may mean little to another market. Producing positive results requires solid effort. It takes a little thought to understand that even if McDonald's is a household name globally, it still spends billions on marketing. Does McDonald's love to spend money? Not really. It has to, for it has many competitors.

Yet doing all the right things is a common challenge facing foreign multinationals in a new market like China. Even giant companies often have to learn the hard way.

VOLKSWAGEN VERSUS BEIJING JEEP

The German company Volkswagen is a success in China. Volkswagen was one of the earliest multinationals to enter China. It arrived in the early 1980s with a Shanghai joint venture to produce the Santana. That German model long dominated China's car market. For many years until recently, its car share was 50% or more.

For many years the Santana was also the number-one choice of Chinese consumers. "Santana" almost became another word for "car." Even today, most taxis are Santanas. Volkswagen is now adding another 10 billion euros and creating numerous joint ventures in China. The company now produces more models and reaches the higher end of the market with the Audi.

What impresses the Chinese most about the German managers may be their love of detail. One policy researcher told me how impressed he was watching the German businessmen as the auto deal was in progress: "They spent so much effort on important issues, yet the same efforts on trivial things. It is a powerful way to produce results. They have even tired down those troublesome bureaucrats in both Beijing and Shanghai."

In the end, the Chinese officials were tired of being the "troublemakers." What a story! More often than not, it is the other way around. To be certain, the trouble-loving bureaucrats have run down countless ambitious businesspeople. It is easy to encounter defeated businesspeople today.

The devil is in the details—in China just as anywhere else. Because of the Germans' commitment to detail they have been given the green light. They have had plenty of room to manage the joint venture in Shanghai since the beginning. All this has paved the way for the German achievement in China's auto market. Volkswagen has been ranked among the top 10 most admired companies in China.[2]

The U.S. executives at Beijing Jeep have shown a different style. They don't even seem to stop doing things that may jeopardize their ambitions.

To be sure, Beijing Jeep has set several records in China. It was the first major China-U.S. joint venture. The two parties were a Beijing auto group and American Motors Corporation, which was later acquired by Chrysler. The joint venture was set up in 1984, a year ahead of the one with Volkswagen. Moreover, it was the first international joint venture in China's auto sector. Beijing Jeep is also known for having had many problems and confrontations within the organization.

One unforgettable event took place sometime after the setting up of the joint venture.[3] Again, a very minor issue led to outsized consequences. Managers on the two sides fought bitterly over management styles and corporate culture, among other things. The disagreements reached a peak with the very personal issue of whether or not the Chinese managers would be allowed to have nap beds in their offices. For many decades, each Chinese manager had had a bed in his office. The U.S. managers viewed this as inappropriate. They demanded that the beds be removed immediately. When the Chinese didn't comply, the U.S. managers stormed the offices and threw the beds out.

Confronted with the U.S. invasion, the Chinese managers were enraged. For a while, the two parties stopped treating each other courteously on a personal or professional level. A turn of events occurred after a government official named Zhu Rongji stepped in. His presence calmed the tension, though he was little known back then with a vice ministerial title. The two parties finally sat down to focus on business, forgetting personal uneasiness. Today Beijing Jeep is still alive. Now its international partner is trying to create more joint ventures in China.

Beijing Jeep had its years of glory, but things have changed. Prior to March 2003, it showed 60 consecutive months of losses. Unlike Volkswagen, it is no longer on the most admired business list. Now Beijing Jeep is working harder toward a comeback. It is trying to introduce more models, for example.[4] Volkswagen has shown steady progress, while Beijing Jeep has been very unstable. Its profitable days were great but short-lived.[5] The company returned to the black only in early 2003.

But the parent company Daimler-Chrysler is eager to expand into China all the way. For now, it even plans to export cars made in China to international markets.

Nonetheless, the experience with Beijing Jeep was a good education for Zhu. He has since become a figure known worldwide for producing quick results. He has put his experience to work on more complex issues. In particular, he was able to influence the bargaining processes for China's WTO entry. His dealings with the formidable WTO negotiators from Washington, DC and other international centers were all needed. So far, so good.[6] In 2004, the German chancellor awarded Zhu a medal for his outstanding entrepreneurial work.

"Capital Is Not Enough"

Conquering a new market certainly takes extra effort. Yet even successful businesses tend to ignore this obvious truth at times. In my professional work, I have often encountered troubling situations. It seems that people, foreign or local, love to repeat the same mistakes. Learning is a painful thing indeed. Perhaps that is why we feel that the ancients were wiser, especially when we read Confucius and Plato.

Once I wrote a small article titled "Capital Is Not Enough."[7] Some investors said, If our money can't bring us success, what else have we got? They were really expecting things to be different in China. China is a market like all other markets in most ways. There are no shortcuts. Business must focus on people. How could capital be enough?

Every so often, businesspeople complain about their difficulties making profits in China. For the most part, they should not blame the Chinese market. Instead, they should ask if they have done the right things.

True, China is no developed market: It lacks transparent rules and regulations, among much else. There are many issues to be resolved. Even so, some players have failed to do what they are supposed to do. Most of the time, market imperfections are not really the reason for unsuccessful ventures. Rather, the players behind them have not performed correctly in the first place.

Most things for which China has been criticized could happen in any market, say, the United States. Japanese investors have learned by heart the cruelty of the American marketplace.

As everyone knows, the Japanese invested huge capital in the United States back in the 1980s and early 1990s.[8] What happened? They lost on a large scale. Could the Japanese blame a stupid U.S. market? They did not. After all, entering a new market demands huge effort and learning. The market is always right, and it was the Japanese who made all the mistakes, not the U.S. market. And not just mistakes: These were simple, obvious mistakes. But people tend to make easy mistakes. These mistakes demonstrate that successful investments take more than capital.

One lesson the Japanese learned in the United States is that not knowing the market situation well enough can lead to disaster anywhere. One notorious deal involved the purchase of Pebble Beach Company with its golf course, though it was one of the smaller failures in dollar terms. For some time it looked like a sweet deal. But troubles soon surfaced. The Japanese found out that there was a stupid local law. It destroyed all their sweet dreams of selling memberships at $750,000 each.

How did the Japanese view these losses? In some ways, they have tried to learn from these experiences. This has certainly helped many Japanese companies achieve success in the United States. Both Honda and Toyota are good examples.

Even so, when these Japanese giants come to China, they must learn the basics again. Is there any alternative? So far, the Japanese executives have also paid dearly in China, though not nearly as much as in the United States. This has not put an end to their desire to stay in China for the long term. They are now doing much better.

Ericsson's Seven Mistakes

Each failure may create a unique lesson, though successes are very much alike. There is an important lesson to be learned when a once glorious brand fails to sustain progress. This has happened with Ericsson, among others. This once high-flying giant has not been successful lately in the global market. It has also run into problems inside China.

Ericsson has made mistakes in China—one report lists seven of them.[9] At its height, Ericsson had a 37% market share. By the end of 1998, it still had about 25%. By 2000, its market share had dropped to 5%. By now Ericsson has become a minor player in this overcrowded market, which included at least 37 players inside China as of 2002.

Ericsson management has made numerous errors that now seem textbook. The company was slow to act in a fast-changing Chinese market. It took too long to get new products to the marketplace, and an even longer time to market them.

At the same time, other players such as Motorola, Samsung, and Nokia all outperformed. One particular mistake made by Ericsson was more costly than many others. It involved a public relations crisis.

It started in May 2000, in a trivial kind of way.[10] A consumer had a bad experience with a product. His Ericsson 18SC model often turned off by itself. In the following 11 months, the consumer went to the Ericsson service center 18 times. Seven repairs were made and four key chips replaced. But still beset with problems, the consumer demanded a refund. He could not get a definite solution from either the service center or the retailer. He was kicked around between the two offices.

Most consumers would have given up completely by now. This young man was an exception. His complaints reached the higher offices of Ericsson, the media, and the official consumer dispute bureau. He attached a demand of $5,435. Furthermore, he demanded that the company withdraw all faulty products and offer a public apology. It refused.

Immediately, the media picked up the story. Still, no action came from the company. Soon a class action suit went to court. Class actions are a new thing in China. In this case, the court rejected the class action suit. But a small step was taken. The court delivered a judgment in favor of the consumer, ordering Ericsson to refund the original purchase price and a smaller penalty amount. The consumer was not satisfied: "I'm sorry I could not trick the elephant."[11]

Ericsson saved some money in the matter. But it lost considerable market share. Things went from bad to worse. Sales dropped sharply and inventories piled up. Some of the assembly lines were closed, and a number of employees were let go.

Since that time, Ericsson has never regained its old glory in China. Despite the setback, though, the company has been improving rapidly ever since. In the last few years, Ericsson has made good progress.[12]

BASHING CARREFOUR

The spring and summer of 2003 were tough for China because of SARS. There were other events as well. One involved the French retail chain Carrefour. In Shanghai, a number of its suppliers of edible seeds went on strike against the store.

Why? The French store demanded numerous fees from the suppliers just for putting goods on the shelves. These fees covered some 20 items. Soon after the strike began, more suppliers showed dissatisfaction with the store. In particular, they complained that the French company often delayed payments.

The news caused wide public debate. The general feeling was not encouraging for the French giant. No resolution occurred for many months, and there was wide media coverage of the dispute. The company was running into a public relations nightmare. This was the second time since 1995, when Carrefour had come to China, that it had experienced trouble. Many business associations supported the boycott.[13]

Some critics feel that the company has built these extra fees into its business model. They believe that Carrefour's business model relies on "high entrance fees" for profits. In their view, the profits are too high.[14]

It is reported that the French retailer ran into similar problems in South Korea. For overcharging and for delaying payments, it was fined three times between 1999 and 2001.[15]

In Korea, it was the government that stepped in and imposed penalty fines. In China, the government does not wish to get involved. After all, it would love to have more foreign players. This may be one reason that the Chinese government behaves differently from the Korean. There may be other reasons. For example, the Chinese government may feel that business parties should handle such disputes on their own. The government wants no part of such troubles. In the end, things have been left for the business partners to resolve.

One thing is worth noting: Consumers continue to shop at Carrefour stores as always. At the same time, the French chain is adding more megastores in a hurry. But there is one additional problem: Wal-Mart and many other global retailers are chasing after its tail.

7 "WHY IS CHINA STILL A DEVELOPING NATION?"

Impressive to many foreign employers is the quality of Chinese employees. Foreign employers have asked why China is still a developing country when the nation has countless talented citizens.

A foreign business executive said to me, "Chinese engineers are truly qualified, especially in research and development. Thousands of them work in Silicon Valley. My company alone has hundreds. They contribute a lot. How come there are no global high-tech companies from China?"

Well, there are no easy answers. For thousands of years, China led the world in technology, prosperity, and the arts of living. Yet in modern times it has lagged behind pitifully. Even in 1820, China took 30% of global production. But it fell to around 1% in Mao era. The creative talents of the Chinese people have been largely unused and even wasted.

Throughout history, China's people have cultivated an ethic of serious learning and hard work. This has become a core value in Chinese life. Yet man-made barriers have stood in the way of China's progress.

It is certainly a great pity that Chinese companies are unable to fully employ the best talents at home. At the same time this has become a great advantage to their international counterparts. This enormous pool of talent has greatly benefited foreign companies in numerous ways. Chinese employees work for these companies not just inside China, but all over the planet.

HIRING BY FOREIGN MULTINATIONALS

Like children who desire sweet, tasty food, multinationals are hungry for talent. It seems that they can hardly get enough of it.

Salaries in China are very low compared to those in the developed markets. With less than $1,000 per month, a company can hire a top software engineer in China. To date, more than 23 million Chinese have worked or are working for overseas companies.[1]

Employers have additional advantages with Chinese employees in comparison to those in the advanced markets. China's labor protection is not yet serious by international standards. Employees are often mistreated, especially blue-collar workers. China does not have the strong unions that exist in Europe and Korea, for example. This offers employers wide opportunities. Indeed, overseas multinationals have enormous choices. They are busy employing any local talent they can find.

"THEY ARE STEALING OUR TOP TALENTS!"

Recently, a survey of new college graduates in China showed that their top 10 choices for employment were the following companies, in order: Haier, IBM, Microsoft, Lenovo, P&G, GE, Motorola, Huawei, China Mobile, and Siemens.[2] Six of these are foreign names. These international players have a great deal of choice.

The U.S. companies have led the waves of hiring. Among these, Microsoft is an active player. Since 1996 Microsoft has had a technology center in Shanghai that has become one of its global research centers. Among other things, the facility handles consumer calls around the clock. Hundreds of Chinese engineers answer all sorts of questions for clients worldwide. The managers are satisfied with their work.

Some time ago, at a conference in Hong Kong, I listened to a talk given by Microsoft's top regional manager. He proudly told the large audience about his work in Shanghai. In the beginning, management worried about whether the center was capable of handling the program. Very soon the managers were happy with the feedback. So Microsoft has been increasing the center's scope of work. And this development is not restricted to Shanghai or China. It extends to all Asia and beyond. By the end of the year 2003, Microsoft was to have added 500 employees in China and India.[3]

Certainly, the Microsoft bosses know the value of a fast-developing China. They have continually increased the scope of work here. When Bill Gates visited China in 1998, he was impressed by the quality of the young students. In the airplane on the way home, he decided to create a research university in China. Soon the company invested about $80 million in setting up Microsoft University in Beijing.[4]

Many Chinese are worried about the powerful foreign giants. Some Chinese feel that the foreign companies are taking away the very best of China: "They are stealing our top talents."[5] This huge "brain drain" is obvious to the Chinese. Many Chinese students studying overseas are not returning. By 2003, China had had 700,000 students studying in some 108 nations. About 172,800 had returned home.[6] In 2000 alone, more than 50,000 students, many of them top graduates in China, went to study in the United States. One thing was sure—most of them would work in the United States. Many Chinese are deeply worried about all this.

Foreign players continue to get the best employees. Certainly there is much more talent in China than any single company can take on. Other IT players such as HP, Philips, Motorola and Intel have also set up research labs in China. The strategy is designed to achieve two objectives. First, the companies want to lower costs through hiring cheap local employees. Second, they want these employees to create their products for the world markets.

These strategies have been producing fruit. Oracle's employees in the United States make an average salary of $80,000 a year. In China, Oracle employees average about $12,000 a year. The savings are huge, but the quality is also high.

ENTIRE LINES OF PROFESSIONALS

Needless to say, all businesses actively search for ways to expand. Many clever multinationals go the extra mile. Some have teamed up with leading Chinese universities and research centers, for example. Their aim is to create all kinds of programs that directly promote their own research and development.

Proctor & Gamble has created a joint research center with Qsinghua University, a top school. This joint venture is one of the biggest research labs of its kind. The aim is to develop new products. Proctor & Gamble has also created a joint venture in medical research with Nankai University.[8]

More business deals have developed in this direction. IBM, Unilever, and Motorola, among others, have also created joint programs with leading Chinese universities.[9] The Chinese universities are interested in such ventures as well. Through these arrangements the universities obtain financial support and additional benefits for doing what they do best.

Japan's multinationals are also active in China. Sony has a research team with 300 employees, designed to be a part of Sony's global research and development. Matsushita is even more ambitious. It has pursued a complex program that aims to combine manufacturing, marketing, and research and development in one basket. The idea is to employ China as a new engine.[10] This idea has become popular among most members of Japan Inc.

By now, these foreign multinationals have set up more than 600 labs. They aim to produce the future generation products for global markets, China included.

NEW ERA OF GLOBAL JOB TRANSFERS

Cost concerns and competitiveness have had many new effects, one of which is job transfers on a global basis. Many jobs from the high-paying markets have been moving to the low-paying regions. These job transfers involve all sorts of industries and businesses—not only global multinationals, but also small and medium-size companies.

It is not just the U.S. companies that are busy extracting the best from China; the competing parties are all doing it too. Some of the most visible of these are Nokia, Nortel, Sony, Hitachi, Volkswagen, Electrolux, BP, Siemens, Philips, LG, and Samsung.

Interestingly enough, some of these businesses are performing terribly in their home markets but are doing fine in China. Examples include Europe's ABB and Fiat, the U.S.'s Lucent, and Canada's Nortel. They make healthy profits over here. In the end, they hope to make more here. Some talk in the street is that they would be better off becoming Chinese companies once and for all. This may not be a bad idea. After all, why should a company lose billions elsewhere when it can make billions over here?

Such job transfers are gaining momentum, even in Asia-based companies. Among these, HSBC is very active, having already set up back offices in Guangzhou, for example. These offices handle credit card transactions and loan paperwork, among other things. Citibank and many other financial service companies are doing the same. Such transfers will help them cut costs and also improve efficiencies. In China, companies can easily get the best low-paid workers for laborious jobs. In addition, work quality is high. There is nothing to lose, and there are millions to gain.

In some ways, what is happening now in China points to a general trend for the future. As never before, all CEOs look closely at the global map. They wish to find the best ways to operate around the world.[11]

The influences flow in both directions. These foreign activities are deeply affected by the culture and traditions of the respective nations. Different multinationals have different behaviors. Each carries its own culture and traditional values to China as well.

To the Chinese employees, the Japanese companies stand below their Western counterparts. As observed by a researcher from a leading Japanese research center, RIETI, the Japanese multinationals are often less attractive to the Chinese professionals. Reasons are numerous. In particular, the Japanese companies have a limited progressive culture within. To many people, these Japanese organizations are overly rigid and lack an atmosphere of freedom. Promotions come slowly. Some feel that the Japanese companies are somewhat like the state companies in China. That is why, in one survey, no Japanese company was ranked among the top 10 employers in China.[12]

How do the Chinese professionals feel about working for the Japanese companies? For many, this would not be among their choices because of the rigid Japanese management system.

In many ways, the Japanese have yet to pursue a more active localization program. Their promotional system is not as encouraging as that of the Western multinationals. This has disappointed many Chinese. In many Japanese companies in China, the highest possible positions for Chinese employees are low-ranking managerial positions. The middle and top country managers are Japanese. In the Western companies' China operations, many general managers and CEOs are Chinese who have studied abroad.[13]

So far, the various multinationals have brought their traditions and cultures to China. In general, different employment policies have been accompanied by differences in performance. Those multinationals with strong localization programs tend to outperform the rest.

JOB WORRIES AROUND THE WORLD

How fresh globalization is to people everywhere! Developing nations like India, Russia, Brazil, and China feel that the developed nations will benefit more from this phenomenon. But the developed nations may not agree. They have worries about changes around the globe.

Behind all the changes, multinationals are most influential. Cost is one powerful force that moves businesses around globally. National borders do not play as important a role as previously. What force is bigger than the desire to create wealth? All businesspeople are eager to compete. They have been struggling hard to cut costs. They are searching around the globe to make ends meet. Job transfers have become a major concern to people living in the developed world today.

Many U.S. IT professionals are worried about their jobs. Legislative measures are attempted in places like the state of New Jersey. State-level governments have introduced anti–job-transfer measures. The U.S. federal government has also created barriers. One way is to limit entry access to international professionals. Many Indian engineers, among others, have had difficulties performing project assignments in the United States. But the surprising fact is that the United States has had a net job increase in the past two decades—of 1 million, according to the TV program *60 Minutes* in February 2005.

Businesses follow their own interests as always. After all, all businesses are profit oriented. Whatever market can bring better profits is where they want to be. Countless U.S. companies have been trying to cut costs and locate job transfers. In so doing, these companies hope to cut costs and increase their competitiveness.[14]

Such job transfers are bound to cause ripple effects. The *New York Times* has reported that by 2015, U.S. businesses will have transferred about 3.3 million professional jobs to developing countries. Countries such as India, China, and Russia will be their new locations.[15]

Europe's situation is similar to that of the United States. Many Europeans fear global job transfers. Some even blame the cheap products made in China and other developing nations. Many European companies, organizations, and trade unions have raised the dumping issue. In their view, stopping cheap imports would eliminate their problems overnight.

In Italy, two government ministers have proposed limiting Chinese exports by law. In their opinion this would be an effective way to protect their national interests.[16] Now five state-level governments in the United States have adopted serious restrictions relating to job transfers.[17] The U.S. government has imposed trade restrictions on China's textiles.[18] Clearly, globalization has new effects around the globe. It has certainly generated new issues, including trade conflicts.[19]

China has different worries. Chinese businesspeople are extremely fearful about the powerful foreign businesses inside. China has become a truly international market. Countless domestic companies have already been forced out.

The fat profits of many foreign businesses trouble some Chinese. In an incident that occurred next to a McDonald's outlet in Beijing, a street vendor proposed kicking out McDonald's, saying "The clever Americans are making big profits out of us." One reporter could not agree, saying "Investments and profits should go together...." In the end, the two men agreed that it was good to have the foreign players in China.[20]

HIRING BY CHINESE PLAYERS

Today China's people have their own worries. A popular expression heard on the streets is "How can you dance with wolves?"

Many Chinese don't look at the new competition as a bad thing. In fact, many feel strongly that China needs competition in order to make progress. In such fashion China's people, for the most part, welcome globalization despite all the worries and tough realities.

"SHEEP" HAVE THEIR WAYS

To be sure, Chinese companies have their unique advantages. The "sheep" have their ways, as they are running faster than ever before. Hot competition is under way between the sheep and the wolves. Who will win? That remains a question.

Chinese companies naturally desire to hire top professionals. But in many respects they have a tough time competing with foreign multinationals. The latter can be more attractive to the best talents. Indeed, as far as hiring is concerned, Chinese companies stand on a lower level.

There are countless other issues facing China Inc. In particular, the

Chinese companies have yet to learn how to create a vibrant and dynamic organization. In this context, global multinationals are more experienced. As a result they can easily attract all Chinese professionals.

Many Chinese are deeply worried by this trend. They believe that without the ability to hire the best talent, Chinese businesses will have no way to compete.

CHANGES IN THE EMPLOYMENT PICTURE

The employment situation is beginning to change. Interestingly enough, it is the professional class that is leading the changes in China.

At this time, many Chinese employees have complex relations with their foreign employers. Yes, their salaries are higher than local salaries, and their office buildings are taller. But they may have different concerns as time goes by.

To some, other issues may be more important than high salaries. They desire more personal satisfaction and greater challenges. They feel that their true value cannot be fully displayed while they are working for foreign players. One common complaint is that foreign managers cannot give talented domestic employees reasonable promotions.

Increasingly, Chinese professionals are jumping over to Chinese companies. Many Chinese companies are increasingly trying to recruit talented professionals from the competing foreign companies. They feel that this will help them quickly decrease the gaps.

There are many attractive foreign employers. Motorola has been active in carrying out a localization program. This has been significant in paving the way for success.

One Chinese commentator says that the management of Motorola has an easy-going attitude, rare among foreign executives: "The Motorola management treats the Chinese clients very nicely regardless how big they are.... Its senior managers seem to enjoy talking to low level client's reps.... The CEO of the Motorola Globe spent much time and efforts to share hot liquor with some partners in Sichuan...."[21] This observer also notes that 83% of the managers for Motorola China are Chinese. This is in striking comparison to the situation with many foreign players.

To date, there have been many conflicts between employees and their foreign employers. A large number of Chinese professionals have switched back to work for Chinese companies. This has attracted much attention and debate. Chinese companies desire to hire foreign professionals as well. Many leading companies have already done so.

In general, foreign multinationals have many more advantages in the job market. In the city of Beijing alone, about 460,000 local employees work for international companies. That is about 10% of the local workforce. Naturally, these people represent the best trained and best informed.[22]

Many Chinese companies are searching for ways to engage the outside markets. This has involved hiring international professionals in large numbers—thousands so far.

One consumer electronics company, Skyworth, has made an impressive move. It has hired some high-profile foreign executives to help with its global drive. In particular, one noted research executive from Japan's Matsushita has jumped aboard. This manager has some 30 years of international experience. He is a leading expert in new-generation TV. Moreover, he has brought with him a number of fellow Japanese engineers. Through this type of hiring, the new employer hopes to gain an edge.[23] How does the company feel about paying high salaries to the Japanese team? To Skyworth, it is the merits that count.[24]

Even the state companies can no longer sit still. They face more challenges than ever before. Many of them have tried to change for the better. Six large Chinese companies in the state sector are now in hot pursuit to hire senior executives around the globe. This has happened under enormous pressures from the marketplace.[25] It signals the beginning of a new era for the state sector.

GLOBAL JOB TRANSFERS: CHINA VERSUS INDIA

In this era of the WTO, good things have benefited more people and nations. If it were otherwise, globalization could hardly have been widely accepted around the world. More and more nations are reaping the benefits in their own ways. Losing some things and gaining others has become a reality in the global economy. Life has finally become a two-way street. Globalization today has new features and meaning compared to Western expansions in the past.

On a global stage, many things happen by design or, more precisely, flow from business interests only. Job transfers are certainly a major example.

Jobs tend to move from the high-cost developed markets to the low-cost emerging markets. This new trend has already created global changes. This tide cannot be stopped. Business needs now dominate the global market in a brand-new way. The matter is one of survival. Those businesses that are able to control costs and achieve efficiency will stay. The less competitive ones may die.

Surely, even great technology and great products do not last forever. More companies and more countries can produce almost anything under the sun. The business world has become fully convinced: Whoever can reduce costs will survive.[26]

New things have emerged around the global marketplace. Both the global giants and the small regional companies in different nations have gained space for development. Emerging companies in many nations are able to produce most of the consumer products. Emerging markets in Asia are already the biggest destination for job transfers.

China and India are leading nations among those that do outsourced work. Both nations can offer what global businesses want.[27] India has certain advantages over China, especially in the software business. India's software success has followed a unique path. It has directly connected India to the global marketplace in multiple ways. India has an educated English-speaking population. It has first-class universities and training centers. It has been able to attract well over 50% of the global 500 companies.[28]

India has built up a powerful software army. It includes players such as TCS, Infosys, Wipro, and Satyam. These emerging Indian companies are powerful enough to compete in the global markets. It is these Indian companies that have helped to make India the second biggest software exporter. In short, India is no longer a developing nation as far as its IT industry is concerned.

Beyond the service industries, India has not developed as fast as China. Indeed, China has not focused on any single industry in the way India has. Instead, China has achieved an overall development. In particular, China has made most impressive progress in manufacturing, enabling China to become closely connected to the global marketplace.

Up to now, China's living standards have been improving faster than India's. Its GDP per capita is more than twice that of India. China had 334 million mobile phone users in 2004, while India had some 46 million. China is already the biggest manufacturer of consumer products globally—an area in which India is seriously lacking.

China's reform has taken steps well ahead of India. Both countries have long suffered under government domination. China took earlier steps toward reform. Its progress has impacted India in a number of ways. India is moving faster now in a new direction. Its economy has been running faster, though a little behind China's. The Indian government is mapping out new strategies to move ahead.[29]

Such different policies have produced different results. On the global stage, China has already become a top trading player. From 1980 to 2004, China's share of global trade grew from around 1% to more than 6.5%.[30] As of 2004, China had surpassed Japan in total worldwide trade.

This expanding trade has attracted further international investments. In particular, the foreign players are helping to widen the international markets for products made in China.[31]

Today, international players treat China as the biggest frontier market. They can't afford not to join the gold rush. With such outside involvement, business in China has achieved further development in a global context.

India's software sector is one exceptionally bright light. China's software companies are tiny, and they lack international experience. But China's software companies can avail themselves of a bigger market at home.

Given all the factors, China will change faster than India. And China will more rapidly attract international capital due principally to its fast-growing domestic market.

Concerning job transfers, India will continue to have a sharp edge in the IT industry for the foreseeable future. The foreign multinationals continue to invest in major ways in their existing operations in India. More foreign players should follow.

Also, more Chinese companies would enjoy investing in India. The Huawei experience in India—which has been completely positive—is spreading outward in China. China's companies also have a lot to learn from the successes of the India software industry.

This sharp Indian edge is producing positive outcomes. The old India is gaining new life. To be sure, like China, India has taken a long path in becoming integrated into the world economy. As with China, this has been the first creative benefit for India from the new globalization processes. This is very meaningful, especially when we view the sad history—thousands of years long—of struggles with powerful foreigner invaders.[32]

Like India, China will increasingly become a central location for job transfers from other countries. Such job transfers will cover even more industry fields, especially IT and manufacturing jobs. This evolution is beginning to take shape.

Two factors are helping China's rapid improvement. One is that China has a bigger domestic market for software. Another is the ever-increasing involvement of international multinationals. Chinese software companies will gain more opportunities as time goes on.

Above all, the competition between China and India is very healthy. After centuries of bitter struggles within and beyond, both nations have finally joined world development, bravely and creatively. Both are late players in the global economy. They are trying hard to run faster and more efficiently.

Very significantly, they have countless resources to share with each other. This increased sharing between the two giant late developers should only increase in the future.[33] Naturally, all nations in the developing world have huge resources to share with each other as well.[34]

More positive things must follow. Globalization has truly reached all corners of the world for the very first time in human history. Every nation, rich or poor, must readjust to it. China and India finally have a place on the map of global development. The development of the established world must also rely on these emerging markets to proceed further. For now, both India and China are proud of their self-transformation to become new engines for global development at large.

Part II

China's New International Experiences

INTERNATIONAL EXPANSIONS; PRICING; STRATEGIC PARTNERSHIPS; OUTSOURCING; SURVIVAL GAMES

8 PRICE, PRICE, PRICE

W hat is the most basic factor in any marketplace? Pricing. All markets move around price. Surely, the emergence of so many late-developing nations is bound to affect global pricing.

Quite frequently here in China, international businesspeople claim that their businesses are not profitable. To most Chinese consumers, that is hard to believe, as shown in a recent survey.[1] Most foreign brands carry a much higher price tag than the Chinese brands. If a foreign company doesn't make a profit selling shirts at $100, how could the Chinese survive selling them for $10?

A CHINESE EDGE

Today, tens of thousands of foreign multinationals operate in China. Confronting these powerful competitors, how can the small Chinese businesses survive? They have their ways. Their biggest weapon is low pricing. They have a price advantage over most global players.

Low cost has become an edge for many small players in developing countries like China and India. Low cost has helped Chinese businesses grow in big ways.

Furthermore, it is consumers who drive such development around the globe. Everywhere they demand the cheapest products and services. Most of them can get by without a Rolex watch. That is how the mega-discount store Wal-Mart racks up $290 billion in sales.

Cheap goods don't mean healthy profits. The fact that China is a new manufacturing hub does not mean that Chinese companies are strong. On the contrary, they are still weak. Without the ability to move to the higher end, they face many tough issues. In particular, their profit margins are small. This has stopped them from achieving a true global reach. Moving to the higher end is easier said than done. This situation will continue for a long time.

Multinationals such as Airbus, Siemens, GE, Unilever, Microsoft, and Intel have a dominance in their fields. This leads naturally to impressive profits. This level of play is beyond the Chinese today. They may send a cargo-loaded ship to the United States and get back a box of chips made by Intel or Texas Instruments. Yet this does not mean that Chinese players don't have a space to play in. In fact, they have gained a large space. They are still growing in their own ways.

GE IN CHINA

The U.S. giant GE learned some long-overdue lessons in China. What was the very first lesson? Pricing. It all started in the early 1990s.[2]

GE's First Lesson

Like many global giants, GE rushed to China in the early 1990s. In 1994, GE set up its first shop in China, to manufacture and sell light bulbs. GE's joint venture in Shanghai focused on making light bulbs. The US company invested about $180 million and had an 89% stake.[3]

GE's light bulbs are said to be more economical than others and to have a longer lifetime. They are supposed to be easier on the eyes than ordinary light bulbs. GE had hoped that the Chinese consumers would rush to pay for its light bulbs.

One problem: There were hundreds of Chinese light bulb manufacturers. Also, there were competing brands like Philips. GE bulbs sold for $1.20 each, while the Chinese bulbs cost only about 25 cents. Many consumers went for the cheap light bulbs. This price difference ended GE's dream of quick profits, among other things.

Before entering China, GE had been successful selling light bulbs in Japan and India, among other Asian markets. The Japanese and Indian consumers favored GE bulbs, to the detriment of the competitors. Naturally, GE made healthy profits in those countries. It came as a big shock to the GE management that China was different.

Naturally, trading takes two parties. This is something the GE people didn't seem to understand for some time. As one Chinese observer noted,[4] the GE people were not without faults. They did not do what they needed to do to make their grand dreams come true. Yet they wanted to make quick profits. They could only be disappointed.

Among other problems, the GE people did not devote enough effort to marketing. They did not tell consumers about the benefits of paying more. Anyway, the Chinese consumers could be as demanding as the US and other consumers around globe.

For many years, GE's approach in China was different from that of other global players. Strangely enough, they did not establish an effective marketing network. In the biggest department store in Shanghai, where the GE factory is located, GE bulbs could not be found. At the same time, many competing players, such as Philips, had been there for years, and had set up special counters with their light bulbs.[5]

OTHER LESSONS FOR GE

But the GE people blamed the situation on a stupid Chinese market. Its bulb business was disintegrating rapidly. Employees were fleeing and the managers did not know what to do. There was a moment of despair for GE management back in the United States.

Action was finally taken. After some serious work, the joint venture survived. Eight years after setup, GE turned a profit. Since 2000, it has been profitable, happily. But its market share is still behind that of Europe's Philips, a key competitor.[6]

GE's initial troubles in selling bulbs produced sharp effects on its management back home. Oddly enough, the managers were not learning the right lessons from the experience. The failure to obtain quick profits had many adverse consequences on GE's China strategy. It seriously affected their confidence. In their mind, China seemed to be a land unfriendly to GE offerings, bulbs included.

Even with its serious doubts back then, GE was expanding in China, though slowly. Over the years there have been both delights and disappointments. GE's medical equipment unit started a serious venture in Beijing to produce X-ray machines in early 1990s. Again, it had a rough start and incurred heavy losses. Once again, the marketing was not right, and GE had not tried to understand market needs. The products were selling at prices that were too high. Whatever could go wrong went wrong. Employees were leaving, and many joined competing companies. Things at GE's factory went chaotic. This mess seemed like one that might have been created by a startup, not a brand called General Electric.

To save the situation, GE called upon a manager from Taiwan. He has been a result producer. He has helped to turn the faltering X-ray venture into a success. Under his management, the medical company started over from the very basics, such as hiring the best employees, doing the right marketing, and talking to as many potential clients as possible. In the end, the company achieved profitability. Doing the right things is a must in order to win over the market. This is true even for a giant like GE.[7]

Following the early mess, GE's senior colleagues in the United States developed different views. They did not feel confident about going to China in a big way. At one point when the manager from Taiwan mentioned his plan to make China the biggest market for GE's medical equipment business—after the United States—his senior colleagues showed their true feelings. They laughed.

This lack of confidence produced consequences. It meant that GE was far behind its competitors in China, especially Siemens, Mitsubishi, and Philips. This slowness on the part of GE lasted for many years, until recently.

Now under the new leadership at GE, things are starting to change, dramatically. GE is aiming big in China. Interestingly enough, the 2002 annual report included a statement to that effect. That said a lot about GE in China today.

Since 2001, GE has become very active in China. It is adding new programs all the time. Among the new activities, GE has moved its three Asian divisional headquarters to China. It has set up a major research and development center in Shanghai. It has been active in making investments and setting up various partnerships. All this has represented a basic change.[8]

For a giant like GE, choices are plentiful. For example, GE has been outsourcing production to numerous Chinese manufacturers for some years. It has been increasingly active in buying cheap products made by Chinese companies and then putting its labels on them for the overseas markets.

By the end of 2003, the new $50 million GE lab was ready for operation in Shanghai. GE's new CEO claimed that this lab would help GE reach $5 billion in sales in China by 2005. In addition, GE would buy $5 billion in products from China by 2005. In short, GE aims to make China its new engine for growth.[9] Interestingly, Philips is well ahead of GE and did $9 billion in China business in 2004.

Today, GE is doing just fine. The stupid Chinese market is becoming terribly interested in all of GE's products. Suddenly it has learned how to make the smart moves. Even a heavy elephant, once it knows where to get the best leaves, can run like a kangaroo. The only problem, seemingly, is that numerous other elephants are also running fast.

JAPAN'S GLOBAL EFFORTS

Japan's global reach has impacted the world in countless ways. In China, Japan Inc. has been playing longer than most Western companies. So far, the performance of Japan's multinationals has been mixed. They have been influential here for well over two decades. Yet in many ways they should have been more influential than they are.

Japanese companies should have gained more market share, but they have lost many opportunities. Today, the Japanese multinationals are reshaping their strategies for China. In particular, the Japanese executives feel that they are ahead of China Inc. at the high end. In their view, they can simply build more plants in China to reduce costs and increase profits. Thus they will be able to acquire leadership over the Chinese.[10]

Many Japanese giants came to China in the 1980s. Their brands have become household names. In many respects, though, they could have achieved greater success than they did. They could even have dominated China's market in a big way. But that hasn't happened.

Events suggest that the Japanese companies didn't anticipate China's quick growth. Now, in this market, they are only one group of players among many. They have lost significant market share to all competing parties, especially the Chinese players. Their problems have been numerous. In the first place, the Japanese demanded huge prices for their products—easily 30% or more higher than those of the Chinese brands.

THREE DESTINATIONS FOR JAPANESE PRODUCTS

In many respects the Japanese did not take China seriously until recently. This is widely felt by Chinese consumers. How do these consumers view Japanese products? Their sense is that the Japanese send the best products to the United States, sell second-rate products at home, and dump the rest on China.[11]

Whether this is true or not, many Japanese businesses have run into problems in China. In particular, their high price tags have not helped. Seemingly, the Japanese have misread the map for a long time. For some decades, they thought that the Chinese would remain too poor to be taken seriously. But the Japanese have been surprised by the rising Chinese purchasing power. For this they paid a price over the long term, even if they made profits in the short run.

Certainly the high Japanese price tags kept Japan from taking a major market share. In the end, this has given rise to a huge space for development for China Inc. By the late 1990s, Chinese companies had succeeded in taking the market lead at the expense of the Japan Inc.

At this time, a continued boom in China has created new Japanese thinking. They are reshaping their strategies. To this point, Japan has had three waves of China investment. Each wave has involved different business aims and strategies.

The first two waves took place between 1985 and 1988 and in the mid-1990s. During those periods, the Japanese strategy focused on employing cheap Chinese labor and shipping products back home.

In the last few years, Japan Inc. has become extremely active in China. Japanese companies, big and small, have increased their investments. This has been viewed as the third Japanese wave in China. This time, Japanese companies have effectively improved upon their previous approaches. In general, they have adopted a new strategy: treating China as a huge factory-market. That is, Japanese companies want not only to produce products cheaply, but also to sell them directly to the Chinese.[12]

Most Japanese businesses now intend to use China as a new engine for growth. In this way they hope to reach the next growth level.

This new thinking has brought new Japanese investments to China. China is now full of Japanese factories and shops. In the words of the chairman of Matsushita Electric (China), the company wants 60% of its profits to come from China eventually.[13]

New Trade

Until 2004, Japan was China's top trading partner, ahead of the United

States and the European Union. Of late, some 50% of Japan's total increase in trade has come from China. Also, with the help of Japanese companies, by 2004 China had replaced the United States as a top exporter to Japan. This was directly aided by Japan Inc.'s Chinese operations. Japan Inc. now employs the strategy of manufacturing a vast range of products inside China and selling them around the globe. Naturally, benefits are tremendous, as currently the average salary for a manufacturing job is only about $115 per month in China.

This type of close trade link within Asia has become a new reality. At this time, all Asian nations have markedly increased trade among themselves. More impacts will occur as intraregional trade increases.

In particular, India's growth will further fuel Asian regional trade. Some people say that if China and India know how to market to each other, they can nicely complement each other's strengths. Indeed, India has a sharp IT industry that can help Chinese business in major ways. At the same time, the Chinese can manufacture all sorts of cheap products that India wants and can afford. The future looks promising. Development in this direction will have tremendous impacts far beyond these two oldest civilizations.

The traffic between China and Japan is certainly two-way. Many Chinese companies are eager to reach Japan. Thousands of them have set up offices there. But their work is just beginning. Tapping into the Japanese market is almost as difficult as landing on the moon. Like all foreign businesses, Chinese companies face countless barriers in Japan. At the same time, China is becoming a global theater with increasingly easy access for all. All the leading Japanese companies are expanding their investment programs in China. In addition, thousands of small and midsize Japanese companies have set up shop in China. They all want to take a dominating market share in China.[14]

CISCO VERSUS HUAWEI

Cisco is not just a global player. It is also famous for charging high prices and gaining impressive profits. Its gross profit margin can reach something like 70%. But such a high profit margin is a double-edged sword. According to *Business Week,* Cisco's huge profit margin has accidentally saved many of its smaller competitors.

One new competitor is called Huawei Technologies. It has been aggressive in selling products in the international markets. Huawei is no Cisco. It is still small, and its key market remains at home. Furthermore, it is not that competitive at the high end of the market where Cisco is the dominating player. Yet Huawei has its space. For there are even bigger markets at the middle and low levels. The telecom markets are growing fast not only in the developed world, but also in the developing countries. Small companies like Huawei are gaining the momentum to jump into these new markets.

Even the developed markets demand high-quality but inexpensive products. So new players like Huawei can gain clients. How does Cisco look at this?

In fact, Huawei is still small compared to Cisco, but its products are of high quality as well as cheaply priced. One foreign observer has been surprised by the low price tags on the company's routers. The foreign competitors' routers sell for a few thousand dollars each, but a Huawei router costs only $600.[15] This Chinese player has been trying hard to reach the overseas markets. Its biggest weapon is, of course, its low prices.

Nothing but cheaper pricing has made room for new players like Huawei. Given all this, several years ago the giant Cisco had to ask itself how it could sit still. How could past glory produce future profits?

As events evolved, Cisco took Huawei to court in New York, charging that its patented codes had been stolen, among other things. What can one expect for the future?[16]

In general, how might Cisco fend off its numerous competitors? Two approaches perhaps stand out. One is for Cisco to adapt to lower margins in one way or another. Another is to take over its major competitors. Otherwise, it will have more competition in the natural course of things. That is, small players will gain more clients and even more space to grow. But companies will not decide all these things in the end. Nor will the courts.

All things considered, the buyers will decide the outcome. They come from everywhere, from rich nations and developing nations. They will have the final say, not Cisco or Huawei. The trend in this direction is moving fast. The small players have lots of room for growth.

Huawei is moving ahead fast. It is the price advantage that is creating an international joint venture between it and 3Com of the United States.[17] Beyond this, Huawei has numerous partnerships with several global names from Japan, Europe, and other places. Even Microsoft has a joint program.

They are all interested in this company's high research capability coupled with low cost.

In October 2003, the court case was over. The parties reached a settlement out of court. A senior manager at Huawei expressed his view to me, saying that the Chinese company was happy about the outcome with Cisco. "As you know, we just had a news conference. We are happy with the latest development." Huawei is now ready to expand further. In particular, it now has high hopes for its partnership with 3Com as well as many other global partners.

So far, so good. Huawei's sales have been climbing steadily. By 2004, it had achieved record sales of $5.58 billion, of which $2.28 billion was from overseas markets.[18] For now, it is accelerating its global expansion programs.

MICROSOFT IN CHINA

Not many companies are as powerful around the planet as Microsoft. Yet Microsoft has run into problems in all emerging markets, including China. There is no easy way to get around such difficulties. Emerging markets like China are growing fast. China is already a top player in the PC market, second only to the United States. Winning China is certainly important. Yet so far, Microsoft has shown lackluster performance in China.[19] (Microsoft had $2 billion in sales in China as of 2003.)

The difficulty in creating more profits is related to the price issue. So far, Microsoft's problems in many developing markets exist largely in this context. In particular, Microsoft has not won many public projects in China. Over the past three years or so, success has not been great.

MICROSOFT VERSUS BEIJING MUNICIPAL GOVERNMENT

One episode in China hit a nerve with Microsoft. It happened in 2002, and the place was Beijing. The potential buyer was the city's local government. China's boom has resulted in a fast-growing computer market. Government offices are certainly significant users. The local government in Beijing is no exception. For a long time it has used all sorts of software products. Very recently, it has tried to implement one unified system. The number of clerks is huge, and they need tens of thousands of copies of documents.

Since 2002, the city government has tried to play the modern game: buying from a public bid. Open bids are rather new in China. This one attracted a lot of public attention. Many small software players rushed in. Naturally, Microsoft was aiming for the deal as well. After some time, the contracts went to some small domestic companies rather than Microsoft.

So, Microsoft gained nothing. Being a global brand, how could the company swallow this bitter pill? Actions naturally ensued. Microsoft changed at least three country CEOs within the past few years.[20] I asked one ex-manager about it. He told me that being a global winner was a way of life for Microsoft.

In a new market like China, gaining a major contract from the capital city would certainly be highly desirable. Huge publicity would follow. But Microsoft did not win the bid. In view of all this, how could Microsoft not worry? It seemed that for Microsoft this was a most serious deal. Yet it could not win over some nameless small players in China.

Its country managers were trying hard. They even brought Bill Gates and Steven Palmer to Beijing. Naturally, businessmen like Bill Gates or Steven Palmer knew the nature of the fight. It was a surprise to the Chinese to see them lobbying in China.

Their trips made hardly any difference with respect to these specific projects. Interestingly, some Chinese officials openly talked about their preference for Microsoft. But one thing stopped Microsoft from winning— price. Microsoft was undersold by numerous players, both domestic and international.

The outcome in Beijing was bitter medicine for these proud people to swallow. It is not only in China that they run into trouble, however, but also in many other parts of the developing world.

Microsoft has many clever employees, however. In China, the company is taking extra steps. It has been creating all sorts of partnerships with government entities and businesses. Through these, the hope is to get supporting partners to sell more products. A brand like Microsoft still has more advantages than most businesses. And this is as true in China as anywhere else.

CHANGES IN MICROSOFT'S STRATEGIES

Global software competition becomes more intense as time passes. The general trend is toward lower price tags. This is so simply because global consumers want the cheapest products and services. Countless Linux-based companies are competing to sell products at far lower prices than the big competitors. Even HP has joined in.

In the middle of 2003, reports surfaced about some new moves by Microsoft. The company had been trying to adopt more flexible marketing efforts. The *New York Times* reported that Microsoft wanted to modify its strategies. In developing markets, it would do whatever was needed to get more business, even if at no cost to the developing countries.[21]

Since early June 2003, Microsoft has taken dramatic steps. The new efforts have been aimed at taking bigger shares in markets like China and other less developed nations. In particular, the company has cut the price of MS Office products by 30%. In so doing it is trying to position itself to better fit the market trends in China.

GLOBAL PRICE REDUCTIONS

In general, the global market is moving toward lower prices for products and services. This trend is beginning to involve more and more markets around the world.

The power of pricing will involve all businesses, not just high-tech. This issue will be as significant as brands, intellectual property rights, and consumer loyalty, if not more so. As time goes by, pricing will become even more significant.

The rapid development in so many emerging markets, especially India and China, will impel more changes. Most products can be produced in more countries. It is increasingly hard for a few global giants to dominate.

Both India and China are among the top choices for job transfers. A software engineer may make $100 or more per hour in the United States. The same job can be done in India for $20 or less. How could the decision makers refuse to go to India or China?

Competition is high in the emerging nations as well. Now the Indian businesspeople are fearful about the low costs in China. They wonder if the Chinese will pay $10 or less for the same job. If and when that happens, it will bring about huge changes.

The developing nations like China and India cannot compete directly in the old ways. Instead, they must focus on things the developed markets may not want to deal with because they are not associated with healthy profits. These low profit margin businesses are what the emerging nations are good at. Even so, their choices and resources are extremely limited.

Multinational businesses mostly welcome globalization. After all, they have become the leading beneficiaries in the process. Choices have become much wider for foreign multinationals today. They can simply choose to do outsourcing, for example. They can also shop anywhere around the globe for the cheapest goods. Wal-Mart is one example—and Wal-Mart can reach $290 billion in sales. GE outsources many projects to India, among other low-cost markets. HP, Dell, and many Japanese computer makers have their products made by Taiwanese companies, which have become the biggest PC makers in the world. These Taiwanese companies are now moving increasingly to Mainland China.

The emerging nations can only focus on their limited resources. They cannot compete directly with the developed nations. Even so, they are operating in an expanding sphere. Through hard work, they are gaining their own share of benefits. In particular, low cost and competitive efforts remain their greatest strengths. India and China are the best examples in this context.

9 WHEN CAN CHINA'S COMPANIES BECOME GLOBAL?

A rising economy will produce some of the biggest multinationals. This has happened in Europe and United States, followed by Japan and South Korea. Now, it is China's turn.

Even so, most international consumers have not encountered Chinese brands directly. Will China Inc. go beyond China? Will Chinese companies act like the Japanese and Korean multinationals?

There are no straightforward answers. All things considered, China Inc. may not follow the Japanese or the Korean model.

WEAKNESS AT HOME

To be sure, many Chinese companies are trying to reach out, but their progress is slow. By 2004, China's total international investment reached around $40 billion. Overall, Chinese international expansion is gaining strength, though there are still tremendous barriers.[1]

So far, the success rate in outside markets is extremely low. One report showed that those companies from the most advanced regions in China had less than a 50% success rate when they tried to expand overseas.[2]

In 2004, China had 15 companies in the 500 club, but they are all in the state sector. Most Chinese companies are still small. What is more, their tiny profits are far below international norms. This is a fundamental weakness for the Chinese. At the same time, their borrowing is rather high. This is made worse by the fact that getting listed in the stock market is difficult. At this point, China has only about 1,400 listings in the domestic stock market and a few hundred listings in overseas markets. Raising sufficient capital is still difficult for most Chinese companies.

Unlike Japan Inc., China Inc. still lacks key resources in all business aspects. To be sure, China Inc. is different from Japan Inc. When the Japanese companies flooded the world with cars, electronics, and home appliances, they had different realities. Above all, they had already made healthy profits at home. With such fat profits, they could spend heavily in the outside markets.[3] But most leading Chinese companies have made only tiny profits at home.[4]

In many ways this should not come as a surprise. Japan has had a different home market. For a long time, its market was basically closed. This helped the Japanese businesses to achieve impressive profits at home. It forced Japanese consumers to buy goods at relatively high prices. A given Japanese electronics product could carry a much higher price tag in Tokyo than in New York. The Korean market is also closed in many respects. Moreover, the Korean multinationals have borrowed heavily. Though highly risky, this has helped them to expand.

China today is a different story. Its market is wide open for all. The home market is already very crowded. Most Chinese companies must compete with everyone, even at home. So generating healthy profits even at home is tough for all.

FOREIGN OBSERVATIONS

Many people around the world worry a great deal about globalization in general and the rapid progress of late-developing nations, especially China and India. Many are now concerned about whether the Chinese companies will expand globally in a big way. Some American and European players want to ban goods made in China.

Any reasonable analysis shows that there is no sound basis in reality for such reactions. Above all, China's economic development carries with it healthy opportunities for the world. In particular, China's export business is more a supplement to the developed markets than anything else. The Chinese companies focus on low-end products. Most Chinese products are not suited to the developed markets.

For the developing nations, such competition is healthy as well. It helps these countries achieve competitive economies in general. Increased competition has brought about greater openness in the developing nations, which in turn helps them better utilize their resources. All such efforts help to improve their living standards, as well as to narrow the gaps between the developed and developing nations.

Many foreign observers clearly see the positive contributions that will flow from a fast-developing China. From their perspective, China's expanding economy has brought numerous benefits to the world, especially the developed nations. Stephen Roach of Morgan Stanley has made some interesting comments. He believes that China's players are the right partners for the West. His view is supported by the fact that 50% of China's exports come from foreign operations in China. An additional 15% of exports come directly from joint ventures. These foreign operations help the participating multinationals in many ways. They can cut costs and directly increase profits. Roach even sees the outside worries as selfish. He believes that China's progress will do much good for the entire world.[5]

Indeed, in 2004, more than 57% of China's total export was carried out by foreign-funded enterprises. China has become a top factory for countless foreign multinationals from around the world. Without them, China's exports would be about 40% less.

According to a report in *The Economist,* China's own export strength is in the areas of bikes, clothes, and toys—in short, the low value-added business. China's companies do not have a way to compete in high value-added items such as semiconductors and autos. Instead, China can offer only the cheapest products to the developed markets.[6]

Numerous trade groups are worried about China's export as a threat to their jobs. But as noted in the *Wall Street Journal,* China's export trade cannot be stopped. The only realistic question is what developing countries it goes to—India, China, or Vietnam.[7] Why couldn't it be stopped? All things considered, such cheap Chinese goods are in the interest of consumers and multinationals. Today, new trends are developing in the multinationals' search for more ways to increase their profits. Big U.S. companies are adopting the strategy of paying Chinese salaries and marking products with U.S. prices.[8]

Yet there have been some troubling developments in trade issues. Both the United States and the European Union have tried to stop Chinese textile exports, for example. In spring 2005, these governments tried to impose bans through quotas. Such actions show that there is a long way to go before a rational mechanism for trade comes into existence. Instead, different nations increasingly employ governmental means to settle trade imbalances, which is not in the spirit of the WTO or GATT. Moreover, these governmental actions could block the road leading to a new, rational world economic order.

LOW BENEFITS FOR CHINA

China's economic strengths remain limited. In fact, the average manufacturing job pays about $115 per month. Such low-income work is left for developing countries like India, Vietnam, and China.

It is fair to say that China is not only nonconfrontational with, but also complementary to, the developed nations. If there is competition, it is among the developing nations. This reality will not be changed easily.

Actually, in many respects, foreign businesses gain more benefits from China than the Chinese do. China is now the biggest manufacturer of DVDs, with some 70% global market share.[9] In 2002, more than 70 million DVDs were sold in the outside markets. Yet most Chinese manufacturers made small profits.

In fact, it is the international technology, component, and chip suppliers that make the higher profits. They sell intellectual rights and components to the Chinese. For each DVD produced, the Chinese have to pay a royalty of at least $6 to the various international patent holders. In the end, they can make about 60 cents in profit. Very few foreign multinationals are interested in such low-profit business. Many Chinese producers feel that making DVDs is not as profitable as selling cabbage on the street corner. But they have little choice.[10]

To be sure, several Chinese companies have already developed their own technology for HVD, the next generation of DVD. But today these machines have to be compatible with DVD. So before DVD is phased out, the Chinese companies must continue to pay royalties.

China's new manufacturing power is very different from that of some other past or current centers. The United Kingdom was the first global manufacturing center. For a long time, the United Kingdom had the biggest companies in the world. It had the biggest banks and manufacturing and trading companies. They all generated healthy profits. With their large profits, they expanded globally as both trading players and investors.

China's economic boom has not created impressive profits for the leading Chinese manufacturers or for most businesses in any sector. This is a key difference between China and the outside world. In the West, global expansion has always given rise to healthy and profitable companies. The rise of U.S. industry has created even more profits and more powerful companies. U.S. products such as cars, computers, semiconductors, drugs, food, and drinks have dominated the world. Indeed, U.S. Inc. has had a world lead for decades.

But China is a different story. China's new development has involved the entire world. Foreign multinationals have directly shared in the expanded sphere of China's economy. Their presence increases competition and reduces profits for Chinese business.

Even when Chinese companies make products, they may enjoy limited benefits. Wal-Mart bought $18 billion worth of goods from China in 2004. But the more than 5,000 Chinese suppliers make tiny profits—not even a fraction of Wal-Mart's. Naturally, the countless consumers are the biggest winners. This fact is a basic feature of the global economy today.

Martin Wolf of the *Financial Times* takes the view that China is more open than Japan already. He feels that even some nations that have a trade deficit with China are benefiting from such trade. Therefore, the outside world should become more rational about China's rapid development. Furthermore, he believes that imposing trade restrictions would be negative for all the parties involved. In fact, a healthy global development needs to bring China in. China's progress should be viewed a positive achievement for everyone. In short, a more cooperative spirit is needed.[11]

Today, the world is deeply connected economically. But the cold war ideology is very much alive. It poses a roadblock to greater sharing and joint responsibilities. In this regard, huge efforts are needed in order for the world to move to the next stage of development.

STATE BANKS: "THE TROUBLEMAKERS"

China has huge problems to resolve at home, especially with regard to weak legal institutional issues. Slow progress in institutional reforms has caused serious problems. One of the most formidable tasks is to turn around the state sector, especially the four big banks.

The core of the problem is that the state sector in general and the state banks in particular are still enmeshed in the bureaucratic framework. The only way out is for them to become truly independent business organizations based on a proper ownership structure and modern management. At this time, there are no easy solutions. Financial numbers tell an important story: Bad loans with the big four banks reached 29% in 2000. By 2002, they were reduced to around 26%.[12]

More recently the banks have been doing better. By the end of 2004, 131 Chinese banks had a nonperforming loan rate of around 13%. Two of the big four banks, Bank of China and Construction Bank, reduced their nonperforming loan rate below 5%—a tremendous improvement—while the other two, Industrial and Commercial Bank and Agricultural Bank, reduced it to the teens.

Despite such progress, the fundamentals remain weak. In early 2004, the government injected more money into two of these banks. The sums were huge: $22.5 billion for each. In 2005, the government injected $15 billion into Industrial and Commercial Bank, the largest state bank. Yet this in no way means that the basic problems are resolved. Many feel that cash injections could become another "free lunch." In the past few years, even though the government has made this move several times, it has failed to turn the banks around.[13]

The banking problems extend to the entire Chinese economy. The biggest risk is that the four largest banks still control around 70% of China's banking assets. These four state banks are now called "troublemakers" by the media.[14]

Their poor performance has a long history starting from day one. Only by 1999, serious banking reform started. In that year alone, they had write-offs of $170 billion. The nonperforming assets had been on their books for many years, even decades. Since then, the banks have made endless bad loans still.

But the problem is hardly only a banking problem. It is simply because these banks are government units. Walking out of the banking mess demands reforming the entire political-economic framework. In particular, these banks must serve market needs rather than the government. They must have a true ownership structure as well as legal protections. After all, it is the existing framework that is directly responsible for the banking mess. Above all, a firm separation of government and the banking sector is a must.

It is true that better management makes a difference even for the Chinese banks. There are some good banks. The relatively new Merchant Bank is certainly one of the better ones. It has taken a nice ride in a rising economy. It has been profitable for many years. Its performance and profits are in line with international norms. Recently, GE in China selected this bank to handle its cash transactions.

Lately, banking reform has been moving ahead much more quickly than in the past. The government plans to list the big four banks in overseas and domestic stock markets as soon as possible. This is a very positive development indeed. It has attracted huge interest in the outside world. In particular, in June 2005, Bank of America spent $3 billion to buy a stake in the third largest Chinese bank, Construction Bank. The U.S. bank hopes to eventually increase its stake to as high as 19.9%, a limit for outside ownership set by Beijing. Furthermore, it wants to become actively involved in helping Construction modernize its management. Naturally, Beijing welcomes such foreign investment, which it views as a positive contribution to banking reform. In fact, such foreign involvement will cause a banking revolution in China.[15]

A LONG WAY TO GO

Today, China remains an emerging market in most ways. Its businesspeople seriously lack management experiences and skills, among other things. They may have insufficient experience to avoid costly mistakes. This is even more true when they step outside China.

As far as international expansion is concerned, more complex issues are involved. These have to do with all aspects of differing markets: Laws, business conduct, and distribution networks are all different. Culture, tradition, and language are all big factors. Managing these issues is still difficult for the inexperienced Chinese companies.

The traditional pharmaceutical players feel that they have good medicines that are needed by global consumers. But getting to the United States and European markets would be next to impossible at this point.

How much of a barrier does FDA approval impose? It is too costly. Hardly any Chinese player can afford to go through it. The testing work takes years and tens of millions of dollars. It is simply beyond the means of Chinese companies.

Importantly, all Chinese companies still lack brands and distribution networks outside. Building brands and networks requires huge capital and effort. How can China Inc. play in the outside world the way the foreign giants do in China?

Western companies have numerous advantages in emerging markets like China. The requirements are few. Their brands are mostly accepted already. Relatively speaking, they face minor regulatory issues. Much less work is required in order for them to take market share. And this is what has been happening in places like China.

In fact, many emerging markets have simply accepted FDA certification at face value. In China, though additional certification procedures are required, they are nothing like the FDA's. The Western drug companies can easily sell their drugs to Chinese consumers.

In addition, as an emerging market China is in the process of setting up new standards that usually follow Western standards closely. The Western players can take an active part in the process. They can therefore gain additional advantages.

Given all this, it would be tough for Chinese drug companies to expand overseas. So far, many have chosen to become suppliers of raw materials and semi-products to the global pharmaceutical industry. This role has been their way to reach out.

ᕫᕬ

For now, Chinese companies have a long way to go to become global multinationals. A wide gap exists between Chinese businesses and the global giants in terms of profits or sales.

In 2002, China's top 100 electronics, home appliances, and IT companies together produced $69.2 billion in sales. This sum was smaller than IBM's sales the same year. The total profits were $2.79 billion, only 52.7% of IBM's. In this group, Haier is the biggest Chinese player; It had $8.59 billion in sales and $326 million in profits—only 1/4 of Samsung's and 1/6 of Sony's. Haier's profit was 1/16 that of IBM and less than 1/23 that of Microsoft.[16]

China's biggest emerging companies are still weak. Having a global reach demands many resources and skills. Given all the facts, the Chinese companies are not able to follow in the path of the Japanese and Korean companies. The Chinese must rely more on resources at home. These facts have shaped China's international reach in general.

Even so, China has created alternate strategies to deal with the global markets. All this takes tremendous effort. It has already produced great results, as shown by the IBM-Lenovo deal. Even Haier wanted to acquire Maytag in 2005, though failed at the end.

10 CHINA'S GLOBAL REACH: ALTERNATE STRATEGIES

In this new era, China's growth started at an extremely low level. But it has gained speed very quickly. As far as going international is concerned, China has taken a unique path. Today, most Chinese companies conduct international business within their home base. This has meant bringing foreign businesses over to China in every possible way. Thus has China emerged as a global business center.

INTERNATIONAL EFFORTS

A few dozen Chinese companies will eventually join the 500 club. This could happen within the next 10 years. At this time, the 15 Chinese companies in the 500 club are all state-run companies. The list in 2003 included several telecom operators, four banks, State Grid, China Food Group, China Life, BaoSteel, and SAIC, the Shanghai-based auto maker.

China is now building a new power plant each and every week. The prize goes mostly to State Grid, which has been the energy monopoly for several decades. Only in this era of reform have private investors and overseas parties been allowed to enter the field. But still, nobody can compete with State Grid. It is everywhere and has been as powerful as the government. Complaining about poor service from this company can invite big trouble. For several decades, its predecessor, State Energy, was an integral part of the government. Moreover, China has almost always faced power shortages. But just as China is changing rapidly, so is the state sector. Only in the last few years has State Grid, willingly or not, begun to behave more like a company. In the new environment, even this company has improved its management and services.

State Grid is already ranked 46th in the club. It will become bigger, as China's energy needs are still exploding. In the last few years, and especially recently, there have been frequent power shortages, even if China is already the biggest energy supplier after the United States. Naturally, this attracts more investment. Also, this giant company comes under criticism for causing pollution. Currently, more than 70% of Chinese power plants still use coal. There are already several atomic energy plants, and more such projects are being added. But the market size is small. Even the hydraulic power market is much smaller than that for coal-burning power.

In the state sector group, at least two companies, China National Petroleum Company (CNPC) and Sinopec, are already global players. How can they be this big? Well, these two companies, together with China National Offshore Oil Corporation, form the state monopoly. Their annual profits could reach $4.5 billion or more.

A booming economy has brought these companies all the perks. Since 1993, China has become a net importer of oil. In 2003, China consumed 7% of the global oil supply. By 2020, its oil demand will more than triple. Fifty percent or more will have to be imported. So these two giants must go outside to acquire both supply and assets.

So far, CNPC has been competing with Sinopec head-on in the international field as well as at home. These two giants have fistfights with each other, especially when they see golden spots for gas stations. CNPC's new management style is reflected in the letter of complaint it sent to *Fortune* magazine when the *Fortune* editors wrongly ranked the company a low 73rd. The magazine had to upgrade CNPC to the 52nd slot.

Both companies have already cut a few dozen deals around the world. Both are aggressive and go everywhere oil resources are located. So, these two giants are ahead of the curve compared to China Inc. as far as international expansion is concerned. But several others in this group are not far behind.

Take China Mobile and Unicom. These companies are the monopoly over China's mobile communication market. China is already the biggest mobile phone market in terms of users. By 2004, there were 330 million users. China Mobile and China Unicom have been the winners in this game. Private Chinese companies are banned from the field. At this time international companies can only sell them hardware and software.

With billions in cash and 334 million consumers in hand as of 2004, these companies can go far. At investor conferences, many investors ask about their plans. But the truth is that China has an exploding mobile market, and these companies will stay at home for a while. They have yet to gain international experience.

The Shanghai-based steel mill BaoSteel is expanding fast outside of China. It is creating a major joint venture in Brazil. China's steel market is already bigger than those in the United States and Japan combined, and China still imports more steel. Its manufacturing expansion is demanding ever-increasing amounts of metals, steel, and cements, among other basic industrial materials. So BaoSteel and many other Chinese companies are reaching out to be near resource-rich places. Canada, Australia, Africa, and Latin America are all natural choices. We should expect more deals from these Chinese companies in the near future.

But today, most Chinese companies are weak and small. Even so, many of them are trying hard to reach out. Going international often means buying existing companies in the outside world. This has become a strategy for Chinese companies as well. The number of deals involving Chinese companies has been increasing. In November 2002, TCL bought the bankrupt European brand Schneider Electronics AG. Less than $10 million was involved, but the deal attracted much media attention. This transaction shows how eager China's business community is to reach out. It represents a popular desire. With abundant production capability, finding new markets is crucial to survival.

In general, only a few Chinese players are ready to go out in a big way. It is not just the small players, but even most leading consumer products players that have difficulty going international. In fact, they do not yet have a strong home base, a necessary condition for meaningful international expansion. So far, international expansion has not really been smooth sailing for China Inc.[1]

BRINGING INTERNATIONAL BUSINESS IN

Yet there are alternatives, as many roads lead to Rome. China has expended much more effort in bringing overseas businesses to China. This has been the dominant strategy up to now—and one that has been successful.

Many pharmaceutical companies have tried to reach overseas markets in other ways. They have focused on the low end of the business chain. They may supply semiproducts or materials. Some sell vitamin products and generic drugs on an OEM basis.

In general, achieving higher levels will take a long time. There are many issues to be resolved before companies can truly compete globally. For example, building global brands will take a long time and great effort. Without reaching out in a big way, brands cannot become global.

SLOW PACE OF INTELLECTUAL DEVELOPMENT

Intellectual development is new to Chinese business. So far, most companies have made limited progress in this area. A lack of cutting-edge technology has many adverse consequences. One fact that has shocked Chinese businesspeople is the size of the profit margins of many global IT companies. International giants such as Cisco, Microsoft, and Intel have gross profit margins between 40% and 70%. Most Chinese companies have tiny profit margins. Moving to higher levels is no easy job.

Overall, Chinese businesses have not expended enough effort on research. There are numerous obstacles. For one, collaboration between academic centers and businesses is weak. Companies confront huge problems in attempting to turn interesting research results into business. Even registering globally for intellectual rights and copyrights is a notable weakness. Companies may lack capital and other resources to do this effectively. Some critics say that they have not tried hard enough.

In reality, foreign multinationals have enormous advantages in terms of intellectual development. They still control most key intellectual products. The Chinese must work with them to obtain these products.

Some Chinese companies have chosen different strategies. They may prefer to focus on end products with borrowed technology. I asked one executive of a Chinese mobile phone maker, "Why is your company not doing much research?"

He answered without a second's delay: "Well, it would be unwise to spend much money on research. It takes too much capital and too long a time. Overall, it may not be sensible for this industry. Once your research is done, other guys may have better products already. What is more, buying technology is much more economical. There are so many suppliers from overseas. They are competing to sell us the latest things. It is pretty cheap to buy directly from them."

This view is not unusual. Many Chinese businesspeople see the issue in the same light. Many have yet to widen their vision. But more and more people are thinking globally. They are painfully aware of their shortcomings, especially in the area of cutting-edge technology and intellectual development. More and more companies see the greater need for research and development.

Some progress has already been made in this direction. Leading the trend are companies like Huawei, TCL, and Haier. They are among the most competitive Chinese brands. They are leading the way toward international expansion. So far, they have had varied degrees of success outside.

They are all eager to move higher, with the idea that controlling intellectual property could mean a bigger space for survival itself. Some of their recent activities have been interesting. Some Chinese businesses are trying to set up their own research centers. A number of Chinese high-tech and home appliance makers are active in this area.

As discussed earlier, Huawei has focused on its own intellectual development with success. The company has independently produced several dozen semiconductors for the telecom industry. By 2004, it held more than 1,500 patents. With its wide product range and research excellence, Huawei can stand up to competition with names like Siemens, Nortel, Lucent, and Cisco.

Huawei for many years has also tried hard to go international. As a first step it has chosen India's Bangalore as a research hub. To the Huawei executives, having a lab in India seems highly economical and sensible. Strange? Not to those who have done their homework. To bring Indian engineers to the home base would be more expensive. In addition, creating a lab in India will enable the company to tap into the resources of the Indian software talent.

There are additional benefits. Creating a lab in India's IT hub will help the company gain international experience. There are many interesting international players in Bangalore. Being their neighbor will have a number of advantages. These players will no longer be strangers. Having a facility in India is a way to enjoy the good things India possesses. So Huawei has avoided other high-tech centers, such as Silicon Valley, for its first international lab. It is happy with India and will be adding more components to its presence there.

Huawei has been active in expanding globally. It has an aggressive, take-no-prisoners management style. Recently, the company sent a marketing team to Russia. Before they left, the top man told them, "Go bring some rubles back. Otherwise, don't come back at all."

REACHING OUT

Reaching outside markets demands a great deal of direct contact and networking, among other things. As a first step, numerous Chinese companies have set up representative offices in many markets. Through such channels the Chinese hope to open windows.

One new trend is to create partnerships with local players in the overseas markets. Chinese companies are interested in doing more along these lines. They hope to widen marketing and distribution channels, for example. Through such partnerships they also want to incorporate into their products the best technology and market intelligence.

Silicon Valley is a major attraction. Several leading Chinese electronics and home appliance makers have set up research labs there. These include the top three Chinese consumer electronics brands, Konka, TCL, and Chonghong.

KONKA

Konka's experience in the United States has been interesting. Konka's lab has been active in helping the company to become more market oriented. One of its innovations is TV models in colors. The television set, in blue, orange, or red, can become part of the home décor. Some of the new models sell well in the United States.

Konka has also tried to expand its markets in other developing countries. It has set up manufacturing facilities in India and Vietnam. The company hopes to become a global player one day.

At home, Konka has been trying hard to move up in the value chain. In particular, it sees a vast market for high-end monitors and is trying hard to become a major player in this area. Like many Chinese home appliance and electronics makers, Konka has also expanded its product lines to include all sorts of consumer products such as PCs and handsets. For now, it is somewhat behind key competitors such as Haier and TCL, but its strong domestic position has already attracted international attention. Recently, the French giant Thomson bought a stake in this company to become the second biggest shareholder.

HAIER

One Chinese player, Haier, has been a leader in reaching out. Haier has built different models for its international programs in different markets. The company has set up plants in the United States, hiring locals to run the local business. It has a U.S. CEO at the helm. Under his leadership, Haier has had some success. Targeting the college market with the subcompact refrigerator has been a clever move. But going beyond this success will require more effort. Moreover, the U.S. operations will depend on continued good performance at home.[2]

So far, Haier has made overall progress both at home and abroad. The company's capabilities in research and development are impressive. On average, it creates one and a half new products daily. This is striking even by global standards. One some occasions when visiting clients asked for certain types of products, these products came into existence overnight. The Haier designers and engineers are very proud of their ability to meet client needs. In this context, the company goes the extra mile to satisfy clients.

Haier is very close to entering the 500 club. In 2004, its sales reached $12.2 billion. Now its business lines have expanded to handsets and consumer electronics. Haier could become a Chinese Philips or Sony one day provided that there is a further improvement on all important matters.

GALANZ

Even if many international consumers are not aware of the name Galanz, they may already own a microwave oven made by this company. It is already the world's biggest manufacturer of microwaves, with some 40% of the global market.

Galanz's international expansion has been successful in another way, involving two steps so far. First, Galanz achieved the dominant position at home. As the second step, the company has searched globally for more markets and partners. The aim is to be the manufacturing center for the world. Galanz has avoided building new factories in other countries. Instead it has chosen to be an OEM player for the global market along with its own brands. The aim is to fully utilize the existing resources at home. The company possesses an impressive collection of manufacturing facilities, human resources, and professional management in China. At the same time, it will try to bring in as much international business as possible.

In this way Galanz hopes to gain the best from both worlds. This strategy has helped the company to fully utilize its resources. Existing resources, including trained low-paid workers, can be employed directly. Furthermore, the company has a complete setup for quality assurance and services.

Galanz has relied on the old trick: the lowest price tag. This strategy has proven successful. The company has attracted a large crowd of international OEM clients by offering the best pricing and efficiency. The low pricing has been attractive to numerous international counterparts. How could they refuse the opportunity to make more profit without jeopardizing anything important?

Numerous international microwave oven producers have shipped their assembly lines to Galanz's home base, which takes care of their production. With this type of arrangement, both parties win.

Through these partnerships, foreign players cut costs more than significantly. Without compromising on quality, they achieve big savings. If it takes $80 to produce a microwave oven in Europe, Galanz can do it for $40 or less. The cheapest models can be produced for as low as around $30. As already noted, Galanz is now the world's number-one producer of microwave ovens. Its international sales have been growing fast. In 1996, it sold about 40,000 sets to the overseas markets. In 2002, production reached 12.68 million—40% of global output. Of this, about 70% went overseas.[3]

The company has successfully created a multichannel distribution network. It focuses on its own brand and on OEM at the same time. It sells its brand products whenever possible, as long as there is no conflict with the OEM clients.

It should be noted that Galanz's profits are tiny—only pennies for each microwave oven. Achieving a higher profit margin is no easy task. For one thing, Galanz has several major competitors inside China. International clients move among all these companies seeking advantages. To attain greater profitability, Galanz must either take greater market share, or innovate more, or do both.

In the last few years, Galanz has been creating more products, notably air conditioners. Progress with this new venture has already been huge. In 2004, Galanz became the number-one Chinese exporter for air conditioners and shipped a total of 1.55 million sets to overseas markets. It is still expanding its production facilities and hoping to become a global leader in air conditioners. Yet, oddly, within China the company is a minor player in the air-conditioning market.

The Galanz model has become increasingly popular. Doing OEM has become very fashionable. China's new manufacturing power and low cost have made China a top place for outsourcing. Global giants like GE, Sony, Siemens, and Nokia have increasingly come to China for contracted work.

Outsourcing has become a key strategy for multinationals. Today, multinationals have many more choices of ways to reduce costs and increase profits. All this has become an important aspect of globalization. China's role as an outsourcing center will only increase in both volume and scope.

INDUSTRIAL PARKS

China's new passion for wealth has many consequences. One is the desire to turn vast farmland into industrial and commercial parks. There are 3,837 industrial parks in China now.[4] Owning an industrial park is a source of pride. It means that one has brought numerous new businesses into the town. And the park may attract more outside investments.

Most parks are owned and operated by government entities at various levels. Owning a profitable park also generates political prestige. This is an even more important reason for government officials to jump into business dealings in general and into industrial parks in particular.

Despite imperfections, the industrial parks are a significant component of the business chain. They have helped foreign players in a number of ways. They have helped to create efficiency and savings. In addition, many Chinese companies also make use of the industrial parks. The owners and developers have gained wealth and power in the process. Therefore, more and more parks have emerged.

Many industrial parks have achieved success. One of their common features is that they are all located around major economic zones. Most are located in major coastal regions such as Guangdong, Shanghai, Beijing, and Tianjin.

The Suzhou Industrial Park has become a major site for multinationals. Its location is a key attraction, as it is within an hour of Shanghai, the economic center for southern China.[5]

Guangdong has even more successful industrial parks. Many of these parks were designed for export companies, both domestic and foreign. One leading group consists of companies from Hong Kong. There are thousands of them, mostly small. Their products can be shipped easily to international destinations.

The industrial parks in Beijing and Tinjian have similar conveniences. They also have the advantage of proximity to the regional markets as well as major ports.[6] So they are also major locations for international companies.

But in fairness, it must be said that there are just too many industrial parks now.[7] Overcapacity has resulted from the fact that the government remains a key investor and operator. The owners are mostly government units or state-owned companies. Some use such parks for housing development, which is against government policies. Critics claim that there is much waste and abuse associated with the industrial parks.[8]

MORE EXCHANGES AND WIDENING CHANNELS

The idea of creating trade platforms has inspired enormous effort. Every city wishes to become a trading center. Shenzhen is a step ahead of others in this respect. Shenzhen has created an annual high-tech fair to attract high-tech players globally. Each year thousands of high-tech companies come to the fair to display their work. Businesses from all regions of China also attend. In a short period of time, many international companies have rushed to the fair. It is one of the biggest shows in China today.

Additional programs are connected with the fair. In particular, the city has created an investment brokerage house: the Shenzhen Hightech Property Exchange. The aim is to provide a brokerage service for asset transactions, a platform for buyers and sellers. Shanghai and Beijing, among other major cities, have similar organizations. Each city has developed its own ways of promoting business transactions.

One Shenzhen insider said to me, "We are better than those in Beijing and Shanghai. Their exchanges are run by the local governments. Ours has many shareholders. We operate as a company instead of a government enterprise." But one Beijing Property Exchange insider told me, "We are located in Beijing, the headquarters for most of the biggest Chinese companies. What is more, by government guidance, whatever asset transactions happen, they must go through an exchange like mine. Therefore, we have all the advantages."

Yiwu

Another interesting model exists in Yiwu, a city in Zhejiang province. This once faceless rural location has emerged as a key center for trade. It has created a vast platform for both foreign and Chinese traders. It focuses on small consumer products ranging from household items to consumer electronics and toys and clothes. It has attracted tens of thousands of international traders in unique ways.

Yiwu is indeed a special place. It offers one-stop shopping for traders. Today, there are some 8,000 international traders living in the city.[9] The city offers a complete range of services. Many major international shipping businesses are stationed there as well. The best feature for international buyers is that all the goodies are in one spot. The pricing for these goodies is highly competitive. Furthermore, the local traders can be extremely flexible in their dealings. No deal is too large or too small. Within such an environment, this tiny place, which is really nowhere in terms of its location, has become a major attraction for global traders.

Yunnan

In the province of Yunnan, efforts have taken a different direction. The people there have adopted a new business model in order to attract companies from both within and outside China. Among other attractions, they have developed a garden and flower fair.

The region is particularly rich in agricultural products. A World Fair was undertaken in 2002 for the purpose of widening the region's marketing channels. After the fair, exchange continued. The aim is for international and domestic traders to trade agriculture and gardening products. So far, numerous international and domestic businesses have set up trading shops there. A new specialized trading platform has been produced.

China's oldest trade show remains the biggest—the Guangzhou Merchandise Fair, held twice a year. For several decades, it was the only platform for international trade. Even today, it is the most important trade show in China.[10] Chinese companies have to fight hard to get into the fair, and only a lucky few get a booth.

Beyond these platforms, numerous other channels have come to life. In every region there are all sorts of business fairs going on all the time. Fairs have become a huge business.

Organizing trade shows has become a new industry. There are already a large number of companies specializing in this field. Many of these are in the state sector. In particular, many business events are still sponsored by government at all levels. Increasingly, though, private companies are rushing into the field.

Many international organizations have also come to share in the growing pie. Together, they make more things happen. Forming connections between China and the outside world has become a big business. Many international government bodies have stepped in. Every year, large government delegations, together with business groups, come to China. All this has been positive in terms of building a global business network.

BUYING INTO INTERNATIONAL MARKETS

In the international markets, China Inc. is particularly interested in three kinds of assets: those that will provide distribution channels, those that can offer leading-edge technology, and finally, industrial and raw materials such as oil and minerals.

One small auto parts maker bought a U.S. marketing company with the idea that this would help it to widen distribution channels. In another case, a Chinese IT company acquired the CDMA research unit from the European company Philips. By buying this unit, the Chinese hoped to develop new technology for their own use.[11]

Such transactions represent new international efforts. On the global stage, they are insignificant at the moment. For the participants to become influential players will take long time. So far, there have been only occasional transactions of this kind. Many difficulties exist for such programs. They require serious capital, to say the least. Furthermore, managing an international business is no small task. Historically there have been plenty of failures.

Back in the 1980s, a major company in the state sector, Capital Steel in Beijing, went out into the overseas market. It set up a company in Latin America. But soon it ran into many difficulties with labor, management, and the government there. This proved to other Chinese players that going international can be very risky. It is not for everyone.[12] In short, going international brings new risks. And most Chinese companies are too small to take large risks.

So far, the Chinese companies have been extremely careful in the overseas markets. By now, they have set up operations in all nations and regions. With regard to the developed markets, the number-one location is North America. Among the developing markets, the top choices are Latin America and Southeast Asia.[13]

Some notable projects involve a number of home appliance and electronics companies. For example, many Chinese manufacturers have set up factories in India and Indonesia. They wish to make India and Indonesia both a manufacturing base and a market. The reason for choosing these nations is that the labor costs are low and the market is growing.

There are already some successful international projects. These projects may be insignificant in the eyes of global companies, but they demonstrate serious efforts on the part of the Chinese.

Going to Japan is of great interest to China Inc. One joint venture with a Japanese company was set up in July 2003. The Japanese company is an established pharmaceutical player. The Chinese player, 999, is a leading pharmaceutical concern in China. The venture will enable the Chinese company to distribute its 100 drugs in Japan. This news created great excitement.[14]

It took more than two years to finalize the deal, although it involved only $1 million. This type of venture has become attractive to China Inc in general. Many experts view such deals as a significant step toward tapping into Japan.

The demand in the overseas markets for traditional medicines is more than $20 billion a year. So far, Japan and Korea are the leading players. China produces these medicines, but the international sales are very small. So all Chinese companies are trying diligently to reach the outside markets. They have advantages, as they have a vast range of traditional drugs with low price tags. Yet up to now, they have had insufficient channels in outside markets. The joint venture with Japan is a serious effort on the part of China Inc. to reach out.[15]

CREATING MORE PARTNERSHIPS

Up to now, the most popular approach to international expansion has been to invite foreign players to come to China. This strategy has worked well so far. When international businesses want to sell their products in large quantities in China, they must come to China to set up plants as required by government policies. Otherwise, they face high tariffs and other obstacles.

To date, things have been going very well for all parties. How could they not? How could 1.3 billion consumers not look attractive to any profit-driven business? If the Chinese can consume 100 million sodas a day, how can Coke and Pepsi refuse to come?

Global markets today face the issue of overcapacity. A booming China means a large opportunity to use extra production capacity. China has already become a new answer to all kinds of international needs, this one included.

Who has benefited the most? Countless foreign players have certainly become winners. With the WTO, China will have to change many old restrictions. There are more choices. For example, international makers in all fields can import their products directly. The overall tariffs decrease significantly. This is one opportunity that has been well exploited by the Korean giant Samsung. Samsung has taken a large share in China's mobile sector without a local plant for many years.

The WTO will certainly widen opportunities as many old restrictions are lifted. More trade and investment will occur. This is bound to be increasingly productive for all participants.

In the past three decades, numerous policy restrictions motivated the creation of joint ventures in China. With the WTO, there will be more choices. Businesses may choose to operate independently or to work with Chinese partners. Creating independent operations rather than joint ventures is currently gaining in significance. In 2002, about 65% new foreign projects chose independent foreign operations in China.[16]

Despite the wider choices, many foreign players are still setting up joint ventures in China. They see advantages in teaming up with Chinese companies. The reasons are simple. Numerous Chinese companies have developed rapidly and have become appealing to outside players. Their strengths have attracted many global giants.

Indeed, joint ventures and strategic partnerships have become very popular, though in a new framework. These have new meanings for many players. Above all, increasingly the Chinese partners can offer great advantages. It is these extraordinary benefits that stand behind the new waves of partnerships.

What can Chinese businesses offer the outside parties? They now have a huge manufacturing capability that can produce nearly any product under the sun. Moreover, they are fast improving in terms of professional quality, fast moving to a higher level. With an exploding home market, they may be able to reach out in the near future in one way or another.

Still, Chinese businesses prefer to create partnerships when possible. They have developed significantly in many ways, but they have done less well with regard to intellectual development, brands, and distribution networks, especially in the outside world. Thus at the moment the best way to move forward is through partnerships. The global trend is in this direction as well.

In 2003, a strategic partnership was created between Thomson SA and TCL. It was accomplished through a joint venture. One of the companies is a global brand, and the other is a leading Chinese manufacturer of consumer electronics and home appliances. The joint venture would produce TV sets, among other things. The partnership nicely combines the brand and research power of Thomson with the manufacturing power of TCL. Therefore, it benefits both parties in obvious ways.[17]

More recently a deal was made by IBM and Lenovo. This agreement surprised the world. Hardly anyone expected a Chinese IT company to become global. In making the deal, IBM got out of a declining PC business. Lenovo became a global player in one shot.

At this point China is becoming increasingly connected to the world economy. One significant result is that China is now more open than Japan is. Japan has been expanding globally without opening its domestic market to foreign players. Interestingly, Japan has held on tightly to its closed network. Even with better and cheaper products and services, foreign companies often find it difficult to play in Japan. But China has become more willing to have foreign involvement. To be sure, foreign involvement can present great challenges to Chinese businesses. Even so, China has obtained benefits from the foreign presence so far. With the WTO, more opportunities will exist for the outside players.

FOREIGN ACQUISITIONS

Foreign companies have been increasingly buying Chinese assets as a way to tap into China. There are many interesting Chinese companies for them to buy. They exist in all sectors.

Most targeted assets are considered strategic. By acquiring these assets, foreign players hope to gain a quick foothold in China. For example, both eBay and Amazon became established in China by acquiring Internet companies in their fields. This trend will continue. For example, Google is busy buying into Chinese search engine concerns.

As of this writing, the year 2004 was the most active in terms of foreign acquisitions. Many high-profile projects were undertaken by multinationals. Among the top 10 deals, the British Bank HSBC spent $1.7 billion buying 19.9% of China's fifth largest bank, China Communication Bank. In mid-2005, this bank became a new listing on the Hong Kong stock market. Also, Anheuser-Busch became the sole owner of a regional Chinese beer maker, Harbin Beer. Two Japanese multinationals rushed in to buy a stake in a food company. All these transactions created another record for foreign direct investment in China. It amounted to over $60 billion.

At the same time, China Inc. went out to acquire overseas assets. In one high-profile deal, Sinopec, one of the three Chinese oil and petrochemical giants, went to South Korea to take over its fifth largest petrochemical company, which had been in bankruptcy since 2001.[18] The acquisition cost $556 million. Sinopec and two other petrochemical companies have cut several dozen deals in the outside world already. At the moment they are increasingly active in addressing the rising demand for oil and petrochemical products within China.

By June 2005, more high-profile merger activities had taken place. While the U.S. giant Bank of America came to China to buy into Construction

Bank, two leading Chinese multinationals made headlines in the United States. Haier made a $1.28 billion offer to buy the distressed Maytag, the third largest U.S. home appliances maker, aiming to employ its brand for global expansion. And China National Offshore Oil Corporation offered $18.5 billion to take over Unocal. All such activities, though failed, have opened up a new chapter for global business.

Part III

China's Reform at Home: The Unfinished Task

OWNERSHIP; TRUST; STATE AND PRIVATE SECTORS; LEGAL PROTECTIONS; CORPORATE RESTRUCTURING; MARKET COMPETITION

11 PROBLEMS OUTPACING SOLUTIONS

Reinventing China is a mighty task. A booming economy coexists with huge problems. For now, China is going through a painful transition.

Currently, institutional weaknesses are causing enormous pain in the society and the economy. The government has yet to become a service provider instead of a market competitor. It is still the dominating operator in the market. In the stock market alone, some 90% companies are under government control. To reform the state sector demands reforming the entire political-economic framework, nothing less.

Why is the government so interested in keeping a huge state sector? Its motivation is political. One reporter writes, "Up to this time, the problems with the state sector are really created by the government to a great extent. In the 608 business sectors, it has dominated 604. It has also created a powerful ideology to go with it. For long, it has firmly believed that the state sector is its very foundation for power. Therefore, all the private business must be completely eliminated. So that its power can be expanded without limits."[1]

Reforming the state sector requires reforming the entire political-economic system in which the government has unchallenged domination. For certain, it means turning the government body into a modern service body.

In the current era, it is the government that has pushed reform. Naturally this has seriously limited decisions about what to reform. So far, it is clear that whenever reform actions might undermine government interests, the government tries hard to stop them. This is the reason for the extremely slow pace of serious legal and institutional reform.

This slowness has also created enormous problems for the government as well. As one policy researcher points out, "As far as the reforming the state sector is concerned, the government policy was already announced in 1993: its goal was to turn the state-owned companies into modern business organizations. Though this program has been going on for long, the state sector is still far away from a modern framework with a well-defined legal structure. Yet, it is a crucial issue, for it is the key of the reform."[2]

Furthermore, according to this researcher, "Also in 1993, the Government determined to establish a 'uniform, open, competitive and orderly' market system. After 10 years, the aspects of 'uniform and orderly' are still far away from the goal." The delay means that China has paid a high price.

STATE ASSETS AND *DEATH ON THE NILE*

China's state sector has existed for thousands of years. The current situation is no more than a new chapter in a long history book. As was true 1,000 years ago, the state sector engages in strange behavior. China's people are constantly surprised by one continuing phenomenon. On the one hand, state-owned assets are said to be divine. On the other hand, the government continually faces foes within. These foes are huge in number, and their destructive power threatens nothing less than its survival. One of the most salient features of the situation is that these parties all utilize the supreme government power for personal gain. Under this cover, it is easy to get away with abuses.

Reforming this failed framework is a monumental task, for the enemies are within the government rank and file. This situation is difficult to grasp. In some ways, it is like the scenario in Agatha Christie's popular detective novel, *Death on the Nile.*

On a paddleboat cruising down the magnificent River Nile, as Christie tells it, a tragic event is unfolding. A beautiful young woman and her new husband are on their honeymoon. Many of the young woman's friends and associates have come along to join in the celebration. The young woman is not only intelligent and very beautiful, but very rich. She has everything her companions value. But at this joyous time, things may not be as they seem.

To be sure, this divine creature knows her power. She can have anything she desires. Sometimes she gets what she wants at the expense of others.

Yet who would have guessed that death travels with her each and every step? She begins to see signs that someone is trying to harm her. Who? Why? How can she protect herself? She pays handsomely for the assistance of the clever detective Hercule Poirot, who happens to be among the passengers on the boat. On a visit to a pyramid, she is almost killed by a falling rock, and from this point on, Poirot is even more intent on guarding her.

The enemy—if there is one—is everywhere. All her companions have the motives, opportunities, and means to make something terrible happen.

And it does. Late one evening, the young woman is found dead in her cabin. In the end, we find out what we would never have guessed—it is her new husband who has killed her. A sad story makes a good book and an exciting film. Yet the central conflict has much in common with what is happening in China. The beautiful victim is like the state sector.

On the surface, the state sector is supposed to be divine. In principle, it is supposed to be protected by the entire society. The reality is just the opposite. Countless people take advantage of the state sector. People are not sure who owns the state assets. There is no guardian like detective Poirot. Even if there were a Poirot in place, there would be no way to safeguard the government's assets, for abusers number in the millions. Worse still, most people don't really know who is responsible for protecting these assets.

Most strangely, it is often the protectors and managers who commit the abuses. Indeed, the foes are within. Today, corruption takes aim largely at the state assets. This has been extremely destructive for China. In 2004 alone, 43,757 government officials were convicted of corruption.[3]

There are countless ways in which corrupt people can exploit the state assets, and few if any true protectors. Some government officials have observed, "The corrupt men not only take corrupt money from the public. They also employ more means to take vast capital and assets into their own pockets. What is worse: they employ the government power and offices to take personal advantages, thus doing destructions to the socialist market system and national economy. If such acts were not stopped, they would create great disasters and even the collapse of China's economy."[4]

Behind the widespread corruption, there is an overwhelming state power that demands the services from the entire society and people. Countless corrupt officials can utilize this supreme state power for personal gains. But up to now, China has yet to find ways to do away with it.

"Two Pockets of the Same Jacket"

The overall environment defines the behavior of human beings. People cannot escape this regardless of how hard they try. In China, the supreme government power has created a particular kind of behavior. Above all, hardly any citizen is sure who owns the state sector companies and banks.

Some time back, I visited a state-owned consumer products company. The company was trying to expand its business but did not have enough capital to do so on its own. Management had its eye on outside assets.

The CEO and I met. I was interested in knowing the financial details, especially how the company would pay off its heavy bank loans. Compared to the small cash flow, these loans seemed too big. "How will you pay back the loans?" I asked. "They seem large."

"Well," the CEO said, looking a bit surprised. "We will not pay them back at all."

I was surprised too. He continued, "Well, we are a state company and so are the banks." He was talking as though this was a matter of $100. "These banks have no reason to demand us to pay. We won't pay them anyway. After all, it is like two pockets of the same jacket."

How can the banks survive if such loans are not repaid? Worse still, how about the bank depositors?

The old framework has done huge harm to Chinese life. Given such realities, banks are very limited in their ability to protect their interests. Many times, this is not through their fault alone, as they face forces beyond their control. In particular, most borrowers are from the state sector and government units. It has been difficult for the state banks to take market measures. Changing this is easier said than done.

Lack of Weapons and True Owners

In real life, Chinese bankers do not have effective ways to protect their interests. Above all, the banks are not independent. They have existed to serve the needs of government. What is the most serious banking headache? Collecting loans. Lending is easy, but collection is tough. Bankers often become helpless when confronting unpaid debts. What happens very commonly is this: Before the bankers agree to lend, they are treated like royalty. As soon as the check is written, they are treated like beggars.

Why does China have such a crisis with trust? Any observer would naturally ask, How about the courts? The answers are troubling.

Seeking the help of the courts has become a tool for the lenders. To be sure, most court judgments are in favor of the debt owners. Yet these rulings may not mean much in actuality. Very often, they have little practical effect, as often these orders can't be executed. Without ways to reinforce such court judgments, how can the wrongdoers be stopped?

The percentage of court judgments that can be executed is a problem. On March 3, 2003, one of the important state institutions, the Chinese National Political Consultancy Conference—which together with the People's Congress is similar to the U.S. Congress—held its 10th national meeting. One major focus of the meeting was the ineffectiveness of the court system—specifically, the fact that about 70% of all court judgments cannot be carried out.[5]

Today, China's courts lack true authority. But they can hardly take all the blame for their ineffectiveness. Court officials may be beaten when they try to carry out court orders. There are many such reported cases.[6]

This weak legal system has created an adverse chain reaction. Many lenders are not willing to go through the courts. Worse still, to some bankers, going to court is no longer a way to find solutions. Rather, it is a way for them to show that they have done all the work required. Such realities have produced a great deal of undesirable behavior in the market.

Many borrowers continue to seek loans without thinking of paying them back. One scenario in particular is very common. People borrow money from the banks and thereafter spend wildly. Under such conditions, it is easy to see why many luxurious hotels are built but then have no business. This does not stop others from building more hotels on the same street. Also, many factories are created to make products that do not sell. Yet more factories are built to make the same products. Spending the banks' money with no thought of paying back creates more and more wasteful investments.

Whose money is really being wasted? If one asks the borrowers, a common answer is that it is nobody's money. Many already bankrupt companies are still eager to borrow. They want to create as many projects as possible. What are these projects for? No one knows. Why do the companies create these projects? They must, because otherwise they have no reason to borrow. Obviously it would be foolish to expect them to pay back the loans.

Many who abuse the system prefer to borrow money from the banks and state companies. This should not seem strange. Borrowing from private parties is much more risky. Private parties would fight hard to get the money back. Borrowing from banks and other state companies is a different story. It involves the least risk. To the borrowers, it is nobody's money. They understand that these lenders often do not try very hard to collect. Thus the state banks become obvious prey.

Bad bank loans are only one problem arising from a lack of true ownership and right legal protection. There are others. One high-disaster area is unpaid salaries for construction workers and contractors, among others. China has had a construction boom, but construction companies often find it difficult to collect payments. There are vast problems awaiting solutions: By 2001, moneys yet to be collected totaled $33.66 billion. Of this sum, 26.7% was related to governmental projects. Among the victims, state contractors represented about 58.2%.[7]

Despite the seriousness of the problems, there have been very limited actions. Naturally, such chaos is deeply rooted in the old bureaucratic framework. Realistic solutions would have to transcend this framework.

The defects in the old government-centered society are obvious to all Chinese. Two scholars engage in a dialogue about the ongoing transitional pains. One says, "To have effective results on economic reform, we must investigate the entire economic system that is in place...though many problems occur in the economic area, they are directly related to imperfections in the existing system as well as proper functioning in a citizen society." As the other scholar sees it, "In a developing nation like China, the government must first function to promote market development. It should put emphasis on building a system as well as a proper education. Moreover, it must try to regulate its own conduct."[8]

Serious discussions such as this have become increasingly open in China. This is a dramatic departure from even the recent past. It suggests an urgency about finding solutions. To be sure, the problems are built into the old government domination. Getting past these problems is nothing short of an essential goal for the Chinese civilization.

12 HOW CAN A MAN STILL WEAR BABY CLOTHES?

China's rapid development has already produced worldly wonders. Lifting living standards for 1.3 billion people is no small task. This achievement is even more meaningful in that it has taken place within such a short time period. It took the United States and Europe much longer to achieve this amount of growth.

Despite very positive progress, there is huge room for improvement. In many ways, China continues to lag behind. Now it stands at a crucial point. The old political-economic framework is broken, while a new one is being introduced only slowly. Naturally, this gives rise to a chaotic market and society.

FACTORIES AND HIGHWAYS ARE NOT EVERYTHING

One significant lesson from China's reform is that economic progress is much more than building factories and hotels. It demands the creation of a modern system.

China's rapid development is highly visible to all. Blocks of new hotels, expressways, and factories are all eye-catching. Stores are filled with goods, and the sales clerks are all smiles. Good restaurants give off delicious aromas that attract passers-by. It is a great era in many ways.

Despite all this, China has an important lesson to learn: Building a modern society based on law is more difficult than building factories, highways, and hotels. China has made vast progress in creating tangible things. However, extraordinary effort is yet required to create a modern framework.

Certainly building airports and plants takes capital. But capital does not build a modern society. It cannot build trust and credit, much less a complete set of modern legal and government institutions. There are many such lessons to be learned in China today.

CREDIT CRISIS AND BANKING PROBLEMS

Due to the failed old system still in place, China's financial system is terribly weak. It does not yet have a practical way to protect its own interests. For example, accurate credit records of business organizations are often unavailable. To fend off potential intrusions, a number of measures have been introduced in the marketplace.

In particular, a credit monitoring system was set up by the central bank in 1997. It covers all regions. All lending information is reported to the credit monitor. By May 2003, the system had records for nearly 4 million companies.[1] It has records for up to 79% of total bank loans. The system now has about 60,000 users. Any defaults are recorded. All banks and financial institutions are required to check on borrowers before entering into a transaction.

Still, this has not stopped bad dealings, as banking frauds have not decreased. On the contrary, they have increased. Even if the credit monitor has been operating, it is no smarter than the people who want to commit abuses. Seemingly they have been able to stay far ahead of all the protective measures.

To change things around will require huge efforts. What is needed is to turn the existing banks into modern business organizations. They will need to have rights of ownership and governance. In particular, they must serve market needs instead of the government.

Yet there is an immense barrier, in that many interest groups benefit from the holes in the existing framework. Increasingly, more abuses are targeted at the state banks. Countless businesspeople have been jailed or executed. Still, China has enormous difficulties containing these widespread problems.

One researcher is deeply troubled by the banking crisis. He feels that unless solutions are found, China's wealth could be destroyed: "Today's Chinese banks face great dangers. They cast a huge shadow over China's sustained development. Without proper solutions, it would not only create giant financial crisis, but also destroy all the progress of China's reform so far. Therefore, it is urgent to reform the banking sector and find solutions for the potential risks."[2]

THE RICHEST MAN IN SHANGHAI

Events in China often happen in unexpected ways. This is true also of the fate of some high-profile businessmen. The big bosses may be enveloped in glory one day and behind bars the next.

One such businessman is Zhou Zhengyi. Zhou once had another name: the richest man in Shanghai. His new wealth was long associated with that glorious city. Within a few years, he became the leader of four listed companies. His story was widely reported as if it were a gospel for the age. Foreigners long regarded people like this man as the best hope for China. Events proved otherwise.

In early 2003, Zhou's father died. Zhou handled the occasion like a business deal. He created the largest funeral parade the city had ever seen. Some 300 luxury cars lined up on their way to the funeral site. The entire city was pleased that one of its sons was so dutiful.[3]

In late May 2003, Zhou was arrested. Shortly afterward, two other high-profile Shanghai businessmen were arrested as well, not to mention some other business associates. These events shocked the general public. People on the streets were not prepared for things like this.

The men who were arrested had much in common. They were all business stars in Shanghai. They all had started from nothing and become bosses. They all controlled large assets. Their assets included companies listed on the stock exchanges in Hong Kong or China or both.[4]

These stories shocked China's people in no small way. Many citizens are terribly confused now. They want to know how so many could steal so much money from the banks. Why could they not have been stopped in the first place? When can corruption be contained?

One citizen asked,[5] "Who would save the rich Chinese? That so many rich men fell into deep troubles, does it mean that our market changes and government regulations are maturing? In this whole process, businessmen must learn how to respect the law and the banks must focus on professional practices, and the government must be corruption free." What might have been the deeper reasons behind the sudden fall of these men? The writer continued, "On deeper levels, maybe the rich people did not originally try to outdo the law or wish to bribe the officials. But they must do all the illegal things in order to achieve their purpose."

How do citizens view such corruption? The same writer stated, "Each and every case involving abusive businessmen has corrupt government officials involved. The real question with the 'sin of wealth' is that it happens with a corrupt power. The real issue is...how to seriously regulate business conducts and be effectively against corruptive partnerships between business and power."

In reality, many businessmen who ended up in jail could hardly have thought about these things before they went forward. Maybe they did not really wish to use illegal means to get ahead.[6] It is no longer a secret that many corrupt officials have partnerships behind them. Such partnerships are the common platform from which they benefit. Putting some people behind bars hardly resolves the deeper issues.[7]

Even in the Party's top magazine, *Qiushi,* one report includes the comment, "Looking at the corrupt cases, we can see the trend: individual corruption is extending to collective corruption; low ranking cadres to higher ranking ones. These officials partner with businessmen to create all sorts of illegal deals...their skills go up from ordinary to hightech, becoming more complex and more undetectable; their partners increasingly involve international crime dealers...."[8]

How might China stop these activities? So far there is no obvious solution. Worse still, vulnerabilities increase faster than solutions. China is continuing to pay a high price.

13 CRISES AND THE FORWARD MOVEMENT OF THE STATE SECTOR

China has had a long history with government domination. The state sector is the key product of an overextended government power. It has existed for ages. The only major difference between now and the distant past is that this government power reached a new height after 1949.

Between the 1950s and 1970s, China's private sector was completely eliminated by force. All shops, banks, farms, factories, and mines were controlled and run by the government. But this government monopoly had the economy and society deeply stuck in the mud.

In the wake of grand failures, the government is currently pushing for reform. One most significant change is that both foreign capitalists and domestic businesspeople are allowed to take an active role in the economy. At the same time, the old state sector remains in place.

The state sector's problems are deeply rooted. In reality, the state sector is a government invention aimed at controlling the society and economy. This desire on the part of the government has little to do with wealth creation. Naturally, only disasters have followed.

China's reform is now reaching a crucial stage. But there are still countless barriers in place. Indeed, turning a government-dominated economy into a law-based modern economy can never be straightforward.[1] To date, China has had bitter transitional experiences.

Rapid Changes in the Managerial Class

Numerous changes have taken place during the reform era. The state sector has been greatly impacted by the new market forces. One change concerns the managerial rank and file. New managers in general are younger and better trained than in the past. Many have received a good education both at home and abroad. Some can speak English and enjoy global traveling.

Today, the state sector has a new kind of bureaucrat-businessperson. These people love Western suits and brand shoes. Most businesspeople and government officials dress alike. In terms of appearance, it is nearly impossible to tell who is a businessperson and who is an official. These people are learning fast, and their curriculum is very broad. Lessons may include things like how to deal effectively with significant outsiders—the international reporters, financial analysts, and businesspeople. This in itself shows the pace of changes.

Corruption and punishment are also common in the managerial class. One reason for the widespread corruption is that the existing system cannot protect the managers' interests. Many managers do find ways of promoting their interests. This often means stretching limits. Countless wrongdoers have been put behind bars or even executed for economic crimes.

At present, the very top business positions may be the most risky. The positions of CEO and chairman of leading state companies and banks are risky. The victims include an ex-president of Bank of China, an ex-chairman of Everbright Group (a state investment company), and an ex-chairman of the biggest tobacco maker. One common feature: They all fell abruptly.

In this reform era, the state sector has gone through tremendous changes. For one, it is fashionable for Chinese companies to hire international employees. These foreign employees often get higher positions than they would overseas. They are often hired as advisors, board directors, and managers. Their international experience is highly appreciated.

One leading insurance company recently brought in six international advisors at one time. In the view of many Chinese businesspeople, adding some foreign faces shows that they are better than their peers.

Another leading insurance concern, Ping An, has gained international equity shareholders. These include minor shareholders such as Morgan Stanley, Goldman Sachs, and HSBC. At the top managerial rank, several managers have previously worked for global professional companies.

LONG LIVE COMPETITION!

The state sector has been going through a painful transition period. Competition has already produced vast consequences, good and bad. Still, the state companies have continued to dominate many key sectors. By government design, the state sector dominates commercial banking, telecom services, postal, rails, oil, petrochemicals, and public utilities, among other sectors. Nevertheless, numerous changes have taken place even in these sectors. By mid-2005, the government had taken further measures to open up private access to these forbidden sectors. This new outlook represents a dramatic departure from the old practices. In fact, it implies that China's reform is reaching a new rational level. All this is highly encouraging.

But that said, changing the old government practices is by no means easy. Basically, the government tries to learn how to dump unwanted troubles while keeping its grip on power. This conflicting desire on the part of government has meant that China's transition to a better society will take endless struggles. So far, the state sector reform has taken place in this context only.

TELECOM BATTLES

China's telecom industry has recently experienced a new form of market competition. It now has six operators instead of the one that existed only 13 years ago. This has involved extensive regrouping and restructuring of the old telecom establishment. The companies are still government controlled, but they now compete with one another. Three of them have listed their major units in either the mainland, Hong Kong, or New York.

Reforming the telecom sector has been a long process, and extremely painful. The reform involved two basic elements, which are more significant in China than outsiders might realize.

The first element, separation between the government and business, has been a giant change, as has the second element, competition. How could the old players face a competitive market? After all, it has taken China some five decades to do so. Now, regulation issues are in the hands of one agency, the Ministry of Information and Telecom. In the marketplace, these companies conduct business independently.

Competition has already changed the telecom landscape. Consumers have benefited greatly. How could consumers be against such competition? For many decades, the word "service" had a different meaning. A few years back, it would have taken weeks and months to get a fixed line installed at home or in the office. Why? The incentives were not there for the installers to be out working. There was no need for management to think about the consumer. Now getting a line installed may take a few days or less. Incentives for the workers are high.

The telecom restructuring has been quite successful. But the success has resulted largely from the booming telecom market. By 2004, China had more than 334 million handset users and 311 million wired phone users. China is already the biggest market in terms of number of users. Sales reached about $80 billion in 2004.

LESS FORTUNATE COMPANIES

In general, if any business sector has a state monopoly, it blocks progress completely. From its beginning, the state sector was built into the government establishment. It was designed to fulfill government rather than market needs. In fact, consumers came into existence only in this era. In the past, there was no concept of consumers as such.

Many business sectors have not made progress similar to that seen in the telecom sector. Unlike the telecom sector, most sectors no longer have a government monopoly. In these competitive markets, the private sector and foreign players more often than not outperform the state companies.

So far, increased competition has taken a heavy toll on the state sector in general. Today, many state companies face deep troubles. They include almost all the old economic sectors. Reforming them has been extremely difficult and painful. One distressing consequence involves the dislocated employees. Layoffs and bankruptcies have been common in the state sector in the past two decades. Competition often implies more business failures.

REFORM DIFFICULTIES

So far, reform of the state sector has been a complex matter. New situations have materialized. In particular, the introduction of competition has greatly impacted the state sector. At the same time, the lack of a modern system has created confusion and vulnerabilities.

One great change is that by now the citizens have gotten used to market measures such as layoffs and bankruptcies. Today, nobody working for a state-owned company feels certain about job security. This represents a dramatic change.

Layoffs and unemployment are a very serious issue for China now. Since 1995, the state sector has let go of more than 50 million employees. At the same time, about 30 million new jobs have been created by the private sector and other entities.[2]

Business failures are common. Even some 100-year-old establishments cannot refuse to die out. What is most surprising about this is that nobody is surprised. Many citizens feel that these badly run businesses should be left to their fate. This represents a huge change indeed. Now consumers vote with their yuan. How can nonperforming companies survive for long?

CONFLICTS BETWEEN MOBILE OPERATORS

China has two mobile phone operators as dictated by the government. No foreign or private parties are allowed to play in this field. Even so, intense competition is going on. All this has taken place in a Chinese way.

China Unicom is a relatively new company, about 11 years old. It has had a tough time growing up within the old telecom establishment. For a long time there were feuds between the two mobile operators.[3] For many years, until recently, China Unicom was badly treated by the entire old telecom establishment.

Given all this, the growth of Unicom has not been easy. Its relationship with the established players has been full of conflicts. For many years, until recently, the old crowd tried hard to deny the company significant access.

One issue involved access for emergency calls placed by Unicom users. This probably seems strange to outsiders. Who would want to block emergency calls? But Unicom's customers encountered problems for many years. They could not understand the difficulties they ran into. The old players were very fearful of intrusion from China Unicom as a competitor and went as far as to deny Unicom access. The fight was so intense that there was no coming to terms. The situation finally demanded government involvement. Some government units, such as Shanghai's local government, had to step in.[4] In other regions, it has taken more time to resolve the conflicts.

Today, such nonbusiness issues are resolved in Beijing. This came about when government and business were separated in 1999. That year, the Ministry of Information and Telecom was created. The ministry became the sole telecom regulator; the government stopped wearing two hats and is no longer both a business player and a regulator. As a result, China Unicom has received better treatment.

"Violence of March 22"

In the last few years, competition has also been introduced into some highly monopolized state sectors. Such new measures have already produced interesting results, mostly positive.

China now has two huge chemical and oil companies, China National Petroleum and Sinopec. They have been fighting with each other intensely. Wherever they meet, they feud.

Some of these competitive behaviors have involved gas stations. Fighting for desirable spots for gas stations has been routine for the two competing oil giants. Each tries to get ahead with whatever means are at its disposal.

A notorious episode occurred in one city on March 22, 2002.[5] One of the companies was working on construction of gas stations along a major highway. It was certainly a good project. The employees were working hard along the highway, day and night. Everything went smoothly until March 22.

The problem was that the other company was trying to do the same thing. More than a dozen of its employees arrived at the construction site. They had come to fight. The two giants were battling for the right places to put their stations. Things at the local level were heated.

More than several dozen employees were involved in the fighting, using their fists and even tools as weapons. Some people got badly hurt. The local police had to come in to put an end to the hostilities. The police believed that the incident was no small accident. They reported the case as "The Violence of March 22."[6]

Things did not stop there. The companies' anger did not subside. It took a long time for them to realize that the public was watching them. In the end, Beijing had to step in. This entire affair was a delight to the media. The general public is totally aware that China's path to a market economy is full of surprises.

PAINFUL LAYOFFS

Unfortunately, the new market-oriented movement has created immense pain. It is made worse by the fact that China does not yet have a working welfare system. Displaced people number in the tens of millions. Each year, millions of employees are dislocated. Urban unemployment is severe. Farmers have their houses and lots, regardless of how poor they may be. But people in the cities depend on a steady income.

This dire situation has brought enormous suffering to urban China. The pain is the greater given that for many decades, myths were built around the state sector. Most people were taught that state companies could not go bankrupt. Today, bankruptcy is a daily occurrence, and countless state companies are gone. Tens of millions of unemployed people now face a cold world. Many have found little help as China has yet to build a social safety net. One popular saying goes like this:

"The most desirable thing is work;

The most frightening thing is unemployment;

Most miserable are those in their 40s and 50s;

The greatest concern is inflation."[7]

A statement from a distressed citizen is equally sad: "All the terrible things have happened to me; what have I done wrong?"[8]

Such suffering can hardly be exaggerated. People are not prepared. Unlike developed nations, China has yet to create a working safety net for people in distress. China is going through a painful period now. The difficulty of such a transition is delaying greater reforms. There are many other obstacles as well.

In the old industrial cities, many employees are employees in name only. They may have difficulty getting paid. Many employers do not require them to work. Even if they do not announce it publicly, the factories are almost bankrupt. Often, employees get next to nothing.

The welfare system is inadequate to alleviate the problem. It is strong family ties that offer hope for survival. People must rely on the help of their family networks. The family network has become a significant alternative to the insufficient welfare system.

Today, with the dramatic changes China is experiencing, criticism regarding all the ills is open and lively. People on the street wish for some kind of magic that could turn things around once and for all. In reality, there is no shortcut. Before things get better, the state sector will go through even more turmoil. Many state companies could go out of business. They will find it very difficult to compete in the marketplace with both private sector and international companies.

GOVERNMENT TRIMMING

To be sure, it is the government that has pushed the current reform. After many failures in the state sector, new thinking has slowly surfaced within the government.[9] It is no longer interested in operating barbershops or noodle cafes. The state has come up with a new strategy—hold the biggest companies and dump the rest. In this way problems can be eliminated and the government can retain its hold on power. This new strategy is one that the government is very interested in carrying out. Especially since early 2003, there have been many developments that reflect this thinking.

At the present time the government does not intend to do away with state ownership. Instead, it favors controlling only the core assets and letting go of countless small assets. Thus it hopes to unload troubles without losing its grip on power.

Interestingly, as soon as the program was announced, serious public discussions of the issues began. Today, the media provides huge coverage on government policies. Many people openly express concerns and even criticisms.

By now, the holes in the state sector in particular and the economy in general are obvious to the public. Clearly, control of fewer companies by the government does not mean a new framework.

Nevertheless, China's development is moving to the next stage. Overall, the reform of the state sector is picking up steam. A significant reason for this is greater openness and the international involvement. To resolve the increasingly competitive pressures from the marketplace, more and more actions are being taken. For example, by 2004, among 2,903 key state sector companies, 1,464 had been transformed into shareholding organizations with diverse shareholders.[10] But still, true reform must aim to separate the government interest from the business sphere, which has yet to happen. In reality, government offices still have countless ways to intrude on the business world.

14 WHEN CAN CHINA ACHIEVE MEANINGFUL RESTRUCTURING?

In this new era, China has finally departed from a shortage economy. In many ways, things have gone to the other extreme. There are too many business players in all sectors. There is an urgent need for this overcrowded market to go through a rational consolidation. Yet enormous problems are in the way. They are often issues beyond the business world.

A SATURATED MARKET

For now, one reality is an oversupply for most manufactured goods. At the same time, there are increasing shortages of water, oil, electricity, and raw industrial materials of all sorts.

Among all market changes, decreases in prices for manufactured goods have been among the most dramatic. To many businesspeople, prices are dropping like a falling knife. Countless businesses, both local and foreign, have been victims. Low pricing has become a worry to all: Some mobile phones were selling for around $1,000 a short time ago but are now selling for $200 or less.[1]

What one paid for a TV in the early 1990s will buy five of the same TV today. With such price drops, making profits takes extra effort. Countless businesses have disappeared. Most businesspeople have lost the feeling of certainty. According to some observers, Chinese businesspeople must immediately learn to fly even though they are just now learning to walk. Confronting this new situation, businesses have entered a new era in terms of survival.

DIFFICULTIES FOR A RATIONAL ORDER

How about rational consolidation? "Why can't it happen in China?" is a question asked by many international executives. They wonder when China will be able to achieve a rational market. Any possible answer is necessarily complex. There are just no small issues where China is concerned. The entire framework must be reformed.[2]

TV WARS

There are several dozen TV manufacturers now. This market is so crowded that all players except Toshiba lost money in 2001. The Japanese company made profits only by selling high-end TVs.[3] Prices have continued to drop as if there were no end. If the trend continues, it will wipe out most players.[4]

Some observers say that these businesses have been their own worst enemies: These companies should have pursued a rational path a long time ago, yet they have done so in only small ways up to now.

One senior executive of a leading Chinese consumer products maker told me, "There are just too many TV makers. It is time to kick most of them out."

"How do you do that?" I asked.

"We don't quite know how. But we know it must happen."

"Why don't you buy some of the competitors?"

"We have tried. But it is not easy at all."

"What is the problem?"

"They mostly belong to the government at all levels. These bureaucrats are afraid to lose their power and benefits. They would prefer to die instead of sell to us."

"How come these companies are still playing even if they have had no profits for many years?"

"Well, they can still get bank loans. They do have their ways, even if it does not make any business sense."

The TV companies should enter into mergers and acquisitions to achieve a rational consolidation. But this has yet to happen. Between 1997 and 2003, the number of TV players only increased, as pointed out by the CEO of a leading TV company. In 1996, only about 30 to 40 players remained. Yet by 1999, more than 100 brands were on the market. Until that time, producing TVs required permission from the government. Now it does not. The change is for the worse.[5]

Don't businesspeople understand the need to protect their market? Of course they do, but the realities are tough. The chairman of TCL feels strongly about the need to achieve a rational order. In his view, the government must adjust its policies so that the leading companies have a better environment in which to develop. In this way they can become truly competitive. This man's hope is that the government will offer easy access to bank loans as well as tax incentives. In addition, a better capital market system should be established so that companies would not need cash but could use equity shares to pursue a rational consolidation.[6]

The market wars are not limited to the TV sector. In almost all sectors, serious redundancies exist. The reasons are complex. Overinvestment has contributed significantly. The situation has been worsening primarily as a result of irrational practices. Above all, there is no clear understanding of ownership. Whoever has access to capital will invest without knowing the market conditions, for example.

The slow pace of reform has created more problems. In daily life, nonbusiness interests, more often than not, control market activities. Finding pure business solutions has been problematic. Countless nonbusiness interests block progress.[7]

U.S. AUTO INDUSTRY

In the early 1900s, the United States had vast numbers of independent auto makers. Most brands of today existed as independent companies back then. Between 1903 and 1926, at least 181 car makers existed. By 1926, only 44 players remained.[8] After the crash of 1929, fewer players were left standing. Today, less than a dozen brands remain, mostly foreign names.

On the global stage, redundancy is everywhere. This is the case in all sectors. There are too many players in semiconductors, mobile phones, and PCs, among others. This situation has caused serious trouble in all markets.

Even companies such as Ericsson, Nortel, and Lucent face the issue of survival today. There are no easy ways out.

To deal with redundancies, different markets respond differently. In Western markets such as the United States, pure market measures play a central role. Such market measures include consolidations and restructuring. The strong swallow the weak. Only a few strong companies survive in the end.

On the surface, China's market is rather similar to the old American market, say 100 years ago. On a deeper level, China's business world is much more involved. It is still affected by numerous nonbusiness interests. Above all, business issues are still decided by the government. Worse still, the market rules are not yet clear. Hardly anyone is certain about what is right or wrong. In daily life, business dealings often turn into bureaucratic dealings.

In general, incompetent companies in the state sector continue to find ways to exist. They naturally cause more harm than good. Very often, they can still get bank loans. At the same time, many competent companies run into problems. All such factors are harmful to healthy development.

For now, there is an urgent need to reduce China's existing 1,300 consumer electronics and home appliance companies to a half dozen or so. The resulting companies would become giant multinationals. Achieving this requires further changes in the economy and the nation.

THE CEO IN CHINA AND ELSEWHERE

To Chinese businesspeople, being a U.S. or European CEO looks easy. These foreign executives need to deal only with business issues, little more. So they can make maximum use of their talents toward business ends.

Chinese businesspeople face a completely different environment. It is almost impossible for them to make pure business moves. China confronts issues beyond the business sphere. In particular, the relationship between the government and the business community is laden with problems. This situation is markedly different from the general situation in many Asian countries like Japan and Korea.

Japan's bureaucratic obstructions are light by China's standards. In fact, a high degree of cooperation exists between the Japanese government and business. Historically this has been a significant element supporting the global expansion of Japan Inc. For example, using complex man-made barriers, the Japanese government has for the most part successfully fended off foreign imports. Even if foreign businesses have competitive products and services, they face enormous barriers to entering Japan. This has become a basic means by which the Japanese government supports Japanese businesses.

In China, businesses face bureaucratic obstructions constantly. There are enormous conflicts between government and business. A meaningful restructuring necessitates reform of the existing framework. In short, businesses must become independent organizations, free from bureaucratic interests. It has taken several decades to reach this realization. One businessman puts it this way: "They don't want to sell the watermelon until it is rotten. Had they wanted to do it in the right way, they would have fewer troubles on their hands."[9]

For ages China has had difficulties containing bureaucratic expansion. This has produced vast adverse consequences for wealth creation. As one reporter writes, "The visible hands of the Government are everywhere."[10]

This was the case with a sugar producer in the state sector. The company badly wanted to update its technology in order to survive. The necessary government permission finally came through after a tough battle that went on for several years. How tough was it? The company had to get approvals 588 times. By the time the permission was granted, it was in distress.[11]

In U.S. history, government has always been limited. This has created a different market behavior. Business organizations are able to pursue their interests independently. Independence has meant effectively avoiding bureaucratic obstruction. It has led to a modern way for wealth creation.

Naturally, in the American marketplace, bulls and bears come and go. So do the winners and losers, as it is the market, not the American political establishment, that decides their fate. This makes for a fundamental difference from China today.

Throughout history, a dominating government in China has produced very different behavior. This problem is not getting better at the moment. All business dealings have become bureaucratic dealings. In the end, wealth creation becomes the biggest victim. The core of the problem is that all business organizations are built around the bureaucratic establishment. The bureaucracy is responsible for the entire decision making for all business affairs even at the company level.

WHO IS RESPONSIBLE FOR WEALTH CREATION?

One fundamental difficulty today is that state assets do not have true owners. Who should be responsible for creating wealth? So far, China does not have clear answers.

State domination has naturally given rise to abuses. As discussed earlier, the foes are within the rank and file. There are many interest groups within the establishment. Wealth creation may be their last concern. The vast state assets have become natural prey.

SELLING ASSETS

Though the government controls vast assets, this does not mean that wealth is being created. In fact, huge waste is common. When does an incompetent farmer sell his watermelons? He sells them only when they become rotten. This is what is happening in the state sector today. The lack of true ownerships as well as legal protections is behind it. More than often, even when state companies are in distress, no decisive actions are taken until things are out of control. In the end, countless companies are bankrupt. Whose fault is this? No one is certain.

Things in China happen in unanticipated ways. Things that were not possible in the 1980s became possible in the 1990s. At the present time, changes are accelerating. A significant reason is the increased involvement of the outside world. Today the pace of changes is faster than ever before.

Worsening situations in the state sector demand decisive actions. In the last few years, waves of actions, especially in selling of the state assets, have occurred in this context.

In mid-July 2003, just after the war against SARS, news came from the Beijing municipal government. Beijing was to have a fire sale of many of the companies under its control. The first selling list included about one-third of Beijing's companies.[12] In all regions, auctions are a popular way of selling state assets.

Such transactions are often seriously affected by nonbusiness interests. The bottom line is that most of the decision makers are government officials. In the end, everyone wins except the nation.[13]

Selling distressed assets has become a new strategy for the government, a way to dump long-standing troubles. There are additional benefits. The various government units can immediately generate income. At the same time, selling these assets may save jobs as well as attract more outside investment. This could mean fewer troubles for the government. So one stone may kill three birds.

With all the benefits involved, it is small wonder that the various government units are actively selling. Such selling is often conducted through public auctions. The sellers hope to widen channels in order to collect money as soon as possible.

Such business transactions may involve few business skills on the part of the government establishment. In most cases, the government officials in charge of these businesses have insufficient know-how. Rather, they act in ways that may make little business sense. In most cases these actions are not planned. Once Beijing gives the green light, all the bureaucrats rush in ready to go.

BUYING PARTIES READY?

Events in China often happen suddenly. These days the businesspeople are excited. Few can sit still, and each and every one wants to get involved.

These sales have taken place all over China by now. Auctioneers are busy and their profits are impressive. This has given many people thoughts of jumping into the profession. Even taxi drivers are tempted to do so.[14]

One party's misfortune may become an opportunity to others. Today, the faltering state sector has delivered a huge space to the private sector and foreign players.

In most cases the transactions are small. Each may involve US$1 million. There have been a few sizable cases. One transaction, involving the controlling stake in Kelon, was a high-profile case. Kelon is China's second biggest cooling home appliance player. It is also listed in both Hong Kong and Shenzhen.

Kelon was a success story for many years. In 1996, it went public in Hong Kong. For several years, Kelon was a high-flying stock. But the good fortune was short-lived. By 2000 Kelon was in complete disarray. Losses totaled about $121 million. The management was chaotic. In short, the company faced problems beyond its control.

Behind the scenes, a township-level government was Kelon's controlling shareholder. The government considered getting out of the mess by selling.

But the transactions took some two years. By the time an agreement was reached, the situation was much worse. The company's performance had hit bottom. Another year of record-breaking losses went by. The asking price had to be reduced to some $42 million, from $67.6 million. By getting some $25.6 million less than the original asking price, the local government got out of the game.[16] But the deal opened a new chapter for the company.

(But the new management has also had enormous problems to turn it around. Now the company is for sale again. This new failure has partly come from that the new controlling shareholder has tried to acquire more companies, going beyond his means.[15] In general, the private businesspeople have yet to become mature and self-disciplined. To achieve this end, huge efforts are still ahead.)

NEED FOR GREATER DETERMINATION

Despite the fact that the various government units wish to resolve the redundancy issue, they are adding more redundancies. In fact, they keep adding new investment projects. These projects may not make much business sense. In the end, much wealth is wasted.

One sector is particularly illustrative: the auto market. The desires and realities do not really match. In many ways, the auto market is even more chaotic than the home appliance sector.

For now, the auto sector is booming. But there are well over 100 small car makers, primarily because most of the money has come from the government at all levels.[16] Easy capital has produced overcrowding.

Why do so many officials love auto plants? Holding such assets gives them a sense of power. How about those regions that do not have a car factory? The officials are unhappy—to the extent that they may do whatever it takes to build one.

In the early 1990s, about three-fourths of 31 province-level governments wanted badly to focus on the auto industry as a way to gain growth. Even if most of these governments had insufficient resources to make it work, they wanted to do it regardless of the outcome.[17]

All things considered, it is this very framework that is responsible for irrational behavior. A true business restructuring will demand a completely new political-economic framework. This means the entire package with all the right components, including true ownership, true protection, and professional management. There is no shortcut.

There are additional issues. For example, in the West, a CEO may work for five companies over the course of his or her career. But a Chinese CEO may work for only one. It is still very difficult to build professional trust. Moving to a rational level is easier said than done. But China is moving forward very fast, due in large part to international involvement. It may well take less time than one might think.

15 EMPLOYMENT AND OTHER TRAPS

China is fast reinventing itself. The best manifestation of this is the fact that Chinese citizens now enjoy much greater personal freedom than in the past. Wealth creation demands a high degree of free flow of goods, ideas, and humans. China has quickly walked out of the old trap.

China has already learned a new lesson: A large burdensome population can become a productive force if a fair and rational platform is present. Even so, there are still all sorts of man-made barriers in place. The room for improvement is still large.[1]

JOBS, PERSONAL FREEDOMS, AND OPPORTUNITIES

It is amazing how much China has gone through in the past half century. In the Mao era, the government viewed the free flow of human beings as a police officer views a suspected thief. An elaborate system was designed to prevent free movement of any sort. In this reform era, life has changed markedly for the better. People are no longer forbidden to move from one place to another, from one employer to another, or from one type work to another.[2]

One area of improvement for the future must focus on a fair and rational environment for both employees and employers. There are many traps for job seekers. Here in China, jobs are few compared to the number of people who want them. The number-one requirement for a good-paying job is your residential permit. With this permit there is also a personal file. This document was at the core of the old system against free movement. For several decades, holding it gave one a huge advantage in life. In the Mao era, it determined the most important things in life: how much food, cooking oil, and clothing you were entitled to buy. Many families were separated for years, even decades, and were not allowed to transfer from one place to another.

In the old era, rural Chinese suffered even more. They had few means of changing their lifestyle. There were ways, but very few people qualified. They had to either enter college or join the army, for example. Even marrying into an urban family often did not help.[3]

Such man-made difficulties existed in Western history as well. The industrial revolution began in the United Kingdom in the late 18th century and developed later in other European nations. The old systems blocked the way to wealth creation. Countless bureaucratic devices prevented the flow of people and business. The various political authorities collected fees—all sorts of fees—whenever possible. According to one scholar, these tactics were often barbaric.[4] Germany was freed only through the creation of an empire in 1870. In France, it took 100 years of bloody revolution to overthrow the old system.

Today, similar things are happening inside China. All the past bloody revolutions have failed to widen personal freedom. Actually, personal freedom suffered the most in the Mao era. Today, China is going through a revolution, peaceful and profound. Hundreds of millions of citizens, especially rural migrants, have found a new life. They are most directly responsible for the economic growth.

This new era has brought tremendous changes. Food and other consumer goods are plentiful. Thus the old resident permit has become less meaningful. Citizens have gained vast freedom for movement and work. Most significantly, this has helped China achieve a booming economy. Yet many man-made barriers are still in place. Most strikingly, laborers cannot truly protect their interests. Therefore rural migrant workers stand at the very bottom of society. All sorts of measures operate against their interests.

There is no way to overstate how little space the old system offered the Chinese people and society. Indeed, nearly every move a citizen made in daily life required government approval. Even when a citizen got married, he had to obtain approval from his employer. The employer was required to offer an opinion first. This requirement was in force for several decades before its abolition in late 2003.

Even today, the old ways have not died out completely. Daily struggles are common. One case involved a computer professional who wanted to change to a better job. His current employer did not want him to leave. The employment contract stipulated that leaving early would mean a penalty of close to a year's salary. To avoid having to pay the penalty, the employee stayed but also worked in secret for the new employer. This went on for nearly a year. After a year, the old employer presented him with a bill for two to three months' salary before letting him go.[5]

Countless abuses target low-skilled workers, especially rural migrant workers. The mayors of New York and Paris sometimes worry about their tight budgets. Maybe their Chinese counterparts could pass on a trick or two. In China today, there are all sorts of fees you must pay just to work in a different place.

How do you get a city's residential permit? It is still a struggle. Different cities have different rules. Fees are involved—big fees by Chinese standards. Permit seekers have a long wait, from a few months to decades, as with the U.S. green card. Without the permit, you may not be able to get a desirable job, among other things. You may get a job nobody wants. Having the proper permit makes all the difference.

LIVES OF THE MIGRANTS

So far, the vast rural population has lagged behind in benefiting from a booming economy. In many ways, the boom is generally an urban phenomenon. Yet some 65% of China's people are rural.

But the rural people are smart. Their desire for a better life has created the greatest movement in China's entire history. Over 160 million rural workers are on the move. In 2001 in the province of Fujian, 4.65 million rural people went to find jobs in urban regions. Among these, 810,000 went outside the province. At the same time, about 2.15 million people from outside the province went in.[6]

Fujian is one of the smaller provinces. More migrants come from provinces like Sichuan, Anhui, and Henan. They are all over China today. In fact, more than 160 million rural people now work in cities as now. Rural workers are mostly young and have little training. They are everywhere today. Guangdong alone has 16 million migrant workers who have held jobs there for six months or longer.

These workers do all sorts of jobs, especially jobs nobody wants. They are the force behind the countless made-in-China products. A large number have jobs in retail outlets of all sorts.[7] The construction field has a high concentration of rural workers. About 30 million of them have jobs in the construction business.

The rural workers are street smart. They have to be, or they could go home empty handed. They must possess the rare capability for survival. Despite countless barriers, they are winning in their own ways. Moreover, they are doing something very significant—raising the living standards for rural people. They wire home large sums of money. Without this money, their families back home could fall into poverty.

I find their devotion to family amazing. Whenever I am in a post office, I see young migrants busy wiring home money.

But this is not all. Millions of migrant workers have become small business owners. They run millions of small restaurants, retail shops, and beauty shops, among other businesses. They are really everywhere there is opportunity of any sort.

This spirit—nothing less—accounts for the endurance of the Chinese civilization. Perhaps it is even safe to say that without this type of strength, the Chinese civilization would have disintegrated long ago. Yes, there are countless man-made obstacles. But people with this spirit have prevailed over all their formidable foes. The fact that they are alive and dreaming demonstrates their triumph.

Mark Twain once said that God must love the rich and the poor equally. God must especially love the poor Chinese farmers, who have been so hardworking, yet voiceless, for ages. Heaven must have given them some great survival skills. Otherwise, they would have been eaten alive by the tigers. As Confucius said some 2,500 years ago, a cruel political environment is much worse than man-eating tigers. But the real triumph of the farmers is that they are dragging these tigers in a new direction.

DRAMATIC CHANGES

Great events are unfolding in China today. The old framework cannot contain the popular desires for a better life. China's business boom has created vast opportunities for average citizens. It has changed the old society in many ways. It is helping to decrease differences in living standards between various regions and between rural and urban China. Thus booming urban regions have produced benefits for the less developed rural population as well. Yet this positive outcome has occurred not at all by design.[8]

In all possible ways, the rural people still live at the very bottom of society. In particular, they are still denied the social benefits that exist in the urban regions. Their children are not allowed access to education in the cities where they work and live. Lifting such barriers has taken center stage in urban China.

FEES AND DIFFICULTIES FOR MIGRANTS

Life is never smooth for people from the rural areas. Today they have new ways to improve their lives, but still they face tough realities. For one thing, without the proper permits, they have difficulty earning a good living. Instead of a permanent permit, the government offers them a temporary permit.

In addition, there are fees attached. In the past these fees were really high in relation to the average income. In a city like Shenzhen, for the average rural girl working on an assembly line, the fees per year were as high as a month's salary.

Such high fees were in effect for many years until very recently. Finally, the rural migrants could take it no longer. There were also public outcries. The voice of the public finally led to positive changes. There are still fees for rural workers to pay, but they have been reduced to a rational amount, such as a day's pay.

Such changes have taken place in many cities, Beijing included. For many years, rural migrants were required to pay about $54 a year to all the relevant government units in their home town and in the city to be able to work. This might amount to a month's earnings.[9] Many rural workers have had problems getting education for their children in the cities. The children have been banned from entering urban schools. As a way of dealing with the situation, many migrants have set up their own schools. But getting a license invites trouble. Also, other benefits such as health care are often totally unavailable to migrant workers.

China's people have lived in conditions like this for centuries. Throughout history, bureaucratic intrusion has been an ever-present fact of life. It has been common for officials to employ state power for personal gain. All this has taken place at the expense of the people at the bottom of society. Even today, such circumstances are widespread.[10]

DAILY ABUSES

For many migrant workers, hard work may not mean bread and butter. They can easily fall prey to abusive employers. At the present time this situation has gone from bad to worse.

How much of what migrant workers earn is stolen from them? Billions. In 2002, unpaid earnings for migrant workers totaled more than $4.83 billion. That year, the various government units stepped in to help. They were able to recover only $169 million. Labor conditions have not improved very much.[11]

These deep-seated problems could cause much bigger disasters. They could undermine social order and peace. But still, no ready solutions are in view.

The public outcry has led to changes in the society, albeit slowly. The various government units have become more responsive. The province of Guangdong is among the regions that have the most migrant workers. It is also a place with all sorts of abuses. The provincial government is considering taking some new measures. How does it plan to handle abuses among employers, say in the construction business? One idea is to expose the employers.[12] Naturally, most laborers doubt that this will have any effect. In truth, the root causes for the abuses remain in place.

EMPLOYMENT DIFFICULTIES FOR OTHER GROUPS

The migrants are not the only people who endure unnecessary hardships. Anyone, even multimillionaires and bosses, may face the same problems. People have to try very hard to get a permit, and very often, luck is what they need most.

For example, in Shenzhen, even some high-profile businessmen have run into problems. The city's government seems to communicate to many of them in strange ways that they are not welcome. These people may be senior managers and business owners. Even so, they can have difficulty getting the needed residential permit.

One marketing manager works for a high-tech company that paid taxes in the amount of $2.29 million in 2002. Yet he could not get a card even though he had worked in the city for five years. Recently, he lost his old card and driver's license and could not get them replaced in the city of his current residency. The only way was to return to his home town to get replacements. It took him a week.

Another businessman, a founder and the chairman of a high-tech company, had different problems. The major one was that he was 55 years old. Why was this a problem? According to the local rule, the ceiling is 50.

Eventually things turned out well for these two businessmen. They got lucky. The city officials made exceptions. The businessmen duly expressed great thanks. The chairman was grateful for his good fortune. He had a lot to say about what had happened. He commented that older professionals should be considered more useful in the business world because they are more experienced and more stable—the city should allow them more opportunities. The fact that this story made the newspaper shows the extent of the problems.[13]

In extreme cases, having a permit can make the difference between life and death. There have been many cases of cruel treatment. Tragic events occur often, and many less privileged citizens experience very serious problems. Countless citizens have suffered physical abuse, imprisonment, and even worse.

DEATH OF A COLLEGE GRADUATE

One recent event shocked the nation. It happened in March of 2003. A new college graduate, Sun Ligong, met a brutal death.[14]

He was in his late twenties. He had been raised in a rural region in Hubei province. His parents were farmers who had worked hard to enable him to get through college. He then moved to Guangdong. There he was lucky enough to find jobs that allowed him to use his education in computer graphics. In February 2003, he moved to Guangzhou, where he worked for a fashion concern. One evening, he left his home to go to an Internet bar. The city police were inspecting the major blocks that evening. They stopped Sun after he had been walking for a few minutes. Because he failed to show proper ID, he was arrested.

What happened thereafter is not unusual. Being a college graduate did not help Sun at all. On the contrary, his sense of pride led to serious trouble. He kept telling the officers that he was a college graduate and had proper employment in the city. The more he protested, the angrier the arresting officers became. They used physical force. His fate was sealed. Someone with more street smarts would have done anything to head off the situation, but Sun was not street smart.

A few days later, in the detention center, he was beaten to death. How many times he was beaten is not known. Sadly, the last few beatings were inflicted by inmates like him, locked up in the same room. There were eight of them, all young. They were having problems trying to get out of detention. Why? Because they were poor and could not afford the fees demanded by the guards. They had alternatives, though. They were ordered to beat Sun. They had to beat him severely to avoid receiving stiff penalties.

Often people can pay cash to get out of detention. The more they pay, the more quickly they can get out. Sun could not come up with enough money. His employer came to help but did not want to pay the required amount.

Sun could not have known that his death would cause a public outrage. His story was widely reported by the media. Why did it cause such an outcry? One legal expert reflected on the message it sent: This event has no outsiders; if we pay no attention to it, the next victim could be you.[15]

The death came at a particularly bad time, during the SARS outbreak. Even so, it caught the public's attention in a big way. The terror of SARS did not decrease the general outcry.

Soon the court issued severe penalties. The penalties targeted many who were involved, but not the individuals behind the scenes. The eight inmates were among those convicted of felonies. They protested, but the courts didn't change anything. So ended this tragic episode.

For a number of years, many citizens quietly expressed the need to change living conditions for rural workers. Hardly anything positive occurred until Sun's death. In reflecting on the situation, one scholar recalled how some years ago a number of young people began to use the Internet to write about the harsh treatment of rural workers. This was an act of bravery indeed. Since then there have been more and more such writings. They have not changed real life much; but because of this public criticism, the problems of the rural workers have become an issue for professional discussion. Bad feelings, the scholar suggested, do not promote change; what is needed is action.

Sun's death has brought about huge changes. Beijing and all other cities are improving, lifting many old restrictions. Only a short time ago, such things could hardly be imagined. Those who might commit abuses have to stop and think a little. Even in relation to the migrant workers, China is improving. Very positively, rural development in general is becoming a top agenda issue. As is true in many other contexts, societal changes are for the better, but the price is often steep.

Migrant workers are winning in their own way. The fact that their life is high on the agenda in China is great progress. This may well be the first time in China's modern history that their plight has become a social and political issue. China's sustained development must include the migrant workers. Reaching this realization has taken many decades, if not centuries.

16 OTHER UNCERTAINTIES FOR THE BUSINESS WORLD

One lesson from China is this: Wealth creation depends on the wealth creators, not government officialdom. Arriving at this new understanding has taken at least a century. For this lesson China has paid a massive price.

The late paramount leader Deng Xiaoping reflected seriously on the existing system. His life was deeply affected by the way things are in China: "A good system stops a bad man from doing bad things, while a bad system would stop a good man from doing good things, and even make him do bad things."[1] This is a powerful understanding of the realities in this nation.

TAILS EVERYWHERE

Once an established framework is in place, citizens can only follow. They have no alternative. People are born the same, but they are made different by different environments. This is how an American, a European, and a Chinese differ from one another.

It has taken ages for China to begin to struggle against bureaucratic entities—the government's tails. These tails have had a powerful existence— they are simply built into the system. They destroy not just time, but much, much more.

Every day, businesspeople must struggle with these tails. Restraining government means nothing less than survival. According to one report, "The private businessmen in Beijing must spend half time to deal with the government offices and the costs are too high. One restaurant owner says that he must 'donate' more than 150,000 yuan ($18,120) a year, of which about 100,000 yuan ($12,100) must be 'tipped' to the various government agencies or their heads. Another businessman in one district of Beijing says that if his store does a promotional sale, he must report to the government 15 days ahead and must also obtain 7 approvals. These agencies are located all over the district. He must run around. He must pay a fee for each approval."[2]

This type of scenario is widespread.[3] In Shenzhen, someone who wants to transfer a commercial liquid-tank truck from one parking place to another must get official approvals 11 times.[4]

LIVING WITH TAILS

Daily, businesspeople run into all sorts of man-made problems. The difficulties encountered by one private chemical company are typical of those experienced by Chinese businesses. In one Chinese New Year, as always, the boss sent out many gift bags. But he forgot an important government unit: the bureau in charge of environmental protection. His troubles came down upon him quickly: His business was shut down on the sixth day following the New Year.[5]

It has been observed that China has two economies. One is the usual economy. The other is the underground economy—the gray economy, as some call it. According to one researcher, this underground economy is a product of corruption. His work shows that in the 20-year period beginning in 1978, China's gray economy produced income amounting to about six years of GDP. How was it created? Corruption.[6]

China is deeply burdened by the government's tails. The more tails, the more corruption. It was corruption that repeatedly destroyed the old governments and brought chaos and civil war in the past.

How can China cut the tails? One reporter asked a researcher: "Prior to China's WTO entry, our Government already started to abolish numerous administrative demands.... What is your idea?"

Government officialdom has a vested interest in the business world, the researcher said. "It is due to such government interests that support its ever-increasing expansion. Such things are done in forms of approvals and the like. It has added huge cost and loads to the business world. Such administrative obstacles have obstructed free business flow and further added unnecessary loads and costs. We should create new [legislation] to reduce such a governmental interference. All things must have a legal basis. In such a way, the personal factors should be greatly reduced."[7]

TAILS AND DEVELOPMENT

This old framework has militated against healthy development. Creative entrepreneurship has suffered greatly. Even in this era, China has yet to find solutions that address the root causes.

Government tails certainly play a role in international trade. Export is a crucial lifeline for all business. However, until 2004, there were innumerable restrictions. Not every company could choose to engage in trade. In 1989, only about 6,000 domestic companies were given the license needed to conduct trade. This number grew to about 60,000 in 2002. Still, not every business that wished to trade with outside markets could do so.[8] Recently, due to the WTO accord, this requirement was finally dropped.

Thus until the WTO, licenses for conducting international trade were hard to get. Yet applicants were countless. Naturally, it became a high privilege to hold the license.

Some businesspeople profited from the situation. They might lend out permits for a profit. They often enjoyed a free ride. The free riders were frequently those who had close connections to the official world. Many were state-owned companies and some were overseas businesses.

LUCKY INTERNATIONAL PLAYERS

In China, one thing has different meanings to different people at the same time. International players have their advantages. Often the Chinese tails do not apply to them.

Even so, foreign players often complain about the general business environment. Most complaints focus on four main issues.[9] First, foreign companies feel strongly that the government should improve further on transparency. In particular, foreign businesses may face quick changes in laws and rules. Rules can change in the middle of the game.

Second, foreign players feel that they are too often subject to complex government regulations, especially in matters that are purely their own business issues. Even in these matters, the government imposes numerous demands. For example, when foreign players need to increase their investment, they must go through lengthy approvals from government offices. The process is very time-consuming and inefficient.

A third concern relates to dealing with governmental units, which can be very confusing. Someone who really needs help often runs into problems.

The last issue relates to favorable treatment granted to companies by the government. These agreements can lose their meaning in practice. Some foreign companies have found that after making an agreement, the official agencies increase the taxes and fees, for example.

The Chinese companies certainly have more difficulties. They all want the same treatment as is accorded to their foreign counterparts. One way to accomplish this is to register a company outside China. With a foreign shell, a company can obtain more advantages.

Many business issues besides international trade are involved. The government has a say in practically all aspects of business life, for example foreign currencies, hiring, investment decisions, and operational and employment factors. At each and every step, business organizations may not be free to make independent decisions.[10]

There are other troubling issues, having to do with schools, housing, and residence of employees and families. All this has greatly increased the power of bureaucrats. It opens the doors wide to abuses.

A law school dean tells two personal stories.[11] One involves a hometown friend who wanted to obtain a business license to operate in the local wholesale shopping center. How did he get the license? It was tough. It took him one and a half years. He went through more than 80 government offices, obtained 112 official approvals, and spent more than $84,540.

The law professor himself had problems with the bureaucracy. One occurred when his daughter was born few years ago. To obtain the ID card for his baby, he went more than a dozen times to different government units as well as to his own and his wife's work units. Why? "Missing any piece of required papers would demand you return."

This framework has cost China dearly over the ages, not just the last few decades. One official puts it this way: "Facts show that power can be abused. The power of government can be utilized by some corrupt officials for personal gains."[12] Few would disagree.

"THE RED BUILDING"

With all the holes in the system, businesspeople have become creative in unique ways.

One businessman followed a particularly problematic path. His business dealings involved people far beyond the business world—a long list of significant public figures in his home province and beyond.

Looking back, China's people are still amazed by how many officials this man turned into his private servants. These powerful figures included police chiefs, regional banking chiefs, tariff chiefs, senior judges, and other significant office holders.

This is a high-profile case that as of this writing had not yet ended completely. It involved not only the nation of China, but also foreign places like Canada. It all started in Xiamen in the 1990s.

Xiamen is a coastal city in Fijian province. It is an elegant seaport on the Taiwan Strait. To visitors, the sun seems to shine every day.

Before 1949, Western businessmen were commonly seen in Xiamen. The city is still full of traces of foreign culture. There are blocks of European-style buildings. Today the city is a regional trade center. Its beauty also brings countless tourists around the year.

The story involves a Charlie Chaplin-type character, Lai Cangxin. He was a farmer by origin. In the reform era, he dived into the ocean of business. He is no ordinary businessman. In a matter of moments, it seemed, he created a vast business empire. It came from nowhere, in a bizarre way. Lai focused on illegal trafficking. His business went wild during much of the 1990s.

Even today, people still wonder how he was so successful. His strategy relied on creating partnerships with corrupt government officials. He successfully enlisted hundreds of bureaucrats in the city and beyond. He also went to other cities such as Beijing to get the protection of figures higher up.

For someone from a rural region to build an empire certainly requires extraordinary effort. Lai understood perfectly that he needed much more than pure business elements. He needed to overcome all the difficulties imposed by the government.

He created everything that was necessary for success. He seemed to be a natural talent. He knew exactly where to get everything he needed.

"You Plant Sesame Seeds and Get Watermelons"

Lai's business endeavors quickly produced huge profits. There are tremendous price differences for numerous products between China and the outside world. There are high tariffs for autos, liquor, and many other popular products. So Lai wanted to ship in foreign products free of tariffs. Then he could sell them for much higher prices.

To get going, he identified the cracks in the official world. It happened that some officials were trying to find partners. There was a natural match. Lai ran into few difficulties in opening the right gates. He quickly formed partnerships with the right people. Several state-owned chemical refineries and marketing companies came to his aid. He also succeeded in areas involving cars, cigarettes, liquor, and home appliances, among others.

But forming partnerships with small companies was not enough. Lai needed more cooperation from the official world. Without such support, no business could be done, big or small.

He did not need to try all that hard. His "generosity" attracted the powerful and untouchable. His ring of associates was extensive. It included all sorts of public figures. Their help was crucial for Lai's business and even his life. Soon these men were acting as his personal assistants. They were formidable figures: police and law officials, tariff officials, bank officials, trade and business inspection officials, and Party bosses, among others.[13]

With such influential help, he would have smooth sailing. It turned out that he was a natural. He did not need to polish his skills. Nor did he need to change his peasant-like appearance. Things were moving so rapidly in some ways that even he was amazed.

Lai found out that these officials were all human. They had same desires and fears that he did. Many businesspeople now understand this: As long as officials have earthly desires, they can become your partner.

To Lai, dealing with the officials was a straightforward task. He easily became the chief among chiefs. These chiefs provided the very best services possible. Furthermore, they provided help that he had not even realized he would need.

A vast business empire was born. Naturally, all partnerships shared in the profits. The price Lai paid was high: It is said that he had to offer the majority of the spoils, say 80%.

But he offered more than cash and material rewards. He worked hard to find the best means of recompense. Along with the spoils, he devised other attractions. He built a building, had it painted red, and filled it with modern niceties and young prostitutes.[14]

He treated the prostitutes generously. They never asked for money from clients. The red building was considered very safe. Inside, business went on undisturbed. The "club" served Lai's ends perfectly. Everything inside the building was designed to make the clients feel like stars.[15] The guests were surprised at all the niceties.

As the story came out, it was shocking to many people to learn that these important guests were willing to take on the roles of Lai's house servants and bodyguards. People who were not important could not get in the building. They knew why: Their bosses were inside. It was a club reserved exclusively for the powerful.[16]

Lai felt that he had invented a powerful growth model: "You plant sesame seeds, but get watermelons." The returns would naturally be impressive.[17] He worked hard in unusual ways. Managing a human business is highly demanding. For a long time, Lai did it perfectly.

From the start, he was convinced that he would be a winner. He believed that the traps in the markets were designed for others, the small and selfish types. How could such people do anything right? To save a little money, they would fall into traps with their eyes wide open and do so over and over again. Lai felt that the bureaucratic traps were never intended for men like him. Having friends was all he needed.

A Mogul's Secret

Yet Lai had one secret. He never truly trusted the government officials who were his partners. He came up with ways to prevent anyone from jumping ship. One method in particular stands out. Hidden cameras in the rooms in the red building recorded every movement. Lai saved the films.[18]

Clearly, all along he had some sense of insecurity. Did he ever find any use for the films? Never. His partners were not the kind who would stop in the middle of the game. They were with him all the way, in glory or in death. Later when some of them actually faced death sentences, they did not show any regret at all.

Everything went smoothly, according to plan. Street rumors referred to profits so big that there was not enough time to count them. But Lai did not stop there. His sudden success may have proven to him that he really was a man with great vision. With leftover spoils, he wanted to try more things.

To fulfill his higher dreams, he worked day and night. There were thousands of employees running around for him. They loved to follow his orders.[19] Still, he chose to do things alone, especially when it came to his bigger dreams. His humble origins did not mean he was willing to compromise in the slightest. On the contrary, he wanted nothing short of the best. He understood that life is not just money, power, and sex. People have bigger dreams. He was fulfilling more meaningful dreams.

Lai's vision was grand, and he wanted what he built to last. He brought in the very best architects and engineers money could buy. One of his most ambitious ideas was to construct a huge plaza in the city's center. This modern plaza would have a combination of shopping, entertainment, a hotel, offices, and apartments.[20]

As is the case with so many newly rich people in China today, Lai's rise and downfall were equally quick. The story has finally ended for most of the participants. Hundreds of felons have been executed or imprisoned. One government official said, "This has been the country's biggest corruption since 1949."[21] He was right: The case involved more than 700 officials from the government, military, and police, among others.

Part IV

Globalization in Light of History

THE RISE OF EUROPEAN POWER; THE AMERICAN CENTURY; JAPAN'S GLOBAL REACH; CHINA'S SUSTAINED GROWTH; GREAT CONVERGENCE; FUTURE CHALLENGES

17 AN UNBROKEN CIRCLE?

Globalization in its current form is new to each and every nation. Naturally, the waves of globalization have already pushed China into completely unfamiliar territory. The new global engagement remains strange to all Chinese. It creates reactions from excitement to fear, from confusion to uncertainty. People prefer certainty as flowers do sunshine. But life is hardly certain: The more one seeks definite answers, the more confused one becomes.

(In the following, our discussion takes the form of dialogue among three fictitious speakers, Tom, Jack, and George.)

THE BRITISH ISLES AS A GLOBAL CENTER

Tom: Jack, you gave a speech recently. What was the topic?

Jack: Globalization. I started with the age of Columbus and the rising British power.

George: Why did you start with such old history?

Jack: It is a natural place to start. Globalization really began there. At that time, Europeans suddenly became restless, after the so-called Dark Ages. People wanted to reach out, exploring unknown places, doing big things, and creating new businesses. That shaped all the future outcomes.

George: In what ways?

Jack: Well, the British outdid the Spanish, Portuguese, and Dutch. The industrial revolution was one direct outcome.

George: How did the British get ahead?

Jack: They created new ways of getting the best out of the situation. Spain and Portugal went ahead of the U.K. and occupied many parts of the Americas, among other places. But it was their governments that benefited directly. In the end, the royal governments gained enormous wealth, and few others did.

George: So they killed the chicken to get the eggs. Is that right?

Tom: More significantly, no new system was created. There were hardly any common interests with the people in the colonies. In the end, governments chose to kill the chicken to get eggs. So after some time there were no more eggs for the colonists.[1]

Jack: The British wanted a continuing supply of eggs. So they provided better conditions in the lands they occupied. It is natural that they got more eggs in the end.

Tom: The British did more than that. Along the way, Britain's private sector came into existence. Its businessmen organized new types of companies with shareholders and independent management. This produced further consequences.[2]

Jack: It gave rise to universal values in the process. The U.K.'s private sector helped to create a new political-economic system at home and abroad. The new system greatly limited the power of the state, and countless barriers were abolished.

George: Do you mean it was the private sector that contributed most significantly to the rise of modern commerce and a market economy?

Jack: Sort of. The U.K.'s private sector made a big difference. Over time, trade created a huge space for private interests. Naturally, the entire British society and government moved in the same direction after the so-called Glorious Revolution of the 17th century. It was under such conditions that the industrial revolution took place in the U.K. rather than in continental Europe.[3]

CHINA'S MISSED OPPORTUNITIES

Tom: China has walked an independent path for ages. China has always experienced tight government domination. For a long time this has stopped China from focusing on modern development. The Western world has seen full development while China has yet to be developed. In fact, China was ahead of the West for thousands of years, up to 1800 at least.

Jack: In many ways, the British controlled new weapons. These weapons were modern institutions, organizations, and professional management. Creating wealth has turned out to be no big secret. Entrepreneurs and managers know how if they have the right environment.

Tom: China lived in a closed world for a long time. Though the world was interested in made-in-China products, especially tea, silk, and china, our businessmen generally were not free to trade. We had the biggest ships and the best navigators in the world in the 15th century. But our traders were not allowed to sail off Chinese waters. They faced death sentences if they did—a new law set by the government for the last few centuries. How could anyone stop China's pitiful decline? Yet impoverished Europe rose to dominate the world. The British were able to rule vast lands and populations like India.

George: But the United States finally took its turn. Why were the U.S. companies able to outdo the British?

Jack: The U.S. businesses have done better. They have greatly improved upon the British. The United States has the biggest private sector in the world, while its government sector is rather tiny. This has meant a greater drive for wealth creation. It has made a difference.

THE U.S. WAY: DUMPING LOSERS

George: Any other reasons?

Jack: One more reason may be this. One person is not much smarter than another. Once you are a leader, everyone else naturally learns from and improves upon your ideas. Students often make more progress than their teachers. That is how I see what made United States the global power over the U.K.

George: What have been the U.S.'s advantages?

Jack: The U.S. success came from advantages over the U.K. People in the U.S. are more practical. They are able to create larger car companies, among other things. In particular, they have shown greater capabilities to dump the losers. They have no feelings for losers. They do it without hesitation.

Tom: Many critics claim that they are hard-hearted to the point of cruelty.

But to the United States, if the losers are not thrown out, the whole ship will sink. That is exactly the view of Al Dunlap, the turnaround executive. He saved several companies by cutting, cutting, cutting.[4]

George: Many Americans dislike him because his strategies caused wide unemployment.

Jack: But you have to appreciate his reasoning. How do you save a sinking ship? What is more, multibillions of dollars are created as a result.[5]

EXPANSION AND WEALTH CREATION, PAST AND PRESENT

Tom: The old Western expansion was quite different, full of blood. They sailed anywhere fit for commercial ships and brought gunships along. They even sailed into our Pearl River,[6] which met with our opposition. What followed was the Opium Wars. But the opium won finally. By that time, everyone recognized the power of gunships. So China spent all its resources learning about guns and such. The Chinese bought many gunships from the West, including the U.K.

Jack: That was a mistake. What made the U.K. powerful was not really just the gunships. It was the whole thing—the entire package. The U.K.'s strength has come from modern organizations, institutions, and professional management. This is something old China seriously missed.

Tom: For ages, China was the richest and most advanced nation around the world. Even so, China has missed all the opportunities in recent history. The West has taken a new path, a market-oriented one. If an entire population is allowed to create, how much wealth can it produce? This is something China has missed for a long time. Naturally, the West got a big step ahead.

Jack: What China really needs is to create an entrepreneurial environment with a limited government. Instead, this bureaucratic power has only intensified. Unfortunately, in the last two centuries, we went for shortcuts. Above all, the entire society had to continue to serve bureaucratic needs. Eventually, China reached a dead-end street. A difficult path!

George: Deng Xiaoping favored the slogan "You can't eat socialism." Should we say today's China is on the right path, finally?

Jack: Yes. China is reinventing itself fast. The Chinese people are quickly learning how to create a modern economy and an open society starting from the very basics. In this era, China's growth started at an extremely low point, but has been gaining rapid progress. That is highly unexpected.

Tom: Everything is at the early stages. But China is fast moving away from the old bureaucratic domination. Between China and the West, the key difference is this bureaucratic power. Under this power, no true private sector can exist. China has had all kinds of reforms and revolutions in the past. But none of them dealt with the problem from the root causes. In fact, after 1949, this traditional bureaucratic power reached a new height. Naturally, the Chinese economy and society were unable to move.

George: How do you compare the United States to China today?

Jack: The United States is more than fortunate. To the Chinese, one U.S. advantage is that it has made the government a service body. Containing bureaucratic power has been its biggest strength. Otherwise, it would have a situation similar to China's. For China, this is what it has yet to achieve.

George: Do you mean that if the government had not been turned into a service body, the U.S. wealth would have declined?

Tom: It would happen in no time. When people's hands are tied, how can they create wealth? There is a little secret about making wealth. A free spirit plus a well-structured organization creates wealth. Even in China now, we have the same land and the same people, but now we are much richer than in the Mao era. Why? We have a vibrant private sector now.

THE GREAT CRASH OF 1929

Jack: The U.S. life is not perfect. In my mind, the Great Crash of 1929 did a lot of good for the market system.

George: How so?

Jack: True, terrible things happened after the crash: At least 15 million people lost their jobs. That was some 23% of its total work force.[7] Even at the auto giant Ford, violence broke out in 1932 when the workers demonstrated to demand that they be able to keep their jobs. The guards killed several workers.[8]

Tom: Europe had even more violence. Many wild political organizations like the Third Reich came into being. And finally, men like Hitler and World War II.

Jack: Without the crash, America could not have created all the modern laws and standards. Plus, without it, how could the American businesspeople have learned to build modern organizations and professional management? Modern standards such as transparency, professional management, and governance were products of the crash in one way or another.

A PRACTICAL PATH

George: In more recent history, China's performance has been terrible. What are the reasons?

Jack: The United States has had one vast strength: the private sector. The private sector has been able to pursue independent interests without government obstruction. It is the small guys who have thrived in big ways. The list of names is long: Ford, Rockefeller, and on and on. The Silicon Valley crowds in our era have only followed them. So many small guys have created unbelievable things.

George: To me, the United States can dump losers much more easily than most nations.

Tom: Well, the U.S. business harshness is balanced by its safety net, its social welfare system. The unemployed and the underprivileged can get help. Without this, U.S. businesses would not be that free. But there is more to it than that. For example, in Western Europe, firing employees is difficult even when business needs demand it. So the United States has overcome this difficulty without causing unwanted trouble.

George: Our state companies cannot really follow the U.S. model, can they?

Tom: True. China has the opposite situation. There are vast redundancies, and often five workers handle the job of one. The bottom line is that it has hardly anything to do with wealth creation. At one major tractor company inland, things have gone really wrong. It's a big company in the state sector and has some 70,000 employees. I asked its president how many people his business needs. His answer was "5,000 at most." Then I asked, "What can you do about it?" "Hardly anything," he said.

Jack: No matter how successful an American CEO is, say a CEO like Jack Welch, would he be able to do much in a business organization in China's state sector? No, definitely not! He would immediately find that managing a Chinese company is more involved than managing GE. He would immediately run into impossible things in the bureaucratic world.

Tom: Not just in China—similar things happen in other nations, including Japan. The Japanese businesses face serious redundancies, inefficiencies, and high costs, for example. Even if they have a good welfare system, they seem rather helpless to handle these issues. Western reporters claim that the Japanese have not been doing the right things for a long time. Twenty-odd years back, when the Japanese took their goods and capital to the United States, people were dumbfounded.

Japan in the U.S.

George: Why were the U.S. citizens so afraid of Japan Inc.?

Jack: I read a book, *Selling Our Security*, by two U.S. intellectuals.[9] They were bitter about foreigners like the Japanese buying their household names. What was behind the pain was almost like the British history. For many decades, the United States had dominated the globe. Yet its success had also brought a lot of ills. The Americans' pride, along with prejudice, had reached a point so high up in the sky that they almost forgot the existence of all other people. When the Japanese went there, the Americans were stunned. They went into a panic.

Tom: The Japanese immediately put many U.S. companies out of business. How did they do it? They offered a wide selection of cheap but highly reliable products. The U.S. consumers wanted them.

George: Why did the United States lose competitiveness?

Jack: The U.S. was taken by surprise. For some time, most U.S. citizens didn't figure out why things happened the way they did. I heard a story about those times. Detroit, being the auto capital, has tens of thousands of auto workers. They were really scared. One terrible event took place in 1982: A Chinese engineer met a fatal end on the streets there. Two men, a father and son, beat him to death for no reason.

Jack: That shows how much pain the United States was suffering. Instead of being able to do things on their own initiative, they were having dramatic actions forced upon them. As always, only under pressure do humans want to change. Huge business restructuring and reform have dominated the U.S. market ever since then.

George: Did these measures produce sound results?

Jack: Yes, they did. Many uncompetitive companies were forced out. It seems that the U.S. public showed little interest in the losers.

George: Even IBM ran into trouble, right?

Jack: IBM is interesting. It was the symbol of U.S. power for decades. But this blue chip company went wrong in the early 1990s and had losses of around $15 billion. It acted almost like a state company in China, with five people doing the job of one. By early 1993, many investors had given up hope. Only a dramatic restructuring turned IBM's fortunes around. But almost half of the employees lost their jobs. For some time, U.S. parents were reluctant to have their daughters marry IBM guys. There were certainly lessons to be learned.

George: Is the IBM-Lenovo deal a smart move for IBM?

Jack: It looks that way. The IBM boys have grown up a bit, certainly. They watch for danger and seem to move ahead with a new level of determination. They badly want to get ahead by dumping low-value things to China. This may represent a future trend: China is becoming a dumping ground.

U.S. STRENGTHS TODAY

George: What is behind the U.S. strengths today?

Jack: To me, the U.S. advantage has something to do with its ability to improve continuously. Dumping losers without hesitation is part of that. This self-improvement is the strength of any organization and nation. As soon as it disappears, you should be seeing the beginning of the end.

George: Do you really think that's such a critical factor?

Jack: Just look at Japan, at the other extreme. Its rise and retreat have both been tremendous. Within a short time, Japan Inc. created vast fortunes. They became a global leader. But seemingly, they lack the capability to improve upon success. Then fortunes quickly decline. When a person has to cut off one of his arms to save his life, can he do it? If not, there's no sense in trying something else.

Tom: I don't know.... What is so perfect about the United States? There are abuses all over the place—involving big bucks. What's more, these things have been going on for a long time. They involve household names such as Enron and WorldCom.

George: All that was a surprise to everyone, especially us Chinese. But what is more amazing is that a long time ago, people invented a big story, that the United States was immune to abuses. Events have shown otherwise. The immunity story was dangerous. But now it's gone.

Tom: True, some people think they are above earthly things. Well, viruses are bigger than humans. Maybe someday we will send people beyond the solar system, but the viruses will go with them, for certain.[10]

Jack: Now the U.S. watchdogs have become active. They are sending out fines to numerous Wall Street and Main Street addresses. They have even gone as far as to prohibit the Citibank chairman from talk directly with his analysts. All this seems a bit funny. Maybe it shows how bad the situation can get.

Tom: Well, this lesson is good for everyone: Like it or not, we are all earthly things.

18 A NEW GLOBAL TREND: MEGA-COMPANIES AND GLOBAL EXPANSION

Today, multinationals take nearly 50% of global trade, and their share is still rising rapidly. The biggest multinationals, such as GE, Siemens, BP, and Microsoft, have more income than many small nations. They even have bigger incomes than some large developing nations. They are everywhere and still expanding. What is behind all this? How will they affect world development ahead?

George: Any new global trends?

Tom: Today, dramatic events happen one after another. What is really behind the doings of multinationals? People seem to lose a feeling of certainty. Bosses can't sit in the offices the way they used to. Why do the big bosses keep running around like salesmen and competing like bulls?

Jack: I see three strategies that dominate the activities of multinationals today.

George: What are they?

BIGGER AND BIGGER MULTINATIONALS

Jack: Globally, multinationals have truly come of age. Today money and power are more concentrated in the hands of fewer organizations and individuals than ever before. Multinationals today lead global economic development in one way or another. They have become much bigger and more influential than ever before. Plus they have found more ways to expand.

George: What ways?

Jack: On the one hand, governments around the globe take a more passive role in the markets now. The wind of privatization has swept over the planet. This means dramatic changes for the world, including developed nations such as the U.K. and Germany as well as later-developing nations like China and India. There are so many market weapons to employ now. Restructuring, consolidations, and global expansion have helped multinationals become even bigger. With such modern tools, they have room to play in. What's more, so many multinationals want to become truly global players. Now they are talking about universal banks and global companies.[1]

George: What sorts of industries are they most active in?

Jack: Almost all industries. The financial sector stands out in particular. Financial companies are more globalized than many others. Clients move globally, so banks have to also. What's more, it is better for banks to go forward globally. That way they can gain an edge. In fact, whichever bank can truly establish a global presence will gain a sharp edge. That is why all major Western banks are trying hard to set up a global franchise.

FIRST STRATEGY: A STRONG HOME BASE

George: So, what are their strategies?

Jack: Their first strategy is to build a strong home base. Each and every bank knows the importance of creating a strong home base. Otherwise, they would not be able to expand at all. This takes place in their established territories.

George: How do they get a strong home base?

Jack: Partly through mergers and acquisitions. In the banking sector, things have also become crowded. All kinds of large-size commercial banks, investment banks, and fund management and insurance companies have tried to merge into megastores. In these ways universal banks are created.

Tom: They have tried to reach all corners of the globe. They have become more viable through mergers and consolidations, right?

Jack: Yes. Many leading banks like Citibank, HSBC, JP Morgan Chase, and Deutsche Bank are all products of those types of deals. They have to have a herd mentality on the one hand and compete with each other globally on the other hand. They are reaching the globe in the truest sense for the very first time in history. Their profits have made new records.

George: Explain.

Jack: These actions have had complex features. In many cases, these mergers have taken place as mergers between equals. Many of the companies were giants even before the current round of mergers. Many business empires were already the products of past mergers. As one example, Chase Manhattan acquired Chemical Bank and HQ, among others. The deal with JP Morgan is the biggest in this direction. Now it gets Bank One. In many other cases, the strong have swallowed the weak. These universal banks have greatly expanded their business lines and scope, handling all financial products and services. What's more, using their home nations as a base, they are expanding into other regions and even around the world.[2]

MERRILL LYNCH

George: Can you give one more example of a giant produced by mergers?

Jack: The U.S. investment bank Merrill Lynch is a company resulting from somewhere around 19 acquisitions since 1980. A recent pick was the failed Japanese investment house, Yamayachi. But it's had problems becoming profitable in Japan.

Tom: One banking deal produces more deals from competing parties. HSBC is a good example. It has gained a strong global position through acquisition. It became a major European bank by acquiring Midland Bank in 1992. It added to its U.S. power by taking over Republic Bank of New York. It didn't stop there. It has been reaching out to get more assets in all regions, especially in emerging places like China.

George: Such expansions are not limited to financial companies, are they?

Cisco

Jack: They happen in most sectors. Growing through acquisitions is certainly a popular practice. Companies like CA and Cisco have been marvels in this context. Today's Cisco is a product of some 100 acquisitions over the past two decades.

Tom: The computer hardware sector is very striking. Though that entire industry has been in existence for only three decades or so, it has been through remarkable changes. Survival is a huge problem even for the biggest. Now only a few global names remain. Even an old giant like Compaq is gone.

Jack: It happens to the old-economy companies, be they auto, food, supermarkets, or other old-type industries. The American companies dominate the top of the list still. A recent survey by the *Financial Times* showed that U.S. brands have some 240 slots on the top 500 list as in 2003. The Japanese took that top seat only 20 years ago. The Japanese power startled not only the emerging markets, but also the established markets like the U.S. and Western Europe. So the U.S. and European multinationals are trying hard to expand globally.

Why Is Being Big So Big?

George: Why do these giants want to get even bigger? They are already mammoth. How big do they really want to become?

Tom: Some observers claim that these businesspeople are preparing with a sense of urgency for the next thing, a great crash. Being big does not mean that they are immune to disaster. The Western world has seen plenty of disasters. Only a few businessmen escaped the Great Crash of 1929 with nothing more serious than bruises.

Jack: The British scholar Alfred North Whitehead lived in a dramatic period. He grew up in England during the Victorian era—an age of great things. The world around him seemed picture perfect. His entire world suddenly changed with World War I. Then more bad things followed—the Great Depression, World War II, and Hitler.

Tom: Well, you don't need to be that old to know that times can get bad quickly. Events of the recent past have been dramatic. Who is not affected?

Everyone remembers the savings and loan crisis in the United States in the late 1980s. Citibank had a rough time as well. Its stock fell to some $10 back in 1991. Citibank was messed up with bad loans in the late 1980s. To be sure, the United States was loaded with investors. But all the friends ran away. Who wants to reach for a falling knife? The depositors in Hong Kong and Taiwan rushed to the doors. Some people believed that the end of the bank was near. Finally, help showed up—a rich Arab prince offered some $1 billion for a 10% share. That saved the day for the bank.

Jack: Not just Citibank, the whole U.S. banking sector was in a mess. Bank of New England and thousands of savings and loans all crashed, causing damages up to $1 trillion.

George: What is another strategy for achieving a global presence?

SECOND STRATEGY: REDUCING PLAYERS AND CREATING A NEW FORM OF DOMINANCE

Jack: The second strategy is an effort to reduce the number of players. This has happened in each industry, each region, and each business line. Through such activities, these huge companies have increased market share, creating a new form of market domination.

George: Is the U.K. a good example?

Jack: Yes. In a place like Britain, almost all the independent investment brokerages have changed owners. The new players are all much bigger banks from the United States and continental Europe. In the U.S., a large number of investment banks have changed owners, like PaineWebber, Republic Bank of New York, DLJ, and Bankers Trust, among many brands on the list. The international buyers are mostly European banks. In an interesting contrast, while these mergers and acquisitions took place in the United States, the Japanese banks were packing and retreating from their earlier global reaching.

George: What would have happened without all these mergers in the West during the recent bear market?

Jack: The companies would have been in worse shape than they are now. These mergers have helped them face a downturn. For example, Citibank is in its best shape ever. Its profits keep reaching new records.

Tom: Once they are strong at home, they can look around and expand into new markets, right?

Jack: That's right, and the timing has been perfect for them. Most nations in Asia have gone through an economic mess, especially in the late 1990s. All this paved the road for the West Inc. to tap into Asia in a big way.

THIRD STRATEGY: A TRUE GLOBAL REACH

George: So their global expansion is the third strategy. Right?

Jack: That's right. This strategy is built upon the first two strategies. The new territories will be the final playgrounds to fight on.

George: Asia is a natural choice for the Western businesses, isn't it?

Tom: Asia has the biggest population. Life in most regions of Asia is also improving. Now China and India are developing quickly. All these things are attractive. Asia has a fast-expanding pie that is most inviting to all outsiders.

Jack: That is very true. No multinational can claim to be a global player unless it is active in Asia. Developing Asia—especially China and India— has become the last frontier. There is nothing to stop them from coming.

George: What are their goals in Asia?

Jack: They are truly discovering opportunities in Asia more than ever before. They originally hoped to find new markets. But Asia has more to offer. In Asia they can do outsourcing and research and development as well. In short, Asia is one big factory-market. All this means more profits.

George: Besides all that, they can establish research centers here in Asia. We have the best talent here. Plus, if something costs $10 in the United States and Europe, here it costs only $2.

Jack: To be sure, multinationals have become homeless. They can put their best assets and operations anywhere on the global map. That is a dramatic departure from the past.

Tom: The rise of India and China has become a new growth engine for the world. It is going to reshape the world. If the average income doubles, the world will feel it. After all, India and China are about 40% of the world population.

George: No wonder the Western companies are rushing to China by the thousands today. They are here to explore all the new opportunities in a country with 1.3 billion consumers.

CHINA'S PARTICIPATION IN THE WORLD ECONOMY

Tom: China offers vast advantages to foreign companies. It can provide a completely sufficient domestic market, not like India, Indonesia and Mexico, for example. Beyond that, there is a complete range of commerce and industry. In addition, there is a huge talent pool and very little in the way of union strikes. These elements must be appealing to all employers.

George: China has become more open than many other developing countries. Is this one key reason China is attractive to global businesses?

Tom: China is improving things quickly. This fast self-improvement puts China a step ahead of many developing nations. In turn, such global participation has further fueled a booming economy in China. It will definitely offer more opportunities for the world. Global investors are smart enough to know all this. Already, China today is definitely more open than Japan. In fact, it is easier for Chinese businesses to play in China than for the Chinese go to Japan.

Jack: What is happening in China has already impacted the global market. This is something people didn't expect 20 years ago.

Tom: In reality, the impact is in both directions. How can dramatic changes in 22% of the world's population not affect everyone else? How can made-in-China products not affect overseas markets?

George: How is the outside world going to affect China?

Tom: China badly needs to get out of the old failing system centered on government. For this, having fuller global participation is a must. The WTO is a powerful way to bring a new set of rules to China. This means that for the first time China has international rules to follow. China is crying out for modern law. The WTO offers a direct link in this context.

George: Is a uniform set of rules that good for the world?

Jack: It is certainly a positive achievement.

Tom: It appears that some nations are afraid to play by the rules for now. Look around and you can see that some developed nations are in a hurry to ban free trade.

Jack: But China is opening up to the world, reaching higher levels year after year.

George: Can't we say that China is deeply convinced by now that an open economy and society are a necessity to bring about true progress and prosperity?

Tom: True. In this respect the outside world has something to learn.

Jack: But the trouble is that some people, especially in the developed world, are reluctant to admit it. Some people are afraid to learn—maybe learning makes them feel they are no longer that superior.

Tom: If that is the case, then China better keep its lessons secret—just kidding.

19 MORE ON THE CIRCLE

The powerful waves of globalization are finally reaching the last corners of the world. No region is left behind. Why does the world need globalization? How is it that Asia's door has opened so wide?

WHO HAS AFFECTED GLOBALIZATION THE MOST?

Tom: Who has really affected globalization most in our era?

Jack: In a big way, Japan.

George: Now that's a big surprise to me.

FIRST FACTOR: JAPAN'S GLOBAL REACH AND RETREAT

Jack: Well, I think actually three major factors led to the right environment for today's global marketplace. First, some 40 years ago, Japan expanded around the world—then, after a while, it pulled back.

George: Can you elaborate?

Jack: It was Japan that first tried to expand globally. Japanese goods and capital are exported globally. Numerous Asian nations and regions have also emerged as international traders. The smaller regions of Asia, such as Hong Kong, Taiwan, Singapore, and South Korea, all tried to copy the Japanese model in one way or another. In particular, they have all focused on export as a growth engine. Finally, the biggest Asian nations, China and India, have joined in the wave started by Japan.

George: But Japan Inc. has been retreating for the last 15 years or so, has it not?

Jack: The retreat of Japan Inc. caused many consequences in Asia and beyond. Everyone agrees that the Asian financial crisis of 1997 was related fundamentally to the crisis in Japan. Asia's gates have been wide open to the Western world for the first time in history. There is another element of Japanese influence. Japan's retreat has further facilitated globalization. The great crash of Japan's stock and land markets coincided with the great jump in asset values in the United States and Europe. This created the global marketplace that we see today.[1]

George: Why is this so significant from a historical perspective?

Jack: For centuries, the world was sharply divided into two hemispheres, West and East. National barriers were more than important. It would have taken political and military means to open doors in the past. Even so, Western business power had some limited activities in Asia in the past. But they could not penetrate deep into continental Asia. Even in Japan and South Korea, where tens of thousands of soldiers were stationed, U.S. businesses could not truly penetrate these markets. The biggest Asian nations have been rather successful in fending off unwanted Western expansion.

George: So Japan's retreat has opened many doors for Western businesses. Right?

Jack: More than that, Japan's retreat has created significant side effects. It has presented vast opportunities for the stronger Western players. During the expansion phase of Europe and the United States throughout the 1990s, the situation in most parts of Asia went bad. Most Asian nations were drawn into deep crises. Economic crises, one after another, started with Japan and spread to South Korea and the Southeast nations.

WHAT IS GOING ON IN TOKYO?

Tom: Japan's quick rise and dramatic retreat are worthy of our attention. Its stock market reached 20-year lows, and the Nikkei index traded in the 7,000s around the spring of 2003. In 1989, it had reached a bubble high of 40,000. What a difference time makes! In particular, Japanese banks have reported terrible losses for a long time. The banking reform efforts have yet to produce positive results.

George: What is really behind Japan's banking mess?

Jack: To me, Japan's problems go far beyond usual business issues. On the surface, their key problem is the cross-holding structure between banks and corporate borrowers. Many Japanese banks hold shares of their clients and vice versa. The declining fortunes of these clients have damaged the health of the banks.[2]

George: Why do the Japanese banks want these kinds of problems?

Jack: No Western banks have this type of practice, of holding shares of their clients while lending them money. By professional standards, it amounts to "insider trading." In short, professional practice would demand that all decisions be business oriented. Being friends may open the door. But making decisions should be completely independent. Banking executives are not allowed to jump on a deal if it seems shaky and risky. These ideas have yet to enter Japanese banking life.

PROFESSIONALISM OF JAPANESE BANKERS

George: What will it take to change the Japanese banks for the better?

Jack: The Japanese bankers do not commit abuses. They are professionals. To many international bankers, the Tokyo bankers are considered the most conservative. Still, their banking issues remain troubling today.

George: If that is the case, why do the Japanese bankers continue to behave in ways that confuse outsiders?

Jack: It is a mystery to us all as outsiders. What really makes them do all the risky things? The *New York Times* publishes many stories on the Japanese banking phenomenon: Their bankers keep lending to bankrupt companies even now. But the Korean bankers have stopped doing it. Why does this still happen in Japan?

Tom: Japan's banking problems should be completely different from those in China. China's banking problems have political causes. The Chinese banks are not independent organizations. But the Japanese banks should have no pressures from the political establishment. Why do they select risky businesses?

Tom: They are still lending to risky businesses, as if they do not care. Well, it seems to me that this behavior on the part of the Japanese must be deeply rooted. No citizen can easily escape the cultural environment, not even the smart Japanese bankers.

George: Do you mean that such business behavior has meanings beyond business?

TRIBAL WARS

Tom: Many people have looked for reasons beyond pure business issues. I think that is the right direction. After all, the business world is not self-contained. Japan's culture has a tremendous component of closed units within the society.

Jack: In Japanese society, an individual hardly exists. Only groups and organizations exist. In history, individual Japanese have belonged to different semi-autonomous political-economic groups on the regional level. Food and land are scarce, and survival may often depend on belonging to these groups.

Tom: Bloody civil wars were fought among these "tribes" over the ages. Some tribes survived at the expense of others. Some merged with others to become bigger. Many citizens depended a great deal on these political organizations.

REPEATED INVASIONS

Jack: China was invaded many times in the past. Tens of thousands Japanese pirates worked hard at invading coastal China and Korea. The invasions went on from the 13th to the 16th century. The Japanese fought bravely and even tried to penetrate into the hinterland.

Tom: We Chinese were more determined.[3] They were kicked out through bloody wars. This was a prelude to the Japanese invasions in the 20th century.

CONTINUING INFLUENCE OF THE "TRIBE" TRADITION

George: Do you think that Japan's "tribe" tradition is still influential?

Tom: How easily can culture and tradition change? In modern times, the old elements are not mentioned often. But traditions and culture don't die out overnight. Given a society with particular cultural elements, nobody can truly avoid them. What is more, individuals now belong to these large business organizations. There is a common interest that binds them together. Without such belonging, individuals feel powerless. This is different from what happens in a society like China. In our society, we are more family centered. Even today, Japanese entrepreneurial activities are much less than in China or the United States. The Japanese citizens prefer to work for the giant companies.[4]

George: What about their business organizations?

Tom: Within their business organizations, the old tradition continues to affect their daily business behavior. Individual Japanese have few choices. All citizens must belong to the same companies for life, body and soul. They must devote their entire life and energy to promoting the interests of their employers in order to better their own existence.

Jack: Truly enough, this tradition is still alive in the Japanese world. Each business group is associated with many companies that act like sisters and brothers. By tradition, they must enjoy the fruits of life as well as the failures together. All these things may require no paper contracts. Indeed, no contracts can express their exact meaning. The clients of the banks are the sisters in the extended family. They may conduct different businesses. They are tied by unwritten contracts whose meanings are not to be measured by Western standards.

George: How do the Japanese operate?

Jack: It happens often that each giant business group has a financial center, the bank. This bank must take care of its member companies. After all, most money in the bank belongs to these member companies. The bank is to serve their needs, in good times and bad. These relationships are common in Japan.[5]

BANKS' LACK OF FREEDOM

George: How does such a tradition affect the Japanese banks?

Jack: The banks are seriously affected. Even in bad times, everyone has to eat. Who are they to judge who deserves food or not?

George: How can the Japanese banks get out of this situation? It appears that their traditional business games are mostly over. They are out of resources for resolving these old problems by their own means. Do you agree?

Tom: The vast losses have largely depleted the capital resources at some Japanese banks. They must rely on capital infusion. But some of them are no longer welcome in the capital market. It is natural for the government to step in. Yet many Japanese bankers are afraid of government obstruction. They would prefer to be independent.

George: It is Francis Fukuyama's view that the Japanese success is due to this traditional system. He claims that only with such a system has Japan Inc. been able to produce the success that it has.[6]

Jack: Well, this is true only on the surface. Deep down, the tradition has undermined professional, merit-based practices. In the end, Japan Inc. has paid dearly. In short, they are their own foes.

George: I understand that the closed Japanese network is powerful enough to fend off foreign interests. Within such a network, businesses take care of each other even if they may not benefit themselves. For example, if an outside business wanted to sell them the best products at the cheapest price, they would not buy. Instead, they would buy based on their relationships even if it did not make business sense.

CANON

Jack: True. The Japanese crisis goes far beyond the banking sector. This tradition issue has undermined reform and therefore recovery. More than 14 years has passed since the peak of the bubble. But this is only a short time in relation to history. Can this short time be compared to the thousands of years of Japanese life? Do you ask Japanese bankers to change things? Even if they agreed, how long would it take?

George: An interesting view. How do you see the fact that the Japanese company Canon recently announced it will close down some plants in China and move them back to Japan?[7] From a business standpoint this is strange. Japanese employees earn many times more than the Chinese. Plus, Canon is rushing to expand its program in China at the moment.

Tom: Well, in Japan the relationship between the employer and employees goes far beyond the usual professional relationship. Saving these Japanese jobs has a spiritual meaning even if it does not make business sense. This is something Canon must do.

George: What can Japan do? Can Japan take a completely new path? Are the Japanese going to deviate from their traditional practices?

Tom: Japan is changing now, albeit slowly. But this is happening because things are in such disarray. Like the United States and every other nation, Japan does not make changes on its own initiative. Changes happen because of pressures from all directions, especially at home.

Jack: Japan has been a closed society for a long time. Inviting foreigners to get involved at the top would be tough. The closed society has had adverse consequences for Japan today.[8]

George: So Japan Inc. also faces the issue of departing from certain traditional practices. Right?

Tom: Traditional practices have given rise to deep problems. But dramatic changes are happening. The survival of Nissan is one case. International involvement is finally viewed positively in Japan. Above all, such new approaches have opened new windows for resolving existing problems.

Nissan

Jack: It appears that Japan is at a turning point. Actually, the worsening situation at Nissan has created dramatic changes for the better. Above all, its restructuring has involved the French. The Japanese managers have reportedly been cooperative. This has helped to save Nissan.

Tom: This Japanese economic slump is a shock to all. Achieving sustained growth is easier said than done. That is a great lesson for the world.

Jack: Changing a tradition takes a long time. One cannot expect to see quick reforms of any sort. Above all, it will take more effort to create an open society. So far, activities inside Japan are still largely a Japanese play. In this regard, China is more determined and therefore more open.

SOUTH KOREA: GLORIES AND BUBBLES

George: Apparently it should be a great lesson that a blind partnership between government and business can bring disaster in the absence of modern law and transparency. Isn't South Korea an example?

Jack: Well said. Japan's economic slump eventually spread over much of Asia. By 1997, once-thriving small economies of Asia were having a bad time. All this resulted in disasters of historical proportions. The Koreans have repeated the glories as well as the bubbles seen in Japan.

Tom: Changes have been dramatic for all Asian nations, including South Korea. The Korean financial crisis of 1997 came as a shock. It offers serious lessons for all of us. Starting in the late 1970s, South Korea Inc. amazed the world by becoming a new power. Several dozen Korean companies have joined the global 500 club. Their cars, steel, home appliances, electronics, and semiconductors have flooded the global market.

George: What is behind all this?

Tom: The chaebols. Furthermore, they have had close ties with government.

George: It is dangerous for a small group of people to control so much wealth, isn't it? Exactly why is that?

Tom: Without a sound framework, things can easily get out of control. The Korean financial crisis has taught us a lesson. Despite rapid development, the Korean companies had serious problems. Within the organizations, professional practices were weak. Often irrational actions followed from the emotion of greed.[9] Behind the crisis, basic professional elements were lacking. Emphasis was not placed on discipline, transparency, and responsibility.

A CLOSED DOOR

George: To me, the Korean society has had a closed door for a long time. As with China, this closed condition has been very negative, has it not?

Tom: True. Once the businessmen crossed lines of rationality, how could they be stopped? Rather, their actions were encouraged. Once this happened, many businessmen felt that they somehow had divine power in their hands. They could turn the world around if they wished.

Jack: Corruption has been a common problem there. Many businessmen used bribery to get help from political officials. Even two ex-presidents were involved. They were sent to prison for taking bribes in the hundreds of millions of dollars. Ties between businessmen and corrupt officials—that is the very best way to create bubbles.

George: How could the bubble last so long? What didn't the bubble burst right after Japan?

Jack: At least two factors contributed. Before 1997, these Korean businesses could not generate a profit. Troubles would quickly follow. They had tremendous power to borrow money at home. But there is a real limit to this. Finally, neither the Korean banks nor investors could give them any more. Another factor was all the debt that businesses incurred to finance their greater ambitions to go global.[10]

KOREAN GIANTS

George: I understand that by 1996, the biggest Korean businesses combined did not earn a profit. Many large companies carried debts of 500% or more. How could this have continued?

Jack: The Korean situation was bound to get out of control. Then a small strike by the auto workers created a chain reaction. Thus we saw the sudden collapse of once-booming Korea.[11]

Tom: A friend told me a story. He is a fund manager working for a U.S. bank. Just before the Korean crash in 1997, he ran into a high-ranking Korean auto executive on the airplane. The executive talked about his ambition to dominate the global auto market. My friend was shocked. He felt as though he needed to dump his Korean stocks as soon as he landed.

Jack: What a story! But the financial crisis of 1997 has taught everyone a lesson. Above all, the Korean society has been following a new path since then. Unlike the Japanese, the Koreans have used heavy dosages of medicine. It looks like the Koreans have reached a common understanding that the doors must open to the entire world. This could enable them to attract international capital that is badly needed.

Tom: As Asians, we often don't wish to admit weaknesses. For example, if we sell our companies, it may be treated as a failure. Asians desire to buy companies, but not to sell them. This is changing gradually.

Jack: Some Koreans who were trying to create funds wanted to raise money badly. To improve credibility, they brought some U.S. professionals into their organizations. In doing so they hoped to convince investors about their commitment to a quality management. This shows how sensitive the Korean public has become.

CHANGES IN KOREA

George: One U.S. MBA graduate of MIT has lived in South Korea for well over a decade. He has gained impressive publicity in Korea as an entrepreneur. He is now on the Korean businesspeople's most wanted list for partnerships.

Tom: The outside world immediately got the signal. International businesspeople everywhere have the best noses. Huge international crowds have rushed in. To be sure, there was a fire sale. There were many bargain assets on the selling block. All sorts of failed assets have been bought. The list is long: First Korea Bank, AmKorea Bank, the auto maker KIA, and auto parts maker Mando, to name just a few. Even recently, one Chinese auto maker in Shanghai went there to buy a controlling stake in a distressed Korean auto maker.

Jack: Crisis can make a big difference. South Korea has walked away from a closed tradition. In this respect South Korea is doing much better than Japan. The Koreans show more determination to an open society than the Japanese. Therefore it is natural for Korea to have had a quicker recovery than Japan.

George: Both Japan and Korea are active in China.

Jack: They now realize that China is their new engine for growth. They are more active than most Western companies now. In this regard, the Japanese are as committed as the Koreans.

Tom: Both want to employ China as a cheap manufacturing center as well as a market. They have been investing heavily. The Koreans are a latecomer. But they are doing better than most foreign players. LG, Samsung, and Hyundai lead the crowd.[12]

SECOND FACTOR: ASIA'S FINANCIAL CRISIS

Jack: In the last 10 years or so, great opportunities have emerged in Asia for Western companies. This Western expansion into Asia had a lucky start. The timing could not have been better. On the one hand, U.S. and European companies had made huge profits in their home markets. Throughout the 1990s, the United States and Western Europe enjoyed a huge bull market. Their asset values reached a historical high. At the same time, most of Asia had a financial crisis in the late 1990s.

Tom: Vast capital inflow pushed asset values to new highs almost every year for a decade in the United States and Western Europe. Then, more consolidations produced much bigger companies. For the first time in human history, individual companies have reached well over $10 billion in profits per year. Their wealth is bigger than that of the small poor nations combined. Two U.S. companies combined, GE and Microsoft, are bigger than China's entire stock market value with its some 1,400 listings. How can anyone believe this?

George: All this has created the right atmosphere for globalization. At the same time, the economic crisis of Asia opened that door much wider than ever before.

THIRD FACTOR: THE WORLD TRADE ORGANIZATION

Jack: It's not only the Asian financial crisis that has opened doors for outside investments. A more decisive factor is that China is developing fast, along with India and other developing Asian nations. This growing Chinese economy is expanding into the global sphere in major ways. Joining the WTO has been a brave act on the part of China to embrace globalization.

Tom: China's growth has already impacted global markets measurably. The results are by nobody's design. They are changing the old economic landscape around the planet. Even at home, changes are accelerating.

George: What exact benefits does the WTO bring to China?

Tom: Broadly speaking, China's new development has involved the world. Two key elements stand out. One is trade. China's total trade has surpassed Japan's since 2004. By 2010, China is expected to increase its share to 10% or perhaps more. China is deeply connected to the global economy.

George: What is the second element?

Tom: The next element is equally striking. The outside world is increasing its interests and investments in China. It must do so in order to share in China's progress. China is a top nation for foreign direct investment. More than $560 billion had come its way by 2004. In the last few years, every year has been a new record. There is no way to stop this. Are you talking about overheating in the Chinese economy? In 2004 alone, some $61 billion new foreign direct investment went there. The speed of development in China means that everyone must come.

George: Does this benefit China?

Tom: Every party is gaining something. This is the nature of the world economy now. Today, more than 23.5 million Chinese work for overseas employers. In addition, more than 70 million are engaged in trade.[13] Joining the WTO is a natural step. At the same time, it is one that allows a greater opportunity for the outside world to share in China's progress.

UNEXPECTED DEVELOPMENTS

Jack: China's new path has already led to great surprises. In the beginning, Beijing merely wanted to revitalize the faltering economy. But strikingly unexpected developments have taken place. It turns out that economic development cannot be compartmentalized away from everything else. It demands changes in all aspects of a nation. Above all, China now demands a completely new framework.

Tom: There is really no way for China to avoid a market economy and a modern society based on law. But what is essential, first of all, is true owners and protectors of wealth.

George: It is a shame that we Chinese still talk about this today.

Tom: This is simply because China has not yet created these things. The ongoing banking crisis, faltering trust, and the failing state sector are the result of the lack of a new framework. Has China paid enough dues?

George: Is China moving closer to resolving these deeper issues?

Tom: Above all, China's sustained growth demands true property owners as well as true protectors. China has created a vibrant private sector. What is missing is true property ownership as well as modern law.

George: How do you view China's new engagement with the outside world?

Tom: China's modernization must involve the entire world. There is no other way. China's openness is already a tremendous achievement.

Jack: That is a crucial point. Foreign businesspeople are only interested in making profits. Maybe they are not aware that they are making other contributions: They are encouraging China, as well as the outside world, to move in a new direction. Above all, China's growth demands an open society. In this respect, China is moving ahead brilliantly.

Tom: China's reform has been going on for a short time from the standpoint of history. By now China is already deeply connected to global development. There are much wider choices today.

20 THE WORLD WATCHES: HOW DOES CHINA ACHIEVE SUSTAINED GROWTH?

China's new engine has been running fast for some three decades without a stop. Thus many people wonder if it can keep going at full speed. What might stop it? Or, what will take China to the next level of development?

A GREAT PARADOX

George: What will take China to the next stage?

Tom: Despite the vast economic progress China has made, every Chinese knows that there are huge problems still. It turns out that there is no straightforward path to a new modern society.

George: Some people feel that China's new growth is simply a restoration of old wealth.

Tom: This is true in only a limited sense. In general, the development is much more than that.

George: What do you mean?

Tom: China is leaving the old framework behind. Over the ages, the entire society and economy have been built around government. The government tries to arrange all things as it wishes. This cannot continue.

George: Why not?

Tom: The system cannot control corruption, but it is so powerful to suffocate the entire people and society.

George: Why can it control corruption?

Tom: Over the ages, corruption has been built into the system. This system may be powerful in fending off outside intrusions. It is weak in dealing with internal foes. Government corruption has repeatedly destroyed peace and wealth throughout history.

Jack: Today, China's key problem continues to be an overextended bureaucratic power. We have a booming market, but the state banks are faltering; there are countless foreign businesses here, but corruption is widespread. What is more, corrupt officials seem to have little to fear. There are so many holes in the system that it is very difficult to catch them.

EFFECTIVE GOVERNMENT, DIFFERENT ROLE

George: Where does China stand now?

Jack: In this era, the creative energy of the Chinese people is evident to all. As a result, great wealth that was destroyed in the Mao era is being quickly restored. So far, the Chinese have been much more productive in an improved environment.

George: Without doubt, China has many highly creative entrepreneurs — nearly 40 million now.

Tom: Still, a better environment is a necessity. There are still countless man-made barriers. But the real issues go beyond that.

George: What exactly do you mean?

Tom: Realities are ironic. On the one hand, China must definitely reduce bureaucratic power. On the other hand, there must be an efficient and strong government.

George: Why so?

Tom: Two basic elements are involved. First, without reducing the bureaucratic power, China cannot build a truly effective government, which is badly needed. But second, without changing the old system completely, China cannot turn this government body into a modern service provider. Indeed, without a fundamental change, the government will no longer possess true political authority. All this would lead to chaos and destruction of wealth.

George: Can one still hope to establish an effective government in the traditional context?

THE BIG PICTURE

Jack: That is no longer possible. Let's look at the big picture. Uncontained bureaucracy has been China's ultimate and persistent problem. China's bureaucratic power expanded for 2,200 years, from the Qin dynasty to the Mao era.

George: How did it keep increasing for that long?

Jack: Well, for one thing, bureaucratic power was able to contain all private initiatives effectively and completely. It reached its height in the Mao era, forcing the Chinese people and society to serve its need exclusively. Since 1978, China's bureaucratic power has been on the decline. This has given birth to a sharp rise in the private sector. It is this private sector that is most responsible for the booming economy. People are happier, more prosperous, and more productive than in the Mao era. What does it take to create wealth? Nothing more than private initiatives and entrepreneurial spirit.

George: Why did this change not happen before? Are there more factors involved?

Jack: Throughout the long search for a better nation over the past 200 years, China has not had real opportunities to resolve the basic issues from the root causes. Instead, there have been many shortcuts. Socialism is nothing but a shortcut that China took in the past half century.

George: Some outsiders argue that China has not had true socialism. Why do you view it as a shortcut?

Tom: Why? Under the cover of the socialist slogan, bureaucratic power expanded in all directions. It finally penetrated the lowest grassroots levels, the household and individual levels. No one was left alone, not even monks. As a result, the society and people were trapped completely. China's economy went dead.

WHO BENEFITS?

George: Who has really benefited from all this?

Tom: The government bureaucrats benefited greatly. Their power expanded in all possible ways and eventually reached the individual level. This had never happened before in China's entire history. Specifically, the dynastic governments had small official bodies. Some 100 years ago, the government had only some 20,000 officials administrating over this vast nation—400 million at the time. But after 1949, the government body grew to several million—8 million by 1996.[1] Under this system, China encountered the biggest man-made tragedies. The people's commune, the Great Leap Forward, and the Cultural Revolution were just a few of these.

George: Why is it so difficult to stop bureaucratic domination?

Jack: You are talking about transforming an entire government-centered society into a modern society based on nothing but law and fairness. How straightforward could that be?

George: Is this type of story unique to China?

Tom: Not at all. For Europe to come out of the Dark Ages took hundreds and hundreds of years. So it is natural for this process to take a long time in China.

Jack: Indeed, this is the first time the root causes of this fundamental issue can be addressed. China didn't have any real opportunities to do so before.

Tom: Even today, it is no small task. This is simply because of the complete bureaucratic penetration since 1949.

George: One ex-prisoner told me that his prison was full of ex-government officials—mayors, magistrates, bankers, and tariff officials. I was shocked.

Jack: Each year now, tens of thousands of officials are put behind bars. Yet corruption is not contained. In 2004 alone, 43,757 government officials were convicted of corruption.[2]

A New Model

George: Here is the general situation: China has always had a vibrant private sector and dynamic market, but it has not given rise to a modern economy. Some 1,350 years ago, Xian, the great capital of the Tang dynasty, had a population of several million. It had vibrant commerce. Tens of thousands of Japanese, Koreans, and Arabs lived there. Its international flavor was something like that in New York or Paris today. Yet in the recent past, China has lagged behind. What has gone wrong? Will China leave the old path?

Jack: Surely enough, the entire society has lost its faith in state domination. This has paved the way for all the changes. Now China is being taken over by great private initiatives. This has helped to turn a government economy into a competitive economy. However, it does not mean that China has a market economy.

George: Why not?

Jack: Today, government bureaucrats still dominate market activities completely. So corruption is common, and for that reason establishing true ownership and legal protection is still difficult.

George: But should we say that China does have many new elements?

Tom: That is not quite enough. An entire package is needed. Otherwise you won't get a modern economy.

George: What do you mean?

Tom: Some 100 years ago, China had an energetic private sector. Shanghai was the great center of commerce for all Asia and beyond. By the early 1900s, it also had a stock market. But this did not lead to a modern economy. Why? Bureaucratic power was able to contain private and independent development. Until only recently, a businessperson who met a magistrate had to bow in the old way. Even today, citizens are fearful of the bureaucrats. Officialdom is thought to hold divine power.

Jack: Only today are people starting to question the very basic issues concerning relations between government and society.

Government Versus Business

George: Why did government want to contain the business community?

Tom: Government fears independent organizations of any sort. Businesspeople possess wealth, organizational abilities, employee bodies, and leadership. They can build powerful organizations. In the eyes of the government, businesspeople are harmful to its domination. Therefore, business must be contained.

Jack: This has been the whole history of China. For several decades in our era, all the private businesses were eliminated. All the business assets were owned and operated by the government. Letting the bureaucrats deal with the business world has been a long tradition. In the end, the entire society was left with only one element, the government. A perfect bureaucratic society was built.

George: Would such tight control bring any benefits to government?

Jack: As a matter of fact, it does nothing but harm the government. Actually, this unlimited power has been the government's biggest enemy. Power carries responsibilities. More power means more responsibility, nothing less. Of course, it is a terrible load to provide all things for 1.3 billion people. There is no way for any government to do this well. In all the golden periods of China's past, a small government body provided very minimal administration. Otherwise there could be chaos.

George: Is this the key reason the government is actively promoting reform now?

Tom: That is exactly the case. The government has initiated the current reform.

George: Is this reform unique? Or has it happened before?

Tom: Fundamentally, nothing much is unique about this reform. It has happened numerous times in the past. As before, the aim has been to get rid of loaded troubles. At the same time, the government wishes to gain more power.

George: Is it a good idea to get rid of problems?

Tom: It is a great idea. But dumping troubles leads to no new society.

TRUE INDEPENDENCE

George: Why not?

Tom: How could it? Very significantly, the ongoing reform has been a way for the government to get rid of its problems, nothing more. Government bureaucrats everywhere love to gain more power. But power invites problems. It is the problems everyone wants to dump, not the power.

Jack: Well, a modern society cannot come directly from a bureaucratic tradition. A modern society consists only of equal members: Nobody stands above the rest, and the law is the only thing above everyone. In short, the traditional government domination must be changed first. There is neither an alternative nor a shortcut.

George: Many people think that the tens of millions of private businesspeople should lead the creation of a new society. Is this so?

Jack: Tremendous efforts are required. After all, our businesspeople are still conditioned within the old system. Their operating space is given to them by the government. In truth, their existence depends on their diligent cooperation with government officials at all levels. They are both beneficiaries and victims. They can only move within the space defined by the government other than law. The private businessmen could not break the government bureaucracy 100 years ago—can they do it now?

Tom: True, the private sector is tightly contained by the old system. But businesspeople always desire true independence. They are interested in pursuing independent work. Given the realities today, they can only grow. What is more, they all desire to have the same environment as in the United States and Western Europe, free of bureaucratic obstructions. That way they can focus on wealth creation.

George: So, breaking out of the traditional bureaucratic domination is the biggest goal for China?

Jack: Absolutely!

Tom: A modern society must be based on law other than government power. Otherwise, modern things like well-defined ownership and true legal protections would be next to impossible.

Getting Out of the Box

George: So, can one say that China is entering an era for building modern legal and political-economic institutions?

Jack: That is what is happening now.

Tom: Well, things are causing dramatic changes for the better. Certainly conditions in China are much better for breaking out than at any time in the past.

George: What do you mean?

Tom: The Chinese society and economy are becoming more open than ever before, and this is happening within a global framework. This new open environment has become the greatest force for promoting fundamental change for the better.

Jack: China has nearly 40 million entrepreneurs now. They are changing everything. In addition, hundreds of millions of people are on the move searching for better opportunities. In short, the new developments have already transcended the old containment. The Chinese people are creative.

Tom: Surely, China is more confident about embracing a better society now than ever before.

George: Now the public has the view that the future direction is "a small government and a big society."[3] Does this make sense?

Jack: That is the right direction. We should have had a serious debate about this a long time ago. But it has been impossible until today.

Tom: All the new wealth is created in a new environment today. China can certainly do better in the future, all under a smaller government.

Jack: The opportunities and the problems are equally impressive. The grave danger is that some people are not willing to resolve the problems from their root causes. They are still hoping shortcuts will work.

Tom: China must now go beyond this. There is no alternative whatsoever.

Jack: This means creating a new society based on law. In particular, the government turns into a modern service provider.

CHINA'S BEST CHOICE: A NEW SOCIETY

George: Earlier you said that China's current development goes beyond a restoration of former wealth. Can you say more about that?

Tom: China is now taking a completely new direction. That is, China is moving past the bureaucratic tradition and a closed society. Instead, China wants to join the world in spirit and practice. In fact, there is a true revolution in the making inside China.

Jack: Our development has already involved the entire world. The outside world is willing to share in China's progress and is actively doing so. This will certainly continue.

Tom: That is certainly the most significant aspect of this true Chinese revolution. As time goes by, China will surpass many other nations in openness and progressiveness.

George: There seems to be an uneasy feeling on the part of the outside world about the quick development in China.

Jack: Much of the world is troubled by the great waves of globalization. Seemingly, many people are worried about a fast-developing China or India.

Tom: For the world to move to the next stage of development is easier said than done. So many nations are unprepared.

Jack: The world today is so connected economically. But ideology lags seriously behind. A car produced in Detroit has an engine made in Europe, wheels made in Asia, and metal and rubber made in Africa, Latin America, and Australia, among other places. Look at China now. Overseas players had 31% of its industrial output in 2003. But some people still have the cold war mentality. This has to change if the world is to move to the next level of development. In short, sharing and joint responsibilities must become the new mandate for the world.

George: Some people still think they can outsmart everyone else.

Tom: Are people today smarter than the people of ancient times? Not really. Actually, if you read Confucius, Plato, and Lao Zi you may feel that we are not as smart as our ancestors.

Jack: I think we can be optimistic. It is wonderful to be alive. We have great hopes as well as challenges.

George: We need Confucius and Plato—in multiple—to resolve the tough issues China and the outside world face today.

Jack: But it is challenges that will give birth to another Confucius.

Tom: It is better to have a great system. Great persons come and go, but a system stays.

Jack: That is definitely what China needs.

George: So does the world.

A GREAT CONVERGENCE

Tom: But there is more to it than that. The new development undertaken by India and China suggests a great convergence of civilizations.

George: What do you mean exactly?

Tom: In the past few hundred years, both India and China, among other late-developing nations, tried hard to fend off the foreign powers by closing doors. But today, they are confident about being open to the world.

George: No one can deny that most developing nations now compete to participate in global development.

Jack: The world has reached the point of recognizing that we humans are about the same everywhere. There is a depth of human interaction as never before.

Tom: Plus, finally, we humans have seemingly realized that there are laws that govern us all. We have to play by these universal laws. Not doing so invites punishment. Shouldn't we see that the world is a great convergence of civilizations?

Jack: Basically, all the best human values and institutions are no more than our best accommodations to these natural laws. Right?

Tom: These laws govern not only the stars, trees, and animals, but also our economy, politics, society, and all the rest of civilization.

Jack: All the great national powers have been defeated in the past, mostly by their own weights. Should the future be any different?

Tom: In the recent past, Western Europe went through defeat. So did Japan. The United States has yet to learn.

Jack: Thank heaven that the United States has a democracy. Otherwise we wouldn't know what crazy thing it might do.

Tom: The United States could not have produced Hitlers. That would have brought ruin not only to the U.S., but also to the world.

Jack: So, the universal laws work. Without a limited government, the United States does not succeed economically. With a limited government it cannot produce Hitlers. Does this make sense?

LAWS

George: What are these universal laws?

Tom: They don't have a name yet. Why should they have a name? After all, they are not our intellectual property. But they are everywhere, invisible but always present. In short, we humans have been trying to express them, with little success. Should we try again?

Jack: Should we think about the ancient Greek tragic dramatists as well as the ancient Chinese sages Lao Zi and Zhuan Zi?

George: So, you claim that this great convergence of civilizations is the best response to the great universal laws?

Tom: What else could it be? Finally, we humans agree that we are all the same. We are all earthly things. So we need to share instead of fighting. Our common enemies are bird flu and SARS.

George: Yes.

Tom: But we have one more powerful enemy.

George: What is that?

Tom: Ourselves.

Jack: Progress is the call of universal laws. We can hide. We can try to outsmart one another. But really we can do nothing but share with one another. Despite all the worries and new conflicts, this convergence must go on. There is no better alternative.

Tom: Mankind is entering a new era, period.

AFTERWORD

BY ANDRE GUNDER FRANK

D r. Gu honors me by his invitation to write an afterword to his marvelously real-life brass-tacks and nitty-gritty examination of China's participation in the world economy today and probably tomorrow. The honor is all the greater, as I am neither Chinese nor a Western "old China hand," or even a new one. I am especially not so at the micro-economic enterprise and institutional levels on which he reports, drawing usefully also on his own wide business experience. Therefore, my afterword must concentrate more on how Dr. Gu's more micro-account fits into China's macro-political economic participation in the world economy and on its historical background and future prospects.

My own book *ReOrient* [1400-1800] and its sequel under preparation *ReOrient the 19th Century*, as well as other recent research on China, establishes that China was predominant in the world economy until at least 1800. Indeed, my most recent research suggests that China did not really "decline" until after the Taiping Rebellion (1851-64) and not the First but the Second Opium War in 1860. And then a major factor in its decline was the weakness of the state. But that means that Western dominance is much more recent and short, only about a century in the world and less in China, and not the millennium, or even half of one, alleged by Eurocentric historiography or rather mythology. And China now gives plenty of indication, much of it reviewed in this book, that it is likely soon to regain its long accustomed place in the world as the so-called Middle Kingdom.

In the 20th century, East Asian economic growth and development restarted from a level both absolutely and even more relatively much lower than it had been a century before. However, over the 20th century as a whole the East Asian growth rate has been faster than that in the West, and in the last half century, since the liberation of China and the end of colonialism, the rate of economic growth in East Asia has been DOUBLE that of the West. It was led first by Japan, then in the flying geese pattern by the First

Four Tigers or little Dragons, and then by the next four, and for two decades now already by the Big Fiery Dragon of China with a nearly 10% annual growth rate. That is enough to double income every six years and quadruple national income in two decades, which is more even than the Japanese miracle.

Moreover, China has become a major player in the world economy and promises to become even more so in the foreseeable future. China's $850 billion foreign trade in 2003 has already put China in fourth place in the world, with 5% of world exports that are swamping markets all over and especially in the United States and 4% of world imports, which has converted China into a major player in the world economy and an increasingly important world marketplace. China also receives by far the most investment among developing countries, and most of it from "overseas Chinese" who have made their fortunes abroad, especially in Southeast Asia.

At the same time, the outside world, especially the United States, has benefited by this new development of China/Asia. Take the United States, for example: It is enormously dependent on East Asian but especially Chinese largesse. The lowly paid Chinese support the Americans in a half-dozen different though related ways. Combined, indeed they make Americans much richer than they would otherwise be, thanks in part to the United States since 1986 having the world's greatest and ever-growing foreign debt.

(1) Over $300 billion, out of the $700 billion of U.S. Treasury bonds, is held by the Central Bank of China, which has therefore already extended THAT MUCH credit to the United States. Its trade deficit is now $550 billion a year and still growing.

(2) Every year China supplies about $100 billion capital to help the United States. About $100 billion more is supplied by Europeans, and this year already over $120 billion by Japanese savings. The rest is supplied by others, especially Taiwan and other East Asians. But the Chinese connection and foreign aid to the United States go way beyond that. First, as Dr. Gu shows, lowly paid Chinese produce real goods as already the leading world producers of 100 manufactures and export—really, *give* many for US$450 billion a year to rich American consumers, who buy them with printed paper dollars.

(3)   So therefore Americans get the $100 billion Chinese goods for
       free, only the cost of printing the paper.

(4)   But that's only the half of it, because the Chinese then turn around
       and use these excess paper dollars to purchase those other paper
       dollar freely printed Treasury certificates, except that on those
       they get a 4-5% yearly interest. Still, what a bargain!

(5)   For an item that costs the Chinese $2 to manufacture, though, the
       workers of course get less and the charge for them is about $3.
       That sounds like a pretty good profit. But it is not. For in the
       United States the final consumer then pays $10 for that same item,
       so that $7 goes to increase the U.S. GNP and taxes, many times
       more than in China! If the same goods were instead sold in China
       itself, Chinese income would more than double; and of course,
       American income would be much lower.

(6)   Not only American consumer and producer income, but U.S.
       government income is also raised thereby, permitting the
       Americans to pay for sophisticated weapons for the Pentagon—
       while they need not make many consumer goods that they get for
       free. And then the United States encircles China militarily and
       threatens it and others politically with these same Pentagon arms
       that China and others themselves paid for!

Interestingly at the same time, some developing nations and especially
China do have other alternatives. Although China has lately begun to use
some of its dollars also to purchase imports from elsewhere in Asia, we may
ask why many foreign nations keep providing this financing to the United
States. The main reason the Chinese give is to keep the dollar up and the
Rmb—and other dollar-linked currencies—down in order to be able to sell
to the U.S. market. But they are not really selling, they are giving. So they
give more in order to be able to give still more.

I suspect that there is another unstated reason for this apparent madness.
It has to do with the inequality in the distribution of income globally and
nationally. Those with the power to do so are *recycling* domestic income
from poor to rich in China itself in a roundabout way via exports to and
earnings from the United States. And something of the same happens in the
United States itself, especially through the financial sector that the Chinese
and Japanese support in the United States and elsewhere. Policies that

would seem to be crazily against the general interest globally and nationally around the world are steadfastly pursued by those in power because they vastly increase their own minority income at the expense of the vast majority nationally and globally. For that way the absolute and relative income of the latter is being pushed down, or to put it in now-outdated terminology, the working masses are thereby obliged to work for the luxury of the ruling classes.

In China at least the "middle class" is growing and in India also (I never understand what is "middle" about them, between whom and whom?), so that this can rally political support for these policies. But Mao's poorer but relatively egalitarian China has already become a country with one of the most unequal distributions of income in the world. Globally, the inequality in the distribution of income has been accelerating so much as to move by one measure from 40/1 in 1960 to 80/1 now. The very structure of the world economy and finance polarizes income, as Samir Amin keeps pointing out. So where is the political policy support coming from to keep this crazy system going in China and the world by pumping ever more savings and goods into the United States and keeping the dollar up—for nothing in return?

For China, there is certainly one bright alternative. This is pointed out by Henry C. K. Liu: China has the power to make the yuan an alternative reserve currency in world trade by simply denominating all Chinese export in yuan. This sovereign action can be taken unilaterally at any time of China's choosing. This will set off a frantic scramble by importers of Chinese goods around the world to buy yuan [who] no longer need to exchange yuan into dollars, as the yuan, backed by the value of Chinese exports, becomes universally accepted in trade. Members of the Organization of Petroleum Exporting Countries (OPEC), which import sizable amounts of Chinese goods, would accept yuans for payment for their oil."[1]

Moreover, there is also a "Greater China," including Hong Kong, Taiwan, and the now tremendously important overseas Chinese, who are key investors on the mainland itself. Additionally, there is the Southeast Asian ASEAN community, and the ASEAN + 3, including Japan, South Korea, and China, in which the latter has now begun to organize economic relations that might be interpreted as a sort of resurrection of the centuries-old "East Asian Trade-Tribute System" that was centered on China and lasted into the 19th century. Additionally, again referring to Henry C. K. Liu[2], but also to my own Foreword to the Chinese edition of my book, it is now possible and likely that East Asians with Chinese participation will build up an East Asian financial fund, among other things. That is in part because of the sad experience of having been *mis*managed by the IMF in the 1997/98 East Asian financial crisis. Indeed for the first time in history, it is the world's greatest debtor who is throwing its weight around. Throughout history, it is creditors who have exercised their power over debtors, and China is now the greatest creditor, and Greater China is even more so.

So, in view of the increasing outside world impact of Chinese international trade and investment, the sharp rise of the private sector, and related institutional reforms of the state sector and banking, which Dr. Gu describes in great detail, its macro-political economic and financial impact may soon be huge as well.

However, neither Dr. Gu's book nor this afterword is meant to suggest that all will be smooth sailing. On the contrary, China's problems are as huge as its 1.3 billion population, and both are still growing, each increasing the other. Increased population, production, and income will further increase pressure on already scarce resources. Land will become even scarcer and more degraded. Water is either too plentiful, with floods in parts, or mostly ever scarcer, further degrading the land. Food will have to be imported, and oil, timber, iron ore, copper, etc. as well. Energy is ever scarcer, and China's reliance on domestic high-sulphur coal will further pollute the air, which is already almost unbearable in big cities that are growing even more and increasing the number of cars and trucks. Indeed, they will increase global warming, which will exacerbate many of the above problems in China itself. Elsewhere and for China itself, the demand for coal and oil imports has recently increased the world prices of both. The already gaping and growing rural/urban and seaboard/interior income inequalities could stretch to breaking points.

Beijing has historically been hard put to exercise control over its richer eastern and especially southern provinces and is so again today, beginning with Hong Kong and Guangdong. Some regions have gone their own way in the past and could do so again. China's neighbors can become wary of the Big Dragon; and the United States, which already fears its challenge, is already again encircling China with military bases. Nonetheless, returning again to a longer historical perspective, it is noteworthy that the economically most dynamic regions of East Asia today are also still or again exactly the same ones as the four China-centered ones before 1800 which survived into the 19th century: (1) in the South, Lingnan, centered on the Hong Kong-Guangzhou corridor; (2) Fujian, still centered on Amoy/Xiamen and focusing on the Taiwan straits and Taiwan as well as parts of Southeast Asia in the South China Sea; (3) the Yangtze Valley, centered on Shanghai and trade with Japan that is already taking the lead again; and (4) Northeast Asia, including Northeast China, Manchuria, Mongolia, Siberia/Russian Far East, [northern?] Japan, and Korea. Its base of ample metallurgical, forestry, agricultural, and even petroleum resources and ample Chinese and North Korean labor can permit regional capital again to develop a very important regional growth pole in itself and a highly competitive region on the world market.

Dr. Gu's important book tells *how* these developments are taking place on the ground level in China. The 21st century will be Asian.

Author of ReOrient: Global Economy in the Asian Age
Luxembourg
August 2004

1.   China vs. the Almighty Dollar, http://www.atimes.com/atimes/China/
      DG23Ad04.html.
2.   http://www.atimes.com/atimes/asian_economy/DG12Dk01.html.

NOTES

CHAPTER 1

1. Wang Zhile (ed), *Report of Foreign Multinationals in China, 2003-2004,* Beijing: China Economics Publisher, 2004.
2. Alain Peyrefitte, *L'empire Immobile ou LE Choc'des Mondes,* Fayard, 1989.
3. *China's Foreign Trade,* July 2003.
4. For discussions see, for example, Gurcharan Das, *India Unbound: The Social and Economic Revolution from Independence to the Global Information Age,* Anchor, 2002; T. N. Srinivasan and Suresh D. Tendulkar, *Reintegrating India with the World Economy,* Institute for International Economics, 2003.
5. For more information see, for example, Hal Hill (ed), *The Economic Development of Southeast Asia,* Edward Elgar, 2002; Chi Lo, *When Asia Meets China in the New Millennium: China's Role in Shaping Asia's Post Crisis Economic Transformation,* Pearson Education Asia Pte, 2003; Foong Wi Fong, *The New Asian Way,* Beijing: Economic Daily Publisher, 1998.
6. For more information see Mark Eric Williams, *Market Reform in Mexico: Coalitions, Institutions, and Politics of Policy Change,* Roman & Littlefield, 2001; Robert J. Griffiths (ed), *Developing World 02/03,* McGraw-Hill/Dushkin, 2002.
7. For more information see Brigitte Granville and Peter Oppenheimer (ed), *Russia's Post-Communist Economy,* Oxford University Press, 2001; Vadim Volkov, *Violent Entrepreneurs: The Use of Force in the Making of Russian Capitalism,* Cornell University Press, 2002.
8. *Beijing Daily,* May 16-18, 2003.
9. CEO & CIO in *Information Times,* #125, June 5, 2003, pp44-47.
10. The company's report.
11. *Beijing Youth Daily,* May 16-19, 2003.
12. See company's Web site: www.konka.com.cn.
13. Luo Qingqi, www.emkt.com.cn, July 12, 2002.
14. Wang Zhile (ed), *Report of Foreign Multinationals in China, 2003-2004,* Beijing: China Economics Publisher, 2004.
15. For various views on China's interactions with foreign retailers, see Editor, Noise in Festivity—the Changing Chinese Commerce, *Economic Outlook,* March 2004, p77.
16. Top Retailers of 2005 in China, Xinhua News, August 4, 2005; also one chapter on retail industry of China is in, Zhibin Gu, *Made in China,* Centro Atlantico, 2005.

17. Nan Chen, BMW's Price Cut Shakes Up the Market, January 13, 2005, *Special Zone Daily*, C1; various reports in *Auto Weekly; Shenzhen Special Zone Daily*, D3-5, November 16, 2004.

18. *Financial Times* Web site, August 4, 2003.

19. *Business Watch*, #14, July 2003.

20. A Reader's Letter on China's 50th Year of Auto Industry, *Business Watch*, #15, August 1, 2003.

21. www.qiche.com.cn, July 24, 2003.

22. Hao Lan, Doing Better Than Number One: An Interview with Pfizer's China CEO, *China Drug Store*, #33, December 2003, pp70-73.

23. Lin Zhijun, *Change: China 1990-2002*, Beijing: China Social Science Publisher, 2003, p49.

24. Lin Zhijun, *Change: China 1990-2002*, Beijing: China Social Science Publisher, 2003, p49.

25. A good source on venture capital is *Asia Venture Capital Journal;* one chapter on venture capital in China is contained in, Zhibin Gu, *Made in China*, Centro Atlantico, 2005.

26. *International Finance News*, September 3, 2003.

27. George Zhibin Gu, Japan's Unfinished Business in China, *Asia Times*, April 22, 2005.

28. *Orient Today*, #1105, May 2003.

29. *Global Times*, July 25, 2003.

30. Huang Weihong et al., *Foreign Advisors' Ideas*, Southern Daily Publisher, 2000.

CHAPTER 2

1. *Global Times*, June 2, 2003.

2. Ibid.

3. China News Agency, July 12, 2003.

4. Wenzhou Government Web site: www.wznw.gov.cn

5. www.zj.xinhuanet.com/wenzhou_2002040101.html.

6. www.wznw.gov.cn/jsdd/wznc1.html.

7. *Xinhua News*, June 26, 2002; Hao Jinzai, *80 Million Migrants*, Beijing: China Social Publisher, 1995, pp186-190; for background information, see for examples, Lian Yuming (ed), *Urban China Report 2004*, Beijing: China Finance Publisher, 2004; Zhibin Gu, *Made in China*, Centro Atlantico, 2005; Pan Wei, *Farmers and Market: China's Grass-Roots Government and Rural Enterprises*, Beijing: Commerce Publisher, 2003.

8. www.wznw.gov.cn./jsdd/wnnc1.html.

9. The Biggest Sports Shoe Export Center, *China Foreign Trade*, #7, 2003.

10. CEO & CIO in *Information Times*, #132, September 20, 2003, pp30-39.

11. *Economic Daily,* August 15, 2002; *Xinhua News,* December 22, 2002; *Southern Daily,* October 11, 2002.
12. *New Fortune,* July 2003.
13. www.qiche.com.cn, August 5, 2003.
14. *International Finance News,* Section 9, September 12, 2003.
15. Interviews with Leading Businessmen, *China Economy Weekly,* March 11, 2003.
16. The Economic Observer, July 18, 2003; Market Daily, September 30, 2002; The Secrets of Galanz, VCDs, Beijing: China Electronics Image Publisher; Zhong Pengrong, Galanz's Experiences to China's Manufacturing Industry, www.dayoo.com, July 16, 2003.
17. *Shenzhen Special Zone Daily,* A12, November 13, 2003.
18. China Statistics.
19. China Statistics.
20. *The Economic Observer,* A4, September 8, 2003.
21. George Zhibin Gu, China's Competitiveness in a Strong-yuan World, *Asia Times,* August 1, 2005

CHAPTER 3

1. *South Metro Daily,* December 31, 2003, A42.
2. *Asia Times,* April 23, 2005.
3. *Financial Times* Web site, September 26, 2003.
4. China statistics.
5. *Financial Times* Web site, September 26, 2003.
6. *Shenzhen Special Zone Daily,* November 16, 2003, D4.
7. *Orient Today,* March 2003.
8. *Sunshine Daily,* January 11, 2005, B16; George Zhibin Gu, Clearer Path ahead for China's Banks, *Asia Times,* July 1, 2005
9. Wang Zaiman, *Destiny of Chinese Brands,* Beijing: Guangming Daily Publisher, 1999, pp8-10.

CHAPTER 4

1. *Zhongguancun,* #4, July 2003.
2. Ibid.
3. *Cankao Xiaoxi,* July 24, 2003.
4. *Zhongguancun,* #2, May 2003.
5. Foreign Education in China, *International Finance News,* August 29, 2003.

CHAPTER 5

1. *Beijing Daily,* August 20, 2003.

2. Ni Jianzhong et al. (ed), *A Study on the Balance between East and West in China* Beijing: China Social Publisher, 1996.
3. Le Zheng (ed), *Blue Book of Shenzhen,* Beijing: China Social Science Document Publisher, 2003.
4. *Nanfeng,* September 15, 2003, pp18-21.
5. *Nanfeng,* September 15, 2003, pp18-21 and pp34-40.
6. *Guangdong-Hong Kong Info Daily,* July 2, 2003.
7. Le Zhen (ed), *Blue Book of Shenzhen,* Beijing: China Social Science Document Publisher, 2003.
8. *Yue Gang Info Daily,* July 2, 2003.
9. *Caijing,* #68, September 20, 2002, pp58-63.
10 Le Zhen (ed), *Blue Book of Shenzhen,* Beijing: China Social Science Document Publisher, 2003.
11. *Shenzhen Special Zone Daily,* July 13, 2003.
12. *New York Times* Web site, July 1, 2003.
13. *Economist,* June 7-13, 2003, p31.

CHAPTER 6

1. *Beijing Business Daily,* June 2, 2003.
2. *Global Entrepreneur,* August 2003.
3. Jim Mann, *Beijing Jeep: A Case Study of Western Business in China,* Westview Press, 1997.
4. *Global Times,* August 20, 2003.
5. He Li et al. (ed), *Talking with 100 Bosses,* pp207-222, Volume 4, Beijing: Economic Management Publisher, 1999.
6. Ye Weirang, *Stories behind China's WTO Entry,* Sichuan People's Publisher, 1999, pp301-350.
7. George Z. Gu, Capital Is Not Enough, *Asian Venture Capital Journal,* January 2001, pp3-4.
8. Bill Emmott, *Japan's Global Reach,* Century Business, 1991.
9. Li Guangdo, Seven Mistakes of Ericsson in China, *China Marketing,* June 2003, #136.
10. One Consumer's Tough Fight with Ericsson, *Beijing Star Daily,* March 14, 2003.
11. Ibid.
12. CEO & CIO in *Information Times,* #132, September 20, 2003, pp44-45.
13. Carrefour's Troubles, *Global Times,* August 5, 2003.
14. The Carrefour's Disputes, *The Economic Observer,* May 23, 2003.
15. Carrefour's Troubles, *Global Times,* August 5, 2003.

CHAPTER 7

1. Shi Guangseng, www.china.com.cn, November 13, 2002.
2. *Global Entrepreneur,* #88, July 2003.

3. *Business Week/China,* monthly issue, #3, 2003.

4. *Global Entrepreneur,* #88, July 2003.

5. Li Cheng et al., *Analysis of Frontier Problems After China's WTO Entry,* Beijing: China Commerce Publisher, pp216-264.

6. *Guangzhou Daily,* February 17, 2004.

7. *Business Watch,* #12, June 15, 2003.

8. Wang Zhile (ed), *Report of Foreign Multinationals in China, 2003-2004,* Beijing: China Economics Publisher, 2004; China's Singapore Diplomatic Mission, *Business Section,* January 9, 2002; www.bizcn-sg.org.sg; www.999.com.cn

9. China's Singapore Diplomatic Mission, *Business Section,* January 9, 2002.

10. *Orient Today,* #1105, May 2003.

11. Guo Wanda and Zhu Wenhui, *Made in China: World Factory is Turning to China,* Jiangsu People's Publisher, 2003; Zhibin Gu, *Made in China: Players and Challengers in the 21st Century,* Centro Atlantico, 2005.

12. Guang Zhixiong, *International Finance News,* May 6, 2003; also www.people.com.cn/GB/paper66/9100/846563.html.

13. *New Capital,* September 2003, pp28-31.

14. *Business Week,* Chinese edition, March 2003; Pete Engardio and Dexter Roberts, China Factor, www.businessweek.com, December 6, 2004.

15. *New York Times,* May 11, 2003.

16. *Asian Wall Street Journal,* September 10, 2003.

17. *New York Times* Web site, May 11, 2003.

18. *New York Times* Web site, November 19, 2003.

19. See also *Fortune,* June 23, 2003, pp39-44.

20. Lin Zhinjun and Ma Licheng, *Five Voices in Present China,* Guangzhou Publisher, 1999; pp250-251.

21. CEO & CIO in *Information Times,* #125, June 5, 2003, pp44-47.

22. *Global Entrepreneur,* #88, July 2003.

23. *Star Daily,* February 20, 2003.

24. *Brains,* August 2003.

25. On Multinationals Practices, *The Economic Observer,* September 15, 2003, pA3.

26. *Business Week,* Chinese edition, March 2003.

27. *Economic Monthly,* September 2003, pp18-21.

28. One good source is the Indian Industry Association: www.nasscom.org; also see, Rohit Verma, China's rise: IT's not a Problem for India, *Asia Times,* June 17, 2005.

29. Reinie Booysen (ed), India Should Catch Up with China in Energy Security, Singh Says, *Bloomberg,* January 16, 2005; also see, Chietigj Bajpaee, India, China Locked in Energy Game, *Asia Times,* March 17, 2005.

30. *World Bank,* Working Paper #3084, June 2003; China Statistics.

31. *Business Week,* Chinese edition, #4, 2002.

32. See, for example, Gurcharan Das, *India Unbound: The Social and Economic Revolution from Independence to the Global Information Age,* Anchor, 2002; T. N.

Srinivasan and Suresh D. Tendulkar, *Reintegrating India with the World Economy* Institute for International Economics, 2003.

33. Ramtanu Maitra, The Energy Ties that Bind India, China, *Asia Times*, April 12, 2005; George Zhibin Gu, It takes Two to Tango, *Asia Times*, February 17, 2005, and, The Late Developers' Trek, *Asia Times*, May 4, 2005.
34. George Zhibin Gu, The Late Developers' Trek, *Asia Times*, May 4, 2005.

CHAPTER 8

1. *Global Entrepreneur,* #88, July 2003.
2. The First Lesson for GE in China, *Business Watch,* #12, June 15, 2003, pp36-43.
3. Fu Dingwei et al. (ed), *The Strategies of Foreign Multinationals in China,* Beijing: China Machinery Publisher, 2002, pp206-209.
4. *Business Watch,* #12, June 15, 2003, p38.
5. *Business Watch,* #12, June 15, 2003, p38.
6. Fu Dingwei et al. (ed), *The Strategies of Foreign Multinationals in China,* Beijing: China Machinery Publisher, 2002, pp206-209.
7. *Business Watch,* #12, June 15, 2003, p39.
8. *Business Watch,* #12, June 15, 2003, pp36-43.
9. *The Economic Observer,* A4, October 27, 2003.
10. Henny Sender, Japan Inc, *Far East Economic Review,* November 2003,
11. *Global Entrepreneur,* #89, August 2003.
12. *New Capital,* #135, 2003, pp10-36.
13. *New Capital,* #135, 2003, pp23-27.
14. *New Capital,* #135, 2003, pp10-33; *The Economic Observer,* A2, September 8, 2003; George Zhibin Gu, Japan's Unfinished Business in China, *Asia Times,* April 22, 2005.
15. *New Fortune,* #31, November 2003, pp88-89.
16. *ChinaByte,* February 12, 2003.
17. *Business Week,* May 19, 2003; Pete Engardio and Dexter Roberts, China Factor, www.businessweek.com, December 6, 2004.
18. www.huawei.com.
19. *Forbes,* February 17, 2003.
20. *Beijing Youth Daily,* April 2, 2002.
21. How Microsoft Warded Off Rival, *New York Times* Web site, May 15, 2003, http://www.nytimes.com/2003/05/15/technology/15SOFT.html.

CHAPTER 9

1. China Statistics.
2. *International Finance News,* September 5, 2003.
3. Gu Zhaoming and Yan Hongyu, *Haier: China's Global Brand,* Beijing: Economic Management Publisher, 2002.

4. Bill Emmott, *Japan's Global Reach*, UK: Century Business, 1991.

5. Stephen S. Roach, *This China Is Different*, Morgan Stanley, 2002.

6. *Economist*, February 15-21, 2003; also, Special Survey on China's Economic Role, October 2-8, 2004.

7. *Wall Street Journal* Web site, July 29, 2003; also see, Max Fraad Wolff, Bye-bye Macro Economy, *Asia Times*, July 1, 2005; Michael A Weinstein, Unocal Bid Highlights Globalist-nationalist Conflict, *Asia Times*, July 20, 2005.

8. *Wall Street Journal* Web site, July 28, 2003; also see, Henry C.K. Liu, The Coming Trade War (ongoing series of papers), *Asia Times*, 2005.

9. *International Finance News*, September 12, 2003.

10. Ibid.

11. Martin Wolf's column, *Financial Times* Web site, November 13, 2003.

12. CEO & CIO in *Information Times*, #129, August 5, 2003.

13. *The Economic Observer*, January 19, 2004, p11.

14. *Global Entrepreneur*, #89, August 2003;

15. George Zhibin Gu, Clearer Path Ahead for China's Banks, *Asia Times*, July 1, 2005.

16. *Business Focus*, June 2003.

CHAPTER 10

1. *Zhongguancun*, June 2003, pp54-60; *New Fortune*, #31, November 2003, pp88-108.

2. Gu Zhaoming and Yan Hongyu, *Haier: China's Global Brand*, Beijing: Economic Management Publisher, 2002.

3. CEO & CIO in *Information Times*, September 20, 2003, #132, pp54-56; George Zhibin Gu, China's Competitiveness in a Strong-yuan World, *Asia Times*, August 1, 2005.

4. *China Construction Daily*, November 19, 2003.

5. Wang Zhile (ed), *Report of Foreign Multinationals in China, 2002-2003*, Beijing: China Economics Publisher, 2003, pp189-196.

6. Wang Zhile (ed), *Report of Foreign Multinationals in China, 2002-2003*, Beijing: China Economics Publisher, 2003, pp153-157 and 170-178.

7. *China Construction Daily*, November 19, 2003.

8. *Xinhua News*, September 6, 2003.

9. *Redian Yanjiu*, #122, 2003.

10. *Global Entrepreneur*, July 2003.

11. *Financial Digest*, August 2003; *China Business*, July 7, 2003; *Global Entrepreneur*, July 2003; *Redian Yanjiu*, #122, March 2003; *The Economic Observer*, January 5, 2004, p10.

12. *Redian Yanjiu*, #122, March 2003.

13. *Global Entrepreneur*, July and September 2003.

14. *Business Watch*, #15, August 1, 2003.

15. *Business Watch*, #15, August 1, 2003.

16. CEO & CIO in *Information Times*, #125, June 5, 2003, p32.

17. *Caijing*, #97, December 5, 2003, pp110-114.

18. *The Investors*, January 2005, p91.

CHAPTER 11

1. Lin Zhijun, *The Change: China 1990-2002,* Beijing: China Social Science Publisher, 2003, p378.
2. Zhang Zhuoyuan, On China's Future Reform, *Economic Monthly,* #57, September 2003, pp52-55.
3. Government report, March 2005.
4. Qiushi, On Needs of Controlling Corruption, *Qiushi,* #365, August 16, 2003, p24.
5. Minute Recording of National Political Consultancy Conference, www.gb18.com/ China/news/economy/2003/03/03/20030303175017.html.
6. Why Are Courts Difficult to Carry Out Orders? www.people.com.cn, May 15, 2003.
7. Xinhua News Agency, February 27, 2003.
8. *Caijing* Editor, Reform or Stagnating Is the Issue: A Dialogue Between Wu Jinglian and Gee Wedong, *World & China,* special edition of *Caijing,* January 2005, pp38-47.

CHAPTER 12

1. *Beijing Business Daily,* May 16, 2003.
2. Yi Xianrong, On the Need of Further Reform, *China Economic Daily,* February 19, 2003.
3. *Caijing,* #86, June 20, 2003.
4. *Brains,* August 2003.
5. A Reader's Response to Corruption, *The Economic Observer,* Section A8, June 16, 2003.
6. *Brains,* August 2003.
7. *The Economic Observer,* Section A8, June 16, 2003; Gu Zhibin, *China Beyond Deng: Reform in the PRC,* McFarland, 1991.
8. Controlling Corruption, *Qiushi,* #365, August 16, 2003.

CHAPTER 13

1. For more discussion see, for example, Gu Zhibin, *China Beyond Deng: Reform in the PRC, McFarland,* 1991.
2. *Economic Monthly,* August 2003, p24.
3. *Market Daily,* November 1, 2002.
4. Zhang Shuguang, *The Natural Roads to Prosperity,* Guangdong Economic Publisher, 1999, p329.
5. *South Daily Weekend,* April 11, 2002.
6. *21 Century Finance,* October 14, 2002.
7. Lin Zhijun, *The Change: China in 1990-2002,* Beijing: China Social Science Publisher, 2003, pp219-220.

8. See note 7 above.
9. See discussions in Lin Zhijun, *The Change: China in 1990-2002*, Beijing: China Social Science Publisher, 2003; Gu Zhibin, *China Beyond Deng: Reform in the PRC*, McFarland, 1991.
10. *Xinhua News*, January 15, 2005.

CHAPTER 14

1. China News Agency, June 23, 2003. Also see *Shenzhen Special Zone Daily*, January 12, 2005, C2.
2. Jorge Nascimento Radrigues (ed), The China Factor and the Overstretch of the US Hegemony, January 2005, GurusOnLine.tv, http://www.gurusonline.tv/uk/conteudos/gu_report.asp.
3. *Business Week*, March 2003, Chinese edition; Chintoz Investment Consulting, *Home-Appliances Sector Analysis*, March 2003.
4. Xinhua News Agency, January 9, 2002.
5. He Li, *Talking with 100 Bosses*, Volume 2, p44, Beijing: Economic Management Publisher, 1999; Zhang Shuguang, Why Does China Lack Qualified Entrepreneurs, Zhengzhou University Press, 2004.
6. *International Finance News*, p9, September 12, 2003.
7. *Market Outlook*, May-June, 2003; *Business Match*, August 15, 2003, pp20-21, 68-70, and 78-81; *Global Views*, August 2003, pp110-115; Chintoz Investment Consulting, *Home-Appliances Sector Analysis*, March 2003; *Business Focus*, #16, June 2003, pp23-27; Xinhua News Agency, January 9, 2002.
8. John G. Glove and William B. Cornell, *The Development of American Industries*, New York: Prentice Hall, 1951, p820.
9. *China Economic News Weekly*, #9, 2003.
10. *Caijing*, #91, September 5, 2003, pp112-116.
11. Lin Cha, *China After Reform*, Beijing: Red Flag Publisher, 1998, p45.
12. *Beijing Youth Daily*, July 18, 2003.
13. *Economic Monthly*, July-August 2003; *Global Views*, August 2003, pp110-115; *Business Watch*, September 1, 2003, pp52-59; *China Money*, March 2003.
14. *Economic Monthly*, July 2003.
15. The End of the Myth of Kelon Management, *Shenzhen Special Zone Daily*, pC1, August 6, 2005.
16. George Zhibin Gu, China's Competitiveness in a Strong-yuan World, *Asia Times*, August 1, 2005; *Business Match*, July 15, 2003; Gao Liang, *Be Firm: Globalization Forces and China's Strategic Industries*, Beijing: Petro Industry Publisher, 2001, pp152-183.
17. Yuan Zhengming et al. (ed), *Picture Stories of Focus Investigations*, Beijing: Beijing Encyclopedia Publisher, 1999, pp682-683; George Zhibin Gu, China's Competitiveness in a Strong-yuan World, *Asia Times*, August 1, 2005.

CHAPTER 15

1. Li Qiang, *Urban Migrant Workers and Social Stratification in China*, Beijing: Social Science Academic Press, 2004.
2. He Qinglian, *Traps of Modernization*, Beijing: Today's China Publisher, 1998; Gu Zhibin, *China Beyond Deng: Reform in the PRC*, McFarland, 1991.
3. Hao Zaijin, *80 Million Migrants*, Beijing: China Social Publisher, 1996.
4. David S. Landes, *The Wealth of Nations: Why Some Are So Rich and Some So Poor*, New York: Norton, 1988, Chapter 16.
5. *China Business Post*, #518, May 31, 2003.
6. *The World of Survey and Research*, #118, July 2003, pp20-22.
7. Hao Zaijin, *80 Million Migrants*, Beijing: China Social Publisher, 1996; Chen Guidi and Chun Tao, *An Investigation on China's Farmers*, Beijing: People's Literature Publisher, 2004.
8. *Caijing*, #73, December 7, 2000.
9. Hao Zaijin, *80 Million Migrants*, Beijing: China Social publisher, 1996; Zhang Xiaoshan, *A Report on Property Ownership Changes in China's Rural Enterprises*, Beijing: Social Science Documents Publisher, 2003.
10. Wu Si, *Bloody Payment Law: Survival Game of China's History*, Beijing: China Workers' Publisher, 2003.
11. *Economic Monthly*, July 2003.
12. *Shenzhen Special Zone Daily*, December 10, 2003, A10.
13. *Guangzhou Daily*, May 28, 2003.
14. The Tragic Event of Sun Zhigan, *Sanlian Shenghuo Zhoukan*, #244, June 16, 2003.
15. Commenting on Sun Zhigan's Death, *Zhongguancun*, #3, June, 2003, p26.

CHAPTER 16

1. Deng Xiaoping, *Selected Works of Deng Xiaoping: 1975-1982*, pp287-292, Beijing: People's Publisher, 1983.
2. Editor, Fast News, *Transition*, Chinese version, China Institute for Reform and Development (Hainan) and World Bank, #24, July 1, 2003.
3. For information see, for example, Zhang Shuguang, *The Natural Roads to Prosperity*, Guangdong Economic Publisher, 1999; Chen Guidi and Chun Tao, *An Investigation on China's Farmers*, Beijing: People's Literature Publisher, 2004; Ma Qingyu, *Farewell Sisyphus: An Analysis & Prospects of Chinese Political Culture*, Beijing: China Social Science Publisher, 2002; and Li Bin, *Overdrafted Power: A Deeper Observation of Misinvestment by the Local Governments*, Hubei People's Publisher, 2003.
4. *Yue Gang Info Daily*, July 2, 2003.
5. *China Business Time*, April 2003, pp24-26.
6. Yang Fan, in *Economic Blue Book: China in 2001: Economic Trends and Predictions*, Beijing: Social Sciences Documentation Publisher, p162.

7. Wang Feng, On WTO Issues, *Legal Daily,* November 12, 2001.
8. Shi Guangseng, www.china.com, November 13, 2002.
9. *Global Entrepreneur,* July 2003, p28.
10. For various discussions see, for example, Wu Si, *Bloody Payment Law: Survival Game of China's History,* Beijing: China Workers' Publisher, 2003; Liu Jiseng and Shi Yongjiang, *Strategy of Transnational Corporations for Chinese Enterprises,* Beijing: Xinhua Publisher, 2003, pp74-83; Gu Zhibin, *China Beyond Deng: Reform in the PRC,* McFarland, 1991.
11. Need a Better Framework and Government Conduct, *Caijing,* #91, September 5, 2003, p113.
12. Can Guangmin, Issues on Building a Corruption-Free System, *Qiushi,* #357, April 16, 2003.
13. Lai's Troublesome End, Liu Zhiwu, Everyday News, *Tianjin Daily,* serial reports, July 1-30, 2002.
14. The Lessons of the Red Building, *CAAC Journal,* June 18, 2001.
15. www.eastday.com, August 26, 2001.
16. The Lessons of the Red Building, *CAAC Journal,* June 18, 2001.
17. Ibid.
18. Shao Daosheng, *The Diseases of the Nation: Reflections on China's Ongoing Corruption,* Beijing: Hualing Publisher, 2000, p3.
19. Lai's Troublesome End, Liu Zhiwu, Everyday News, *Tianjin Daily,* serial reports, July 1-30, 2002.
20. China News Agency, October 15, 2002.
21. Shao Daosheng, *The Diseases of the Nation: Reflections on China's Ongoing Corruption,* Beijing: Hualing Publisher, 2000, p3.

CHAPTER 17

1. For more information see, for example, Angus Maddison et al., *The World Economy: A Millennial Perspective,* OECD, 2001.
2. For more information see, for example, the above book and Niall Ferguson, *Empire: The Rise and Demise of the British World Order and the Lessons for Global Power,* Basic Books, 2003; Gao Yingtong, *The Sunset of an Empire: Declining Britain,* Jilin People's Publisher, 1998.
3. For more information see, for example, Andre Gunder Frank, *ReOrient: Global Economy in the Asian Age,* University of California Press, 1998; David S. Landes, *The Wealth of Nations: Why Some Are So Rich and Some So Poor,* New York: Norton, 1998.
4. For more information see, for example, Sarah Kaplan and Richard Foster, *Creative Destruction: Why Companies That Are Built to Last Underperform the Market and How to Successfully Transform Them,* Currency-Doubleday, 2001; John A. Byrne, *Chainsaw: The Notorious Career of Al Dunlap in the Era of Profit-at-Any-Price,* HarperBusiness, 2003.

5. For more information see, for example, Sarah Kaplan and Richard Foster, *Creative Destruction: Why Companies That Are Built to Last Underperform the Market and How to Successfully Transform Them*, Currency/Doubleday, 2001.
6. For more information see, for example, Ni Jianzhong et al. (ed), *Goodbye to Hong Kong's British: Two Destinies and Two Centuries*, Beijing: China Social Publisher, 1996; Alain Peyrefitte, *L'empire Immobile ou LE Choc'des Mondes*, Fayard, 1989. Chinese translation by Wang Guangqing et al., Beijing: Sanlian Books, 1995; David S. Landes, *The Wealth of Nations: Why Some Are So Rich and Some So Poor*, New York: Norton, 1988, Chapter 9.
7. Eric Foner, *The Story of American Freedom*, New York: Norton, 1998.
8. Douglas Brinkley, *Wheels for the World: Henry Ford, His Company and a Century of Progress, 1903-2003*, Viking Press, 2003.
9. Martin and Susan J. Tolchin, *Selling Our Security*, New York: Alfred A. Knopf, 1991.
10. For information see, for example, Frank Partnoy, *Infectious Greed: How Deceit and Risk Corrupted the Financial Markets*, New York: Times Books, 2003; Paul Krugman, *The Great Unraveling: Losing Our Way in the New Century*, Norton, 2003.

Chapter 18

1. For more information see, for example, Bruce Wasserstein, *Big Deal, The Battle for Control of America's Leading Corporations*, New York: Warner Books, 1998; Stuart C. Gilson, *Creating Value Through Corporate Restructuring: Case Studies in Bankruptcies, Buyouts, and Breakup*, New York: Wiley, 2001; Chen Baoseng, *Global Competition of American Multinationals*, Beijing: China Social Science Publisher, 1999.
2. For more information, besides those books above, see also Gary A. Dymski, *The Bank Merger Wave: The Economic Causes and Social Consequences of Financial Consolidation*, M.E. Sharpe, 1999; Charles R. Geisst, *Deals of the Century: Wall Street, Mergers, and the Making of Modern America*, Wiley, 2003; Robert E. Rubin and Jacob Weisberg, *In an Uncertain World: Tough Choices from Wall Street to Washington*, Random House, 2003.

Chapter 19

1. For more information see, for example, Tim Callen and Jonathan D. Ostry (ed), *Japan's Lost Decade: Policies for Economic Revival*, International Monetary Fund; Wang Lingao and Gao Yintong, *Challenges of Economic Islands: The Emotions of Japan's Political Feelings*, Jilin People's Publisher, 1998; Chen Baoseng, *Global Competition of American Multinationals*, Beijing: China Social Science Publisher, 1999; Foong Wi Fong, *The New Asian Way*, Beijing: Economic Daily Publisher, 1998; Zeng Huaguo and Sun Yiqu, *Crises of Nations*, Jiangsu People's Publisher, 1998; John Naisbitt, *Megatrends Asia*, Touchstone Books, 1997.
2. For more information see, for example, *Caijing*, #52, January 20, 2002, pp56-60; Wang Lingao and Gao Yintong, *Challenges of Economic Islands: The Emotions of Japan's*

Political Feelings, Jilin People's Publisher, 1998; Chen Baoseng, *Global Competition of American Multinationals,* Beijing: China Social Science Publisher, 1999.

3. For more information see, for example, Tang Gang and Chu Yuanyi, *A History of Ming Dynasty,* a volume in the series of *China's History,* Shanghai Ancient Books Publisher, 1998, pp159-167. In a way, here is the large picture: No matter how ambitious these warriors were, the invaders failed in the end. They loaded their boats with wounded warriors and peddled away back to their islands. This historical attack turned out to be a prelude to the modern invasion by Japan in the 20th century. This time, Japan carried not just some tribes of invaders; it carried entire empire of invaders. Not only China was invaded; America and many other nations were as well. Ni Jianzhong et al. (ed), *China and Japan: One Century Conflicts and Exchange,* Beijing: China Social Publisher, 1996; Ray Huang, *1587: A Year of No Significance,* Yale University Press, 1981.

4. For various discussions see, for example, Francis Fukuyama, *Trust: Human Nature and the Reconstitution of Social Order,* New York: Free Press, 1996; R. H. P. Mason and J. G. Caiger, *History of Japan,* Charles E. Tuttle Co, 1988; Yoshio Sugimoto, *An Introduction to Japanese Society,* Cambridge University Press, 2003; Noriko Takada et al. (ed), *The Japanese Way: Aspects of Behavior, Attitudes, and Customs of the Japanese,* McGraw-Hill, 1996; and Curtis Andressen and Milton Osborne, *A Short History of Japan: From Samurai to Sony,* Allen & Unwin, 2003; Chen Baoseng, *Global Competition of American Multinationals,* Beijing: China Social Science Publisher, 1999; Foong Wi Fong, *The New Asian Way,* Beijing: Economic Daily Publisher, 1998; John Naisbitt, *Megatrends Asia,* Touchstone Books, 1997.

5. An interesting discussion appears in Francis Fukuyama, *Trust: Human Nature and the Reconstitution of Social Order,* New York: Free Press, 1996; also see Ma Ping, *After Meiji Restoration: Japan's Economic Jump after World War Two,* Nanchang: Baihuazhou Publisher, 1997; Chen Baoseng, *Global Competition of American Multinationals,* Beijing: China Social Science Publisher, 1999; Zeng Huaguo and Sun Yiqu, *Crises of Nations,* Jiangsu People's Publisher, 1998.

6. Francis Fukuyama, *Trust: Human Nature and the Reconstitution of Social Order,* New York: Free Press, 1996.

7. *Beijing Business Daily,* February 12, 2003.

8. For more information see, for example, Eisuke Sakakibara, *Structural Reform in Japan: Breaking the Iron Triangle,* Brookings Institution Press, 2003; Chen Baoseng, *Global Competition of American Multinationals,* Beijing: China Social Science Publisher, 1999.

9. For more information see, for example, Tat Yan Kong, *The Politics of Economic Reform in South Korea: A Fragile Miracle,* Routledge, 2000; and Kenneth L. Judd and Young Ki Lee (ed), *An Agenda for Economic Reform in Korea: International Perspectives,* Hoover Institute Press, 2000; Francis Fukuyama, *Trust: Human Nature and the Reconstitution of Social Order,* New York: Free Press, 1996; Chen Baoseng, *Global Competition of American Multinationals,* Beijing: China Social Science Publisher, 1999; Zeng Huaguo and Sun Yiqu, *Crises of Nations,* Jiangsu People's Publisher, 1998.

10. *Caijing,* #60, May 20, 2002, pp36-39.

11. For more information see, for example, Eun Mee Kim, *Big Business, Strong State: Collusion and Conflict in South Korean Development, 1960-1990,* State University of New York Press, 1997.
12. *Financial Times* Web site, November 27, 2003.
13. China Statistics.

CHAPTER 20

1. Ma Qingyu, *Farewell Sisyphus: An Analysis & Prospects of Chinese Political Culture,* Beijing: China Social Science Publisher, 2002, p172.
2. Government report, March 2005.
3. For various discussions see, for example, Zhang Shuguang, *The Natural Roads to Prosperity,* Guangdong Economic Publisher, 1999; Chen Guidi and Chun Tao, *An Investigation on China's Farmers,* Beijing: People's Literature Publisher, 2004; Ma Qingyu, *Farewell Sisyphus: An Analysis & Prospects of Chinese Political Culture,* Beijing: China Social Science Publisher, 2002; and Li Bin, *Overdrafted Power: A Deeper Observation of Misinvestment by the Local Governments,* Hubei People's Publisher, 2003.

INDEX

ISBN 141206911-4

9 781412 069113